# Ridesharing Law and Liability

Zachary B. Pyers and
Kenton H. Steele

AMERICAN BAR ASSOCIATION
Tort Trial and Insurance Practice Section

Cover design by Jill Tedhams/ABA Design



Printed in the United States of America.

24 23 22 21 20 5 4 3 2 1

A catalog record for this book is available from the Library of Congress.

Discounts are available for books ordered in bulk. Special consideration is given to state bars, CLE programs, and other bar-related organizations. Inquire at Book Publishing, ABA Publishing, American Bar Association, 321 N. Clark Street, Chicago, Illinois 60654-7598.

www.ShopABA.org

# Contents

# Preface

Approximately five years ago, we began receiving requests to speak on and write about the rise of ridesharing litigation and the liability issues surrounding ridesharing companies. Although these requests continue to come in, we started to receive additional requests for consultations from practitioners regarding the increasing nuances of ridesharing litigation, ranging from jurisdictional issues for ridesharing companies, insurance coverage, novel liability theories, and the effects and impacts of changing regulations. This book serves to encapsulate and provide practitioners the information that we have been providing in seminars and articles on a much broader and thorough scale.

We hope that this book can serve as a resource to the practitioner who is examining both the liability and regulatory issues surrounding ridesharing companies. We also hope that this book can serve as a resource for those practitioners who are examining new and emerging technologies. Our goal is that this work will shed light on how some of the issues and theories that are used in the ridesharing context can be applied to cases involving other emerging business models. What has become clear in recent history is that the world and business are changing at ever increasing speed and the law must adapt to these changes. We are excited to be producing this first edition and are already looking forward to preparing a second edition as the relevant issues are given further consideration by courts throughout the nation.

This work has been a labor of love and is the product of the input and insight of many people who have our gratitude. We cannot thank our contributors, Karen Moury, Ken Germain, and Sean Owens enough. We are also truly blessed to be so supported by Reminger Co., LPA, and all the leadership who supported us in this endeavor. Our sincerest thanks is also owed to all of our law clerks who so greatly assisted with the research and preparation of these materials, including Travis Huffman, Emma Mulvaney, Megan Nelson, Courtney Pyatt, Melanie Walters, and Jason Woyce.

We hope this book serves you well, and we look forward to seeing you with the second edition.

Zachary B. Pyers
Kenton H. Steele

# Note on the Impact of COVID-19 on the Ridesharing Industry

The global impact of COVID-19 is unprecedented. COVID-19 has caused countries to lockdown, people to stay home, and businesses to create new remote working strategies that were previously believed to be impossible. Although staying home and working remotely became a new norm for many, some businesses could not adapt as easily. Ridesharing companies are a prime example, as they heavily rely on people needing transportation to and from. When people are voluntarily staying at home or are staying at home as a result of local emergency mandates, the need for ridesharing plummets. Moreover, the unique business model that ridesharing uses—having individuals provide transportation using their personal vehicles—poses difficulties for preventing the spread of COVID-19. Consequently, Uber and Lyft were forced to promptly respond to COVID-19 and its impact not only on its drivers but also on its users.

Initially Uber and Lyft responded by sending their drivers notifications regarding health and safety. Uber directed its drivers to stay at home if they felt sick and wash their hands frequently.[1] Whereas, Lyft advised their drivers to keep their cars clean and wipe down surfaces that are touched frequently, like door handles and seat belts.[2] But as the spread of COVID-19 progressed, Uber and Lyft's responses also had to evolve.

Then, in April 2020, Uber launched its "Uber Stop Moving" campaign. Through this PSA-style campaign, Uber urged

1. Alex DiPrato, *Uber, Lyft Tell Drivers to Clean Cars to Prevent Coronavirus* (Mar. 2, 2020), https://whdh.com/news/uber-lyft-tell-drivers-to-clean-cars-to-prevent-coronavirus/.
2. *Id.*

people to stay home and stop moving, if possible, in order to end COVID-19.[3] Subsequently, Uber launched a second part, "Thank You for Not Riding." In commenting on the campaign, Uber's vice president of global marketing stated: "Our message with this campaign is pretty simple: Stop Moving. We felt it was particularly relevant for a company whose brand stands for movement to reinforce this message. And we don't think you can repeat it enough."[4] Although an unprecedented move, Uber's campaign goes to show the seriousness of COVID-19 and the fact that some things are bigger than the business itself.

In May 2020, as cities reopened and things began to return to "normal," Uber and Lyft continued their fight in the COVID-19 battle. Both companies provided their drivers with access to cleaning supplies and face masks, and implemented a safety commitment, or checklist, for drivers and riders.[5] As a part of the safety procedures, the companies made wearing a face mask a requirement for drivers and riders,[6] and granted both parties the ability to cancel the ride penalty free if the face mask requirement or another safety procedure was violated.[7]

Supplementing their commitment to drivers and riders during the coronavirus outbreak, Uber and Lyft also took to supporting local communities and organizations as a whole. Lyft, for example, offered free 30-minute scooter rides for critical workers in select cities and used its LyftUp program to provide access to free rides for low-income seniors, young families, health care workers, and individuals with disabilities.[8] Likewise, Uber

---

3. Wieden + Kennedy, *Uber: Thank You for Not Riding* (Apr. 2020), https://www.wk.com/work/uber-thank-you-for-not-riding/; Uber, https://www.uber.com/us/en/coronavirus/ (last visited July 13, 2020).

4. Wieden + Kennedy, *supra* note 3.

5. Dara Khosrowshahi, *Your Second First Trip*, Uber Newsroom (May 13, 2020), https://www.uber.com/newsroom/your-second-first-trip/; *Helping Lyft's Driver Community*, COVID-19, https://www.lyft.com/safety/coronavirus/driver (last visited July 13, 2020).

6. *Id.*

7. *Id.*

8. *Supporting Critical Workers and Providing Free Scooter Rides*, Lyft Blog (April 3, 2020), https://www.lyft.com/blog/posts/LyftUp-Scooter-Critical-Workforce-Program.

pledged ten million free rides and food deliveries for frontline health care workers, seniors, and people in need around the world.[9] Additionally, these programs teamed up with organizations like United Way Worldwide, Mastercard®, Feeding America, and Save the Children, to name a few.[10] Finally, both Uber and Lyft used their drivers to help deliver and transport essential supplies, including medical supplies.[11]

It is unclear what the true impact of COVID-19 will look like years down the road. However, recent data suggests it may be detrimental to Uber and Lyft's current business models. Large cities, including San Francisco, New York City, Paris, Buenos Aires, and many more, have closed streets to most vehicle traffic to allow for social distancing and ways for people to get around without cars or public transit.[12] And, if remote work becomes a more permanent staple for companies, lessening the need for and distance of commutes, these trends may continue.

In addition to cities closing streets to implement more green space and bike lanes as means of transportation, experts foresee a jump in private vehicle use.[13] Although mass transit like subways provide an easy way for large crowds to travel quickly in the same direction, mass transit is not conducive to social distancing or other good public health practices suggested in response to the COVID-19 outbreak. Consequently, experts believe a certain number of people in large cities where mass transit was the

---

9. Uber, *Community-Recovery*, https://www.uber.com/us/en/coronavirus/community-recovery/ (last visited July 13, 2020).

10. Lyft, *LyftUp*, https://www.lyft.com/lyftup/programs (last visited July 13, 2020); Uber, *Community-Recovery*, https://www.uber.com/us/en/coronavirus/community-recovery/ (last visited July 13, 2020).

11. Uber Freight, *Moving What Matters When It Matters Most*, https://www.uber.com/us/en/freight/coronavirus/ (last visited July 13, 2020); Lyft Blog, *Supporting Our Community* (March 20, 2020), https://www.lyft.com/blog/posts/supporting-our-community.

12. Cheryl Katz, *The Pandemic Has Taken Cars Off Urban Streets. Will It Last?*, Yale School of the Environment (June 1, 2020), https://e360.yale.edu/features/the-pandemic-has-taken-cars-off-urban-streets.-will-it-last.

13. *Id.*

primary mode of transportation, pre-pandemic, will purchase private vehicles to avoid overcrowded buses or subways.[14]

Further perpetuating the idea of an increase in private vehicles is the fact that COVID-19 has caused a surge in the number of people looking to move away from urban areas where rideshare programs like Uber and Lyft are a prominent mode of transportation.[15] As rideshare programs are less likely to have a heavy presence in the suburban and rural areas in which people are looking to move, other means of transportation are necessary. If the exodus from densely populated urban centers continues, the demand for rideshare services will continue to be impacted. Therefore, Uber and Lyft may need to look at changing their current models to sustain their growth.

Predictably, Uber and Lyft have remained proactive. On March 23, 2020, Uber's CEO Dara Khosrowshahi wrote a letter to the White House and the president.[16] In this letter, Khosrowshahi outlined the steps Uber had already taken to combat COVID-19 while lobbying for the protection of rideshare and delivery drivers. He detailed how Uber was the first rideshare program to offer financial assistance for drivers and delivery people who were diagnosed with or placed in quarantine due to COVID-19, and how they were working to provide free disinfectant supplies, waiving delivery fees for over 100,000 restaurants, and regularly communicating safety tips to their customers.[17]

Khosrowshahi did not stop there. He also urged the president to include independent workers in the stimulus package and any future legislative response to COVID-19.[18] In an effort that can be described as an effort to not let a crisis go to waste,

---

14. *Id.*

15. Katelyn Newman, *Survey: Amid the Covid-19 Pandemic, Ubanites Are Eyeing the Suburbs*, U.S. News (May 6, 2020), https://www.usnews.com/news/cities/articles/2020-05-06/a-recent-survey-suggests-the-pandemic-has-urbanites-eyeing-the-suburbs.

16. Letter from Dara Khosrowshahi, CEO Uber, to Donald Trump, president of the United States of America (Mar. 23, 2020) (on file at https://blogadmin.uberinternal.com/wp-content/uploads/2020/03/UberLetter.pdf).

17. *Id.*

18. *Id.*

Uber's CEO also lobbied for the federal government to create a third classification of workers.[19] Khosrowshahi noted that while employees are provided with protections that independent contractors are not, employees do not enjoy the flexibility of independent contractors.[20] Thus, Khosrowshahi argued, the need for a third category is evident. The basis for the argument is a purported desire to ensure that independent contractors are not disproportionately affected by unforeseen circumstances like COVID-19.[21]

Days after Khosrowshahi's letter to the president, the Coronavirus Aid, Relief, and Economic Security (CARES) Act was passed. The CARES Act was a more than $2 trillion economic relief package that "provide[d] fast and direct economic assistance for American workers, families, and small business, and preserve[d] jobs for our American industries."[22] Because the CARES Act offered "unemployment assistance to self-employed individuals who traditionally have not been eligible for such benefits" "gig-economy" workers—short-term, temporary, or independent contractors for one or a variety of employers—were included.[23] The inclusion of gig economy workers in the CARES Act was a major step by the federal government in recognizing that gig economy workers are a large and growing sector of the economy.

In sum, COVID-19 has caused great uncertainty as to what the future holds, especially for rideshare programs like Uber and Lyft. Large cities are reshaping available modes of transportation, and evidence suggests people are moving from urban to suburban and rural areas, decreasing the need for rideshare programs and increasing the need for private vehicles. Despite the negative impact COVID-19 has had on Uber and Lyft, the companies have

---

19. *Id.*

20. *Id.*

21. *Id.*

22. U.S. Dep't of the Treas., *The CARES Act Works for All Americans*, https://home.treasury.gov/policy-issues/cares (last visited July 13, 2020).

23. UberLyftDrivers.com, *The CARES ACT and the Self-Employed: A Primer* (Apr. 14, 2020) https://uberlyftdrivers.com/2020/04/14/the-cares-act-and-the-self-employed-a-primer/.

both been proactive in response. Uber's CEO wrote the president lobbying for a new category of worker to provide protections not previously afforded to independent contractors. The inclusion of gig-economy workers in the CARES Act relief programs could be an initial step toward major changes to how the federal government views, and regulates, ridesharing drivers. Ultimately, the full scope of the impact of COVID-19 on the ridesharing industry is unknown. However, it is certain that this industry, like many others, will be forced to adapt to respond to the post COVID-19 world. We will continue to follow these changes and analyze how these shifts play a role in the application of legal concepts in the context of ridesharing litigation.

# About the Contributors

**Zachary B. Pyers** (editor and author) is a partner in the Columbus, Ohio, office of Reminger Co., L.P.A., and practices throughout Ohio and West Virginia. His practice focuses on complex commercial, professional liability, catastrophic tort, and class action matters. Mr. Pyers is a graduate of Ohio University (BBA management and strategic leadership and business pre-law, 2005) and Capital University Law School (JD 2008 and LLM 2009). He is a member of the American Bar Association, Federal Bar Association, Ohio State Bar Association, West Virginia Bar Association, District of Columbia Bar Association, Ohio Association of Civil Trial Attorneys (Young Lawyers Committee Chair), and the Defense Trial Counsel of West Virginia.

Mr. Pyers is also a passionate educator, having taught more than 75 CLE programs and authored over 20 articles, many focusing on ridesharing litigation and the intersection of technology with modern day tort law. In addition to the education of legal professionals, Mr. Pyers also serves as an adjunct professor at Capital University Law School where he has developed and taught several courses. He and Kenton Steele co-teach a newly developed course on ridesharing and autonomous vehicle litigation. Mr. Pyers also teaches cross-disciplinary experiential classes in depositions and expert witnesses. He teaches a course in E-discovery and advises the school's mock trial competition team.

Mr. Pyers has been recognized as a Super Lawyers Rising Star, is AV Preeminent rated by Martindale-Hubbell, is an associate fellow to the Litigation Counsel of America, and a fellow to the American Bar Foundation and the Ohio State Bar Foundation. He was awarded the Young Alumnus of the Year Award by Capital University Law School in 2016 and was awarded the Outstanding Young Lawyer for the Ohio Association of Civil Trial Attorneys in 2019.

**Kenton Steele** is an associate in the Columbus, Ohio, office of Reminger Co., L.P.A. He practices in Ohio and West Virginia. His practice is focused on personal injury and professional liability, including long-term care and medical malpractice litigation. Mr. Steele is graduate of the University of Southern Indiana (BS in philosophy 2013) and the University of Akron School of Law (JD 2017). While in law school, Mr. Steele received a certification in litigation and trial advocacy.

Mr. Steele's focus on trial advocacy has continued into his professional career. He has coached student advocates in national mock trial competitions for the University of Akron School of Law and currently works with the mock trial competition team for Capital University Law School. Additionally, Mr. Steele has presented multiple CLEs on pretrial motion practice and evidentiary issues in trials of personal injury claims. Mr. Steele and Zach Pyers co-teach a newly developed course on ridesharing and autonomous vehicle litigation at Capital University Law School.

**Karen Oill Moury** is a member in the Harrisburg, Pennsylvania, office of Eckert Seamans Cherin & Mellott, LLC. Previously, she held various staff, management, and executive level positions at the Pennsylvania Public Utility Commission (PaPUC). In one role at the PaPUC, she focused on regulation of the transportation industry. While in private practice, Ms. Moury led efforts to obtain an experimental license from the PaPUC for Raiser-PA, LLC, a subsidiary of Uber Technologies, Inc. She is a 1982 graduate of the Dickinson School of Law, Carlisle, Pennsylvania, and a 1979 graduate of Thiel College, Greenville, Pennsylvania, with a BA in political science.

**Ken Germain** has more than 45 years of varied experience in the trademark/unfair competition field and is a former full-time law professor. He focuses his practice on trademark counseling, consulting, and litigation, including early neutral evaluation. He is often retained as an expert witness on issues relating to trademarks and unfair competition, working on cases involving some of the nation's largest companies in high-stakes, cutting-edge cases. He has testified in court more than 15 times.

Mr. Germain has been an active speaker on trademark and unfair competition, lecturing at national, regional, and local conferences 300 times. In addition, in 1990 Ken founded, and until 2014 chaired, the All Ohio Annual Institute on Intellectual Property seminar. This seminar is in its 30th year, provides two-city programming (Cincinnati, Cleveland) covering all aspects of IP, and is the largest (over 250 attendees per city) full-day IP CLE program in and around Ohio.

After 15 years as a full-time professor at the University of Kentucky College of Law, Mr. Germain served as an adjunct professor at the University of Cincinnati College of Law for many years, teaching trademark/unfair competition courses. Later, Ken served as the Distinguished Professorial Practitioner in the University of Dayton Law School's Program in Law and Technology. Over the years, Ken has been honored by The Best Lawyers in America, Ohio Super Lawyers, Chambers USA, and Who's Who Legal.

**Sean Owens** is a partner at Wood Herron & Evans LLP, a full-service IP boutique located in Cincinnati, Ohio. With Ken Germain, he has previously published and lectured on potential liability for trademark owners in the sharing economy. Mr. Owens also serves as an adjunct professor at Northern Kentucky University's Chase College of Law and has previously taught at the University of Cincinnati's College of Law. He graduated from UC's College of Business in 2005 with a BBA in marketing and finance and obtained his JD from UC's College of Law in 2008.

CHAPTER ONE

# The Rise of Ridesharing

After only nine years in business, on July 24, 2018, Uber announced its company had reached a milestone—ten billion completed trips.[1] After six years, on September 18, 2018, Lyft announced its company had completed one billion rides.[2] These companies are changing the way we travel.

In 2014, there were approximately 160,000 active Uber drivers in the United States.[3] By 2019, there were more than 3,900,000 Uber drivers worldwide.[4] With more ridesharing[5] drivers on the road, the number of car accidents involving ridesharing drivers has grown. Not only are there more drivers on the road, but these ridesharing drivers are spending a significant amount of time on the road without passengers—only having passengers in the car 59 percent of time they are active on the application.[6] When a ridesharing driver is involved in an accident with no passenger

---

1. *10 Billion*, UBER (July 24, 2018), https://www.uber.com/newsroom/10-billion/.

2. *1 Billion Rides. 1 Billion Connections*, LYFT BLOG (Sept. 18, 2018), https://blog.lyft.com/posts/one-billion-rides [archive site: http://web.archive.org/web/20190102134159/https://blog.lyft.com/posts/one-billion-rides].

3. Biz Carson, *Why There's a Good Chance Your Uber Driver Is New*, BUS. INSIDER (Oct. 24, 2015), https://www.businessinsider.com/uber-doubles-its-drivers-in-2015-2015-10.

4. Mansoor Iqbal, *Uber Revenue and Usage Statistics 2019*, BUS. APPS (May 10, 2019), http://www.businessofapps.com/data/uber-statistics/ [archive site: https://web.archive.org/save/https://www.businessofapps.com/data/uber-statistics/#4].

5. Ridesharing is a term commonly used to describe companies like Uber and Lyft. Other times, these companies are referred to as Transportation Network Companies or Mobility Service Providers.

6. John M. Barrios et al., *The Cost of Convenience: Ridesharing and Traffic Fatalities* 8 (Becker Friedman Inst., Working Paper No. 49, 2019).

in the vehicle, the issues related to apportioning liability between the ridesharing company, the driver, and their respective insurers can be even more difficult to parse than if a passenger were in the vehicle at the time of the crash. These issues are becoming increasingly important as the claims arising from ridesharing crashes can be significant. According to one study, the rise of ridesharing is associated with a 3 percent rise in fatalities for both pedestrians and motor vehicle occupants.[7]

As accidents involving ridesharing drivers become more common, finding the correct way to allocate liability between drivers and ridesharing companies for injuries caused in car accidents is becoming a pressing necessity. A ridesharing company acts as an intermediary—connecting consumers with the desired goods or services—rather than keeping an inventory of its own. With this intermediary business model comes the employee or independent contractor classification battle, one that Uber was staving off prior to its initial public offering. This is evidenced by Uber's announcement of a settlement with tens of thousands of its drivers over their status the day before Uber went public with an estimated total payout of $146 million to $170 million.[8]

Defining the relationship between a rideshare driver, the parent company such as Uber or Lyft, and the insurance companies for these respective parties, will have a significant impact on who is responsible for any financial liability that stems from a crash. However, there are legal theories that could result in a ridesharing company being held directly liable for injuries caused by its driver, regardless of how the relationship between the driver and the company is defined.

Although the issues presented by ridesharing appear novel, and in many ways are unique, the litigation that arose from the introduction of taxis helps frame our approach to allocating liability. Taxi companies have experimented with different

---

7. *Id.* at 17.

8. Kelly Phillips Erb, *Worker or Independent Contractor? Uber Settles Driver Claims Before Disappointing IPO*, Forbes (May 13, 2019), https://www.forbes.com/sites/kellyphillipserb/2019/05/13/worker-or-independent-contractor-uber-settles-driver-claims-before-disappointing-ipo/#53325c703f39.

models, from traditional company-owned cars to a dispatch model with employee-owned cabs. Even in the more modern dispatch model, courts have found an employment relationship to exist, dispelling the notions of taxi drivers as independent contractors.[9] However, because ridesharing companies offer a technology platform beyond the traditional car service, it is not as simple as assuming courts will follow the paths set by prior courts addressing taxi service litigation.

## I. What Is Ridesharing?

We are now in an ever-growing "sharing economy." Companies are using technology to offer goods and services in real time. Some of the most well-known of these companies are ridesharing companies, like Uber and Lyft. Similar companies offer food delivery, home rentals as an alternative to hotels, or even freelance handyman-like labor, from cleaning to furniture assembly. These online services are becoming more common. In 2015, 72 percent of American adults used at least one shared or on-demand service.[10] Similarly, ridesharing is quickly growing in popularity. In the United States, between 2015 and 2018, the number of people who used ridesharing services more than doubled, growing from 15 percent to 36 percent.[11]

Ridesharing is a private people-to-people transportation service, where riders are connected with drivers that use their own cars. Unlike traditional taxi or car services, ridesharing exists inside a smart-phone application. To utilize ridesharing, a rider must download the application and create an account. Through the platform and the smartphone's GPS, the rider may digitally hail a car. This digital hailing offers features that traditional

---

9. Agnieszkja A. McPeak, *Regulating Ridesharing Platforms through Tort Law*, 39 HAWAII L. REV. 347, 364 (2017).

10. Aaron Smith, *Shared, Collaborative, and On Demand: The New Digital Economy*, PEW RES. CTR. (May 19, 2016), https://www.pewresearch.org/internet/2016/05/19/the-new-digital-economy/.

11. Jingjing Jiang, *More Americans Are Using Ride-Hailing Apps*, PEW RES. CTR. (Jan. 4, 2019), https://www.pewresearch.org/fact-tank/2019/01/04/more-americans-are-using-ride-hailing-apps/.

services do not. Riders may share their ride's location and status with others, allowing a friend or family member to follow along with the smartphone's GPS and the suggested route for the driver.[12] Additionally, if sharing a car, one may split the fare with other passengers through the application.[13]

This book is designed to serve as a guide to the practitioner that deals with ridesharing services, and the evolving nature of ridesharing. We will first explore the regulations that impact ridesharing companies. These regulations were often an afterthought, sometimes put in place after the ridesharing companies were already providing services in a given market. As such, we see a significantly varying regulatory landscape. This landscape can be governed by municipal or state regulations, which may vary from jurisdiction to jurisdiction, and some federal regulations. The impact these regulations have on ridesharing companies and, by extension, ligation involving ridesharing companies can be significant.

This book also explores the nuances of tort litigation involving ridesharing companies. When a ridesharing vehicle is on the road, it can find itself in several different "phases" of operation, whether there is a passenger in the vehicle, the driver is on the way to pick up a passenger, or the driver is waiting for a ride to be requested. In the event of a crash, consideration of the phase in which the accident occurred can all impact both liability for the ridesharing company and insurance coverage. Further, the long-standing dispute as to whether ridesharing drivers are independent contractors or employees will be explored. Outside the context of an employee/employer relationship, several alternative theories of liability have developed by which injured parties have sought to hold the ridesharing applications liable using various tort theories.

---

12. *5 Uber App Features You May Not Know About*, Uber (Feb. 2, 2018), https://www.uber.com/en-AU/blog/5-features/ [archive site: https://web.archive.org/web/20200228153534/https://www.uber.com/en-AU/blog/5-features/].

13. *Id.*

One of the most impactful issues related to ridesharing litigation is reaching a conclusion about the insurance coverage that may apply to an accident involving a ridesharing company, and those who drive for the company. We will discuss the insurance coverages that are available for drivers from the ridesharing companies, as well as through primary insurance providers, and the applicability of the various insurance coverages in various phases of ridesharing.

This book also provides practical guidance for litigating a ridesharing case. This includes issues attorneys should consider from the outset of a case, such as issuing effective evidence preservation letters. It also provides examples of effective complaints for different types of claims and a framework for discovery requests to obtain the information needed to prepare a ridesharing case for trial. These materials and discussions will provide attorneys who are new to addressing ridesharing cases with a firm understanding of the unique issues. For attorneys who have previously addressed ridesharing cases, these materials may provide some additional insights to make their practices more effective.

Finally, one of the biggest issues facing ridesharing companies is the ever-increasing drive to utilize and deploy autonomous vehicles. In seeking to use autonomous vehicles, ridesharing companies hope to someday eliminate human drivers and their associated costs, thereby driving up revenues. Some have proposed that a switch to "robot" drivers would also increase safety. However, the use of autonomous vehicles on the road, whether by ridesharing companies or individuals, has created more questions than answers. As regulators have been left to scramble to address autonomous vehicles, several theories and potential solutions addressing liability issues have been raised. We will explore various outcomes of potential liability theories as if they were adopted.

CHAPTER TWO

# The Regulatory Landscape of Transportation Network Companies (TNCs)

## I. Introduction

Transportation network companies (TNCs), or ridesharing companies, first started operating in the United States in early 2011.[14] TNCs use a digital network or application (app) to match drivers using personal vehicles with members of the public who need transportation services. For more than a century, state and local governments throughout the country have regulated "common carriers"—companies providing transportation services to the public for compensation.[15]

To many regulators, TNCs initially looked like common carriers, which are often subject to myriad state laws and sometimes burdensome rules. Incumbent common carriers—taxicab companies—were particularly vocal in their opposition to the entry of TNCs. A persistent theme was that the TNCs had not endured the arduous vetting process nor demonstrated compliance with

14. In the regulatory arena, most state laws refer to the companies as TNCs rather than ridesharing companies. One reason for this is that in some jurisdictions, "ridesharing" connotes a different meaning such as carpooling or employer-provided transportation and, as such, is already exempt from regulation. *See, e.g.*, 66 Pa. Cons. Stat. § 2602 (2019). In other circumstances, the terms "ridesharing company" and "TNC" are interchangeable. However, because of the prevalence of the term TNC in regulations, this chapter will use the language of the regulations.

15. *See, e.g.*, 66 Pa. Cons. Stat. § 102 (definition of common carrier by motor vehicle) (2019).

the safety and other regulatory requirements that taxicab companies must adhere to.

TNCs generally resisted the notion that they were common carriers, claiming that they were not providing transportation but rather were technology companies connecting drivers and passengers.[16] Some TNCs also contended that since they were only accepting donations from the public, they were not receiving "compensation," and therefore were not common carriers. TNCs further pointed to the many steps they were taking to provide safe, reliable, and affordable service, arguing that regulation by the market is sufficient. Their theory was that if they did not deliver services in the manner demanded by the riding public, they would fail as businesses.

The difficulty with trying to regulate TNCs under traditional laws governing common carriers is that their business model does not fit neatly into that framework. The principal areas where TNCs operate differently than common carriers are in vehicle ownership, control over drivers, and charging fares. When TNCs first entered markets across the country, these notions that set them apart from common carriers were challenging for regulators to accept. For decades, regulators have been holding taxicab companies responsible to ensure the safety of the vehicles being used to serve the public. However, since the TNCs do not typically own or lease the vehicles that drivers are operating on their platforms, regulators were challenged to find a way to ensure that the vehicles were safe. Similarly, regulators have traditionally required common carriers to directly oversee the operations of the drivers. Yet, after vetting the drivers' criminal backgrounds and driver histories, TNCs generally take a hands-off approach, unless consumers complain or incidents involving drivers occur that cause them to take action. In the area of fares, regulators have often required taxicab companies to obtain agency approval for the rates that are charged to consumers and publish them in tariffs. By contrast, TNCs use basic principles of supply and demand in setting their prices.

16. *See infra* Chapter 3, Section IV.B.

TNCs were often not willing to wait for legislators and regulators to catch up to technology. Instead, they entered many jurisdictions without licenses or permits, facing cease and desist orders, the threat of civil penalties, and more. Especially in areas where taxicabs were not accessible or reliable, the public got a taste of how convenient it is to use TNC services. People needing transportation quickly learned that if they downloaded an application on their smartphones, entered their payment information, and indicated where they needed to be driven, a driver usually arrived within minutes and took them to their destinations in cashless transactions. While the passenger waited for the driver to arrive, he or she received information about how far away the driver was and approximately when the driver would arrive. Passengers no longer had to stand outside in inclement weather attempting to hail a taxicab or wait for a dispatched taxicab to arrive, having no idea when that would happen.

Naturally, when regulators began to take steps to ban TNCs, to demand compliance with archaic rules designed for taxicabs, or to threaten their continued ability to operate effectively, the public responded. Consumers demanded access to the services being offered by TNCs. Regulators responded to the public demand. Recognizing that the TNC business model does not neatly fit into the traditional regulatory framework for common carriers, regulators developed TNC-specific rules. They also found ways, such as through provisional or temporary authority, to permit TNCs to operate legally while awaiting passage of new legislation.

## II. Early Focus of Regulators

Regulators initially focused on three primary areas—vehicle safety, driver integrity, and insurance.[17] This section uses

---

17. *See, e.g.*, PUB. UTIL. COMMISSION CAL., ORDER INSTITUTING RULEMAKING ON REGULATIONS RELATING TO PASSENGER CARRIERS, RIDESHARING, AND NEW ONLINE-ENABLED TRANSPORTATION SERVICES, RULEMAKING 12-12-011 (2013) [hereinafter CAL. 2013 ORDER], http://docs.cpuc.ca.gov/PublishedDocs/Published/G000/M076/K998/76998666.PDF; PA. PUB. UTIL. COMMISSION, APPLICATION OF RASIER-PA LLC, A WHOLLY OWNED SUBSIDIARY OF UBER TECHNOLOGIES, INC., FOR EMERGENCY TEMPORARY AUTHORITY TO OPERATE AN EXPERIMENTAL RIDE-SHARING NETWORK SERVICE BETWEEN POINTS IN

examples from California and Pennsylvania to discuss the processes that were followed, the priorities of the regulators, and how they struck a balance between protecting the public and allowing technology-driven TNCs to enter their markets. Both agencies determined that TNCs were operating as "common carriers" but devised TNC-specific rules for them to follow, recognizing that the traditional rules applicable to common carriers were not feasible to impose on TNCs.

On the common carrier issue, the California Public Utility Commission (CA PUC) rejected the concept that TNCs were merely an application on a smart phone or technology platform, explaining that TNCs perform essentially the same function as a common carrier's dispatch office.[18] The agency said that TNCs do not fit neatly into the conventional understandings of either taxis or limousines but "that does not mean that this Commission's responsibility to public safety in the transportation industry should be ignored and/or left for individual companies or the market place to control."[19]

The CA PUC also dismissed arguments by TNCs that payment is voluntary and therefore the transportation is not being provided for "compensation." Even if transportation was free, the CA PUC determined that the organization receives a business benefit. It does not matter whether money is received in consideration for the transportation; it is enough that the company receives an economic benefit. The economic benefit identified by the CA PUC is that each ridesharing company was receiving "increased patronage with the growth of their businesses."[20] Also, a donation can be considered a form of compensation.[21]

Similarly, the Pennsylvania Public Utility Commission (PA PUC) found that it had jurisdiction over TNC services. In doing so, the PA PUC explained that the innovative technology

---

ALLEGHENY COUNTY, PA PUC DOCKET NO. A-2014-2429993 at 12 (2014) [hereinafter PA. JULY 2014 ORDER], http://www.puc.pa.gov/pcdocs/1299363.doc.

18. CAL. 2013 ORDER at 12.

19. *Id.*

20. *Id.* at 19.

21. *Id.* at 20.

incorporated into the service does not change the fundamental nature of the service—transportation for compensation.[22] The PA PUC also declined to exempt a TNC from its jurisdiction based on the receipt of only donations.[23]

## A. California

Following the initiation of a rulemaking, the receipt of comments, and the scheduling of workshops, California was the first jurisdiction to regulate TNC services by adopting regulations in September 2013.[24] It was the CA PUC that coined the term "transportation network companies."[25]

Noting its awareness that TNCs are a nascent industry, the CA PUC emphasized that innovation does not "alter the Commission's obligation to protect public safety, especially where, as here, the core service being provided—passenger transportation on public roadways—has safety impacts for third parties and property."[26] The CA PUC expressed confidence in its "ability to protect public safety in the face of rapid technological change."[27] The CA PUC further explained that the purpose of the rulemaking was "not to stifle innovation and the provision of new services that consumers want, but rather to assess public safety risks, and to ensure that the safety of the public is not compromised in the operation of these business models."[28]

The CA PUC stated that "[r]egulatory bodies must always look to update their rules and regulations in order to keep pace with time and technology." The Commission sought to strike the "proper balance between safety and innovation, so that

---

22. Pa. July 2014 Order at 11.

23. Petition of Bureau of Investigation and Enforcement for Cease and Desist Order Against Lyft, Inc., pa puc docket no. p-2014-2426847 (2014) at 17–18.

24. Ken Yeung, *California Becomes First State to Regulate Ride-Sharing Services, Benefiting Uber, Lyft, Sidecar, and Instantcab*, Next Web (Sept. 19, 2013), https://thenextweb.com/insider/2013/09/19/california-becomes-first-state-to-regulate-ride-sharing-services/.

25. Cal. 2013 Order at 2.

26. *Id.* at 3.

27. *Id.*

28. *Id.* at 7.

regulation provides a safety net that the public can rely on for its protection while new businesses innovate and use technology to better the lives of Californians."[29]

Under the CA PUC regulations, the TNCs had to obtain a permit, perform criminal background checks, and conduct driving record reviews. They further had to require drivers to be at least 21, possess a valid driver's license, and successfully pass a TNC-developed training program. Each TNC was obligated to set up and adhere to a zero tolerance policy on drugs and alcohol. Insurance coverage of no less than $1 million per incident was mandatory.[30] The agency further required the digital network to contain a picture of the driver and vehicle, and the license plate number. In addition, the TNC was required to inspect the driver's vehicle or have it inspected at a licensed facility to verify that the vehicles passed a 19-point inspection.[31] TNCs were obligated to allow passengers to indicate whether they require a wheelchair-accessible vehicle.[32] The CA PUC also required the TNC vehicles to display consistent trade dress.[33]

The early emphasis by the CA PUC on driver integrity, vehicle safety, and adequate insurance carried through to its statewide legislation. It also became a model for other jurisdictions to follow in establishing the requirements that would be applicable to TNCs.

## B. Pennsylvania

In Pennsylvania, the PA PUC embraced the entry of TNCs, recognizing the substantial benefits to be derived from the initiation of a competitive service.[34] Referring to the services as allowing for a "wider-ranging, faster and more user-friendly scheduling of transportation services," the agency committed to ensuring

29. *Id.* at 62.
30. *Id.* at 40.
31. *Id.* at 28.
32. *Id.* at 30.
33. *Id.* at 31.
34. PA. JULY 2014 ORDER at 10.

that "its current regulatory structure is not a barrier to technological advances and desirable changes in the transportation industry."[35]

Due to an existing classification in its passenger transportation regulations for "experimental service," the PA PUC was able to forego the initiation of a rulemaking.[36] Instead, it devised temporary rules that would apply to TNCs, pending the passage of legislation, through orders addressing the TNCs' applications to offer experimental service.[37] In July 2014, the PA PUC approved the applications of Lyft and Uber for emergency temporary authority while their applications for two-year experimental service authority were pending.[38] In December 2014, the PA PUC conditionally approved the applications of Uber and Lyft for two-year experimental service authority.[39] While the orders generally focused on the same issues, the orders granting two-year experimental service authority also required the TNCs to submit compliance plans addressing a number of areas, including insurance, driver integrity, vehicle safety and recordkeeping, and reports and audits.[40]

Similar to the CA PUC, the PA PUC emphasized that in an era of rapid technological advances, it must be "mindful that its traditional regulatory framework should be interpreted with reasonable flexibility to account for changes in technology and to accommodate a more competitive environment and its attendant

---

35. *Id.* at 12.

36. 52 Pa. Code § 29.352.

37. *See, e.g.*, Pa. Pub. Util. Commission, Application of Rasier-PA LLC, A Wholly Owned Subsidiary of Uber Technologies, Inc., For Right to Transport, by Motor Vehicle, Persons in Experimental Service of Shared-Ride Network Service, pa puc docket no. A-2014-2424608 (2014) [hereinafter Pa. December 2014 Order], http://www.puc.pa.gov/pcdocs/1330208.docx.

38. Pa. July 2014 Order.

39. *See also* Pa. Pub. Util. Commission, Application of Lyft, Inc, For Right to Transport, by Motor Vehicle, Persons in Experimental Service of Shared-Ride Network Service, pa puc docket no. A-2014-2415045 (2014), http://www.puc.state.pa.us/pcdocs/1333203.docx.

40. Pa. December 2014 Order, Appendix A.

public benefits."[41] However, the regulator stressed that in making room for these changes, it "must also keep in mind its statutory obligation to protect the safety of the traveling public" and "cannot compromise in requiring compliance with reasonable driver integrity, vehicle safety, and insurance requirements."[42]

In their applications, the TNCs presented proposals that reflected their existing practices for ensuring safety of the vehicles and integrity of the drivers, which the agency found to be generally acceptable. The PA PUC determined that annual inspection requirements, coupled with a rule to use vehicles that are not more than ten years old, were sufficient to ensure vehicle safety. Similarly, the agency was satisfied with the TNCs' plans for driver integrity, which included four important components: (i) conduct criminal background checks and disqualify individuals convicted of specific crimes from driving on the platform; (ii) review driving history records and disqualify individuals convicted of specific moving violations from driving on the platform; (iii) require drivers to meet minimum age requirements and possess a current, valid driver's license; and (iv) establish and follow a zero tolerance policy on the use of drugs or alcohol.[43]

With respect to insurance, this is the area where the PA PUC and TNCs had a larger gap to bridge. Some TNCs proposed to provide only contingent coverage and to primarily rely on the driver's own personal insurance during the stage when the driver opens the app and is soliciting rides. However, the agency saw the driver as already being on the "clock" and determined that the TNC's insurance must be primary during that time.[44] This issue continued to be litigated in Pennsylvania until the general assembly enacted legislation, resolving it in favor of the regulator.[45]

---

41. Pa. July 2014 Order at 12.

42. *Id.*

43. Pa. December 2014 Order at 30–32, 35–37.

44. Pa. July 2014 Order at 17–18.

45. 66 Pa. Cons. Stat. § 2603.1(a)(2) (2019). Note that under Pennsylvania's statewide legislation, the PA PUC regulates all TNC services in

The PA PUC accepted the TNC's proposal for the driver's insurance to be primary if the driver was operating the vehicle for personal reasons and the app was not turned on. However, the agency imposed a requirement on the TNC to direct drivers to notify their insurer, in writing, of their intent to drive on the platform.[46] One TNC sought a modification of this requirement in the PA PUC order, describing it as unduly burdensome and unnecessary.[47] Ultimately, through legislation, this issue was also resolved in favor of the regulator.[48]

Three areas where the PA PUC was more flexible than in the past include a showing of "public need" for the proposed service, approval of rates, and ownership or control of the vehicles. The agency had traditionally required common carriers to show a public need for the proposed service. Applicants typically presented supporting statements of witnesses for each portion of the Commonwealth they wished to serve. However, for TNCs, the agency accepted sample and anecdotal evidence as sufficient to show public demand for the proposed service.[49]

Similarly, the regulator had always required common carriers to submit proposed rates for review and approval. Nonetheless, the PA PUC accepted a TNC's proposal to explain its pricing methodology and offer customers an estimate in advance, upon request, in lieu of fixed rates "in view of the competitive nature of the TNC market."[50] However, it required the TNC to submit

---

Pennsylvania except those provided in Philadelphia, which are under the domain of the Philadelphia Parking Authority. This format follows the framework that was already in place for taxicabs and limousines. Importantly, both agencies administer statewide laws that are nearly identical. *See* 53 PA. CONS. STAT. §§ 57A01–57A22 (2019).

46. PA. JULY 2014 ORDER at 18.

47. PA. PUB. UTIL. COMMISSION, PETITION FOR MODIFICATION: APPLICATION OF RASIER-PA LLC, A WHOLLY OWNED SUBSIDIARY OF UBER TECHNOLOGIES, INC., FOR EMERGENCY TEMPORARY AUTHORITY TO OPERATE AN EXPERIMENTAL RIDE-SHARING NETWORK SERVICE BETWEEN POINTS IN ALLEGHENY COUNTY, PA (2014), http://www.puc.pa.gov/pcdocs/1317377.pdf.

48. 66 PA. CONS. STAT. § 2603.2(b)(6)(i) (2019).

49. PA. DECEMBER 2014 ORDER at 12–14, 21–26.

50. PA. JULY 2014 ORDER at 21.

a tariff describing the basic means by which rates will be determined. The PA PUC also mandated that the receipt contain a notice to the customer of the agency's telephone number and website to be used to lodge a complaint.[51]

As to ownership of the vehicles, the regulator had long required a structure in which the transportation company owns or otherwise controls the vehicles. The purpose of this requirement was to ensure accountability for the vehicle safety. However, the agency recognized that this structure would not work for the TNCs and waived its regulations. In doing so, the PA PUC stressed that it was still holding TNCs accountable for the safety of the vehicles operated on their platforms, and that by waiving the vehicle ownership/lease requirement, it was "able to make room for a new and innovative service, while still ensuring the safety of the passenger using this service."[52]

## III. Statutory Requirements Applicable to Transportation Network Companies

### A. Overview

Since the onset of TNC services when regulators were scrambling to devise rules under which TNCs could operate legally and safely in their jurisdictions, most states have passed statewide legislation that has clarified and expanded the applicable requirements. Through legislation, states have typically carved TNCs out of the definition of common carrier and created a new classification for this novel service, along with a set of standards developed for TNCs. Even the states that include TNCs in the common carrier category have generally exempted TNCs from complying with the laws applicable to common carriers that do not fit their business model.

The statutory requirements are frequently the product of negotiations among various stakeholders, often including the TNCs, the taxicab industry, the insurance industry, and the regulators. Similar to the early focus of regulators, the key requirements the states have imposed on TNCs through legislation

51. *Id.*
52. *Id.* at 16.

relate to driver integrity, vehicle safety, and insurance. Particularly in jurisdictions where local government regulates transportation services, the passage of statewide legislation has been helpful in ensuring that TNCs are required to follow a uniform set of rules. Despite the focus on these areas, state laws address a host of other issues, including accessibility and nondiscrimination, privacy of customer information, overall operations, customer service, and placards.

The negotiation process is evident through the many similarities, as well as the differences, in the laws that legislatures have passed throughout the country. While TNCs were successful in negotiating minimal regulatory requirements in some states, it appears that in other states they had to agree to more onerous provisions in order to get the laws enacted. Areas that differ widely across the states relate to recordkeeping by the TNCs, inspections and audits by regulators, and the production of documents or reports by the TNCs. Yet, even in those areas, a common theme throughout the statewide laws is that any information that TNCs share with regulators is confidential and often expressly exempted from disclosure under state laws governing the right to know or freedom of information.

Whereas California was the first state to recognize and develop rules for TNCs,[53] Colorado was the first state to enact legislation.[54] The District of Columbia was also an early adopter.[55] As of the writing of this book, the only state that has not passed statewide legislation is Oregon where TNCs continue to be regulated exclusively at the local level.[56] Four other states—Hawaii, Louisiana, Minnesota, and Washington—have

53. Yeung, *supra* note 24.

54. *See* Colo. Rev. Stat. §§ 40-10.1-601–608 (2020); Patrick Hoge, *Colorado Becomes First State to Pass Law Embracing Uber, Lyft et al.* (June 6, 2014, 7:47 AM), https://www.bizjournals.com/sanfrancisco/morning_call/2014/06/colorado-uber-lyft.html (last visited Apr. 5, 2020).

55. *See* DC Code Ann. § 50-301.29a (2020); Sean Slone, *State Regulation of Rideshare Companies*, Council St. Gov't (Apr. 14, 2016), https://knowledgecenter.csg.org/kc/content/state-regulation-rideshare-companies.

56. Dirk VanderHart, *Proposal to Regulate Uber, Lyft Spurs Debate in Oregon Capitol* (Mar. 18, 2019, 2:31 PM), https://www.opb.org/news/article/uber-lyft-oregon-capitol-debate/ (last visited Apr. 5, 2020).

passed legislation that addresses only insurance requirements while establishing no other statewide requirements for TNCs to follow.[57] Any other regulation of TNCs in those states is left to local government.[58]

The regulations applicable to TNCs throughout the United States have many similarities but also follow many different frameworks. This discussion is intended to offer the reader a description of the types of requirements that statewide laws impose on TNCs. It is not designed to present a comprehensive summary of all jurisdictions but rather to identify the standard rules that many or most states impose on TNCs. It also highlights some less common rules that state laws mandate, whether more or less onerous for the TNCs to follow. Notably, the regulatory landscape involving TNCs is rapidly evolving, and citations to statutory provisions and regulations are only accurate as of the writing of this book. Also, many state agencies have promulgated regulations imposing additional standards on TNCs on issues where statutes are silent. This book focuses primarily on state legislation. Prudent practitioners should consult the laws of their jurisdictions for the most up-to-date information.

## B. Common Terminology

Statewide legislation across the country generally uses the same or very similar terminology in describing the services offered by TNCs. For example, the laws typically define transportation network service as matching a passenger and TNC driver through a digital network in advance of a prearranged ride.[59] Legislation commonly defines TNC driver as a person who receives connections to potential passengers from a TNC in exchange for a fee and uses a personal vehicle to provide a prearranged ride upon connection through a digital network.[60] Digital network is normally defined as any online-enabled application, software,

---

57. Haw. Rev. Stat. § 431:10C-703 (2020); La. Rev. Stat. § 45:201 (2020); Minn. Stat. § 65B.472 (2020); Wash. Rev. Code § 48.177 (2020).

58. *See, e.g.*, Wash. Rev. Code § 46.72.160 (2020).

59. *See* 66 Pa. Cons. Stat. § 102 (definitions) (2019).

60. *See id.*

website, or system utilized by a TNC that enables the prearrangement of rides with TNC drivers.[61] The standard definition of a prearranged ride is one that begins when a TNC driver accepts a ride requested by a passenger through a digital network, continuing while the driver transports the passenger, and ending when the last passenger departs from the personal vehicle.[62]

The vast majority of states exclude TNCs from the definition of common carrier or a for-hire transportation service. Examples of such states include New Mexico and Tennessee.[63] States that place TNCs within the definition of common carrier are Maryland and Washington.[64] In the District of Columbia, the law refers to TNCs as "private vehicle-for-hire" companies.[65] Many state laws, including Arkansas, expressly exempt TNCs from commercial vehicle registration requirements.[66]

## C. Oversight of Transportation Network Companies

### 1. Statewide Regulation

At the state level, legislation designates different types of administrative agencies as the regulator. Often, it is the state's department of transportation or the public utilities commission. Other agencies with this authority include secretaries of state, departments of insurance, departments of revenue, professional licensing bureaus, public safety agencies, commerce or economic development departments, consumer affairs or protection agencies, and corporation commissions.

Although some states do not have a requirement for licensure, a typical model is for the state to require TNCs to obtain a permit or license from the regulatory agency before operating.[67] Various approaches exist among the states, but a common

61. *See id.*

62. *See id.*

63. N.M. Stat. Ann. § 65-7-3 (2020); Tenn. Code Ann. § 65-15-301(4) (2020).

64. Md. Code Ann., Pub. Util. §§ 10101, 103 (2020); Wash. Rev. Code § 48.177.005 (2020).

65. D.C. Code § 50-301.29a (2020).

66. Ark. Code Ann. § 23-13-703 (2020).

67. *See, e.g.*, 66 Pa. Cons. Stat. § 2604 (2019).

practice is for the law to require annual fees for permits, with the fee amounts varying widely. For example, Colorado assesses an annual permit fee of $111,250,[68] while New Jersey requires a $25,000 annual permit fee,[69] Arkansas imposes a $15,000 annual fee,[70] and Maine charges a $10,000 annual permit fee.[71] Other annual permit fees are $5,000, which are charged by several states, including North Carolina and Mississippi.[72] On the other end of the spectrum is New Hampshire with a $500 annual fee[73] and Pennsylvania with a nominal initial filing fee of $350 and no annual renewal requirement.[74]

Some states do not specify the amounts. For instance, Rhode Island's annual renewal fee varies from $5,000 to $30,000, depending on the number of drivers operating on the TNC's platform.[75] A few state laws, such as Texas and Utah, are silent on the amount of the permit fee, leaving that to the regulator.[76] In Nebraska, the TNC may choose to pay either an annual fee of $25,000 or a fee to be determined by the regulator in an amount not to exceed $80 per vehicle.[77] Under Michigan law, the fee depends on the number of vehicles that are registered, following the same process that is required for limousines and taxicabs.[78]

## 2. Funding

A primary reason for the wide variation in permit fees among the jurisdictions is that various approaches exist for funding the oversight of TNCs. Some states fund the administration and enforcement of the TNC operations through annual permit

---

68. Colo. Rev. Stat. § 40-10.1-606 (2020).

69. N.J. Stat. Ann. § 39.5H-4 (2020).

70. Ark. Code Ann. § 23-13-704 (2020).

71. Me. Stat. tit. 29-A, § 1672 (2020).

72. N.C. Gen. Stat. § 2-280.3 (2020); Miss. Code Ann. § 77-8-5 (2020).

73. N.H. Rev. Stat. Ann. § 376-A:3 (2020).

74. 66 Pa. Cons. Stat. § 2604; act 164 of 2016—Implementation of Chapter 26, pa puc docket no. l-2016-2574379, Appendix A (2016).

75. 39 R.I. Gen. Laws § 39-14.2-5 (2020).

76. Tex. Occ. Code Ann. § 2402.052 (West 2020); Utah Code Ann. § 13-51-104 (West 2015).

77. Neb. Rev. Stat. § 75-305 (2020).

78. Mich. Comp. Laws § 257.2104 (2020).

fees. For instance, the express purpose of these fees in Colorado, Michigan, and Nebraska is to cover the regulator's cost of TNC oversight.[79]

By contrast, Pennsylvania law funds the regulation of TNCs by the imposition of an annual regulatory assessment on the TNC, which is based on the TNCs' gross operating revenues.[80] In Alabama, the regulator's costs are recovered through assessment fees charged by the TNC equal to 1 percent of the gross trip fare.[81] Under Connecticut law, each TNC pays a 30-cent fee for each ride to fund the regulator's operations.[82] New Hampshire law imposes a 50-cent surcharge on every ride to cover the costs of the regulator, but allows the TNC to impose only half of that amount on the rider.[83] Other states, including Delaware, use monies collected through the imposition of civil penalties to enforce the legal requirements.[84] The law in New Mexico establishes a fund that consists of fees, fines, gifts, grants, and donations, which may be used by the regulator to cover the costs of administration and enforcement.[85]

### 3. Local Regulation

A common approach throughout the United States is for statewide legislation to declare that it is the controlling authority and to prohibit local government from imposing additional burdens, such as charging fees or requiring licenses, on TNCs. Examples of states that have gone this route include Delaware, Idaho, and New Hampshire.[86] However, many of the states that generally ban local regulation permit airports to impose reasonable tolls and fees. This is the approach followed in Michigan, Florida, and

---

79. Colo. Rev. Stat. § 40-10.1-607 (2020); Mich. Comp. Laws § 257.2104 (2020); Neb. Rev. Stat. § 75-331 (2020).
80. 66 Pa. Cons. Stat. § 2610 (2019).
81. Ala. Code § 32-7C-23 (2020).
82. Conn. Gen. Stat. Ann. § 13b-121 (2020).
83. N.H. Rev. Stat. Ann. § 376-A:3 (2020).
84. Del. Code Ann. § 1921 (2020).
85. N.M. Stat. Ann. § 65-7-19 (2020).
86. Del. Code Ann. § 1922 (2020); Idaho Code § 49-3715 (2020); N.H. Rev. Stat. Ann. § 376-A:17 (2020).

North Carolina.[87] Some states also allow airports to impose reasonable rules (in addition to fees), such as Ohio, Rhode Island, and Texas.[88] The Ohio law specifies that the statewide legislation is controlling, and the Texas statute provides that the airports' regulations cannot conflict with the state law. In Maine, airports may impose rules on TNCs, but they have to be consistent with the treatment of taxicabs.[89]

West Virginia is among the states that declare state law as being the controlling authority. However, while making it clear that local government cannot regulate TNCs in any way, West Virginia's law contains a comprehensive list of items that local government is prohibited from and not prohibited from doing. For example, the West Virginia law expressly prohibits local government from imposing an excise tax, sales tax, use tax, business and occupation tax, or any other tax or fee on TNCs or drivers, or to require a license for a TNC, a TNC driver, or the driver's personal vehicle. It also bans the imposition of any tax on the consumer related to the prearranged trip.[90]

The West Virginia law further clarifies that these prohibitions are not intended to affect (i) the imposition of a property tax on the personal property of a TNC or driver; (ii) the imposition of a state corporation or personal net income tax on the TNC or driver; (iii) the imposition of a motor fuel excise tax on fuel purchased by a TNC or driver; (iv) the requirement that TNCs and drivers obtain a business registration certificate; or (v) the application of state laws with respect to the licensure of drivers and registration of vehicles.[91]

By contrast, some state laws permit local government to regulate or ban TNCs. For example, in Alabama, TNCs are governed exclusively by state law, but municipalities can pass an

---

87. Mich. Comp. Laws § 257.2116 (2020); Fla. Stat. § 627.748 (15) (2020); N.C. Gen. Stat. § 2-280.9 (2020).

88. Ohio Rev. Code Ann. § 4925.09 (2020); 39 R.I. Gen. Laws § 39-14.2-18 (2020); Tex. Occ. Code Ann. § 2402.003 (West 2020).

89. Me. Stat. tit. 29-A, § 1677 (2020).

90. W. Va. Code § 17-29-19(a)–(d) (2020).

91. *Id.* § 17-29-19(e).

ordinance prohibiting TNCs from operating within their boundaries.[92] In New York, every county and any city with a population of 100,000 may ban TNCs. An exception to that rule is that a county containing a city with a population of 100,000 or more may only ban outside the boundaries of the city. The county or city banning TNCs must notify the Department of Motor Vehicles, which maintains a list on its website. Notably, this ability of local government in New York to ban TNCs does not apply to a city with a population of one million or more.[93] Under Nevada law, local governments can require TNCs to obtain a business license or pay a fee.[94] In South Dakota, the law provides that nothing limits further regulation of TNCs by local government except that they may not enact further regulations relating to insurance requirements.[95]

The Washington law includes TNCs in the category of "for hire vehicles," which cities, counties, and port districts may license, control, and regulate.[96] The oversight by local government includes regulating entry, requiring a license, controlling rates, regulating routes, establishing safety and equipment standards, and any other requirements to ensure safe and reliable for hire vehicle transportation service.[97]

## D. Driver Integrity

### 1. Zero Tolerance Policy on Use of Alcohol or Drugs

An almost universal requirement across the country is that TNCs must adopt and enforce zero tolerance policies on the use of drugs and alcohol while a TNC driver is logged onto the platform. The typical provisions call for the immediate suspension of a driver who is the subject of a reasonable passenger complaint alleging a violation of the zero tolerance policy. The suspension must continue until the complaint investigation is complete.

---

92. Ala. Code § 32-7C-36 (2020).
93. N.Y. Veh. & Traf. Law § 1700 (McKinney 2020).
94. Nev. Rev. Stat. Ann. § 706A.310 (2020).
95. S.D. Codified Laws § 32-10-23 (2020).
96. Wash. Rev. Code § 48.177.010 (2020).
97. *Id.* § 46.72.160.

Most laws require the TNC to post notice of this policy on its website and to provide procedures for reporting a complaint about a driver with whom the passenger was matched and whom the passenger reasonably suspects was under the influence of drugs or alcohol during the course of the ride.[98]

### 2. Criminal Background Checks

Nearly all jurisdictions require TNCs to conduct or have a third party conduct a criminal background check before permitting drivers to operate on the platform and to disqualify individuals who have been convicted of certain crimes.[99] Going further than most states, Massachusetts requires a two-part background check, whereby the TNC completes a background check and is then required to obtain the driver's consent for a background check to be performed by the Transportation Network Company Division of the Department of Public Utilities (MA DPU).[100] The two-part background check involves the submission by the TNC to the MA DPU a driver roster, which, for each driver, includes first name, middle name, last name, former names, address, city and state of birth, driver's license number, driver's license state, date of birth, last six digits of Social Security number, electronic mail address, and the driver's consent. New Jersey's process involves the Office of the Attorney General in the criminal background review.[101]

State laws that require criminal background checks universally prohibit individuals who appear on the U.S. Department of Justice National Sex Offender Registry from being TNC drivers.[102] As to other crimes, a common approach among states is to disqualify persons who have been convicted of or plead guilty to designated felonies, violent crimes, acts of terrorism, crimes involving property damage, theft, and sex offenses over the past

98. 66 Pa. Cons. Stat. § 2604.1(b)(4) (2019); D.C. Code § 50-301.29a(9) (2020).

99. *See* Vt. Stat. Ann. tit. 23, § 751(b) (2020).

100. 220 Mass. Code Regs. § 274.06 (2020).

101. N.J. Stat. Ann. § 39:5H-17 (2020).

102. *See, e.g.*, Ark. Code Ann. § 23-13-713(b) (2020).

seven years.[103] In addition to these types of crimes, the District of Columbia law also disqualifies individuals who have been convicted within the past seven years of aggravated reckless driving, fleeing law enforcement in a vehicle, leaving after a collision, negligent homicide, driving under the influence of alcohol or drugs, and unauthorized use of a motor vehicle.[104] Another common approach is to look back ten years for violent crimes or sexual offenses while requiring a seven-year look back for theft, fraud, and drug offenses.[105] A variation on the time frame for review is five years for certain types of criminal convictions.[106]

Several states forever disqualify individuals who have been convicted of specific crimes. For example, Kentucky bars persons who have been convicted of Class A or Class B felonies or a sex crime, as well as leaving the scene of a traffic accident, causing a fatality through negligent operation of a vehicle, and using a vehicle in the commission of a felony involving the manufacture or distribution of a controlled substance.[107] Also, in Delaware, a person may not be a TNC driver if he or she has ever been convicted of certain violent felonies, any crime against a child, any felony sexual offense, and any felony homicide.[108] Similarly, in Kansas, the law permanently bars individuals who have been convicted of designated felonies, any sex offense, or identity theft from operating on the digital network.[109] Under Nebraska law, individuals who have been convicted of, or plead guilty or nolo contendre to, any offense involving fraud, use of a motor vehicle to commit a felony, a felony crime involving property damage, theft, acts of violence, or acts of terror are barred from being TNC drivers.[110] In New Jersey, a driver can overcome the

---

103. *See* Ohio Rev. Code Ann. § 4925.04 (2020).

104. D.C. Code § 50-301.29b(c) (2020).

105. 66 Pa. Cons. Stat. § 2604.1(b)(5) (2019); 220 Mass. Code Regs. § 274.21 (2020).

106. Fla. Stat. § 627.748(11)(f) (2020); Mich. Comp. Laws § 257.2107(2)(b) (2020), Mo. Rev. Stat. § 387.420(2)(b) (2020).

107. Ky. Rev. Stat. Ann. § 281.6301 (2020).

108. Del. Code Ann. § 1913(b) (2020).

109. Kan. Stat. Ann. § 8-2720 (2020).

110. Neb. Rev. Stat. § 75-325 (2020).

disqualification for certain crimes if he or she produces a valid certificate of rehabilitation.[111]

Massachusetts is another example of a state that permanently disqualifies individuals for numerous prior convictions, felony robbery, multiple driving offenses, serious bodily injury offenses, sexual conduct and abuse offenses, or any violent crime punishable by ten or more years in state prison. Further, the Massachusetts law sets forth a comprehensive list showing each crime that bars a person from driving on a TNC's platform for seven years. Also, the law in Massachusetts permits an individual to be disqualified if reliable information demonstrates that providing TNC services is not consistent with the public interest.[112]

### 3. Driver History Records

Most states also mandate TNCs to perform reviews of driver history records before allowing individuals to become drivers. Typically, these reviews consider three years of records and disqualify persons who have been found guilty of more than three moving violations or a major moving violation during that period.[113] Examples of major moving violations include fleeing or attempting to elude a law enforcement officer, reckless driving, and driving with a suspended or revoked license.[114] Kentucky law specifies that a person with four convictions in the past three years for operating a motor vehicle in excess of the speed limit or for any offense that requires the assessment of points may not operate on a TNC platform.[115]

### 4. Ongoing Reviews of Criminal Background and Driver History

Requirements vary on whether the TNC must review criminal and driving history on an ongoing basis. They also differ on the frequency with which these reviews must occur. Some state laws impose no rules to subsequently check these records, whereas

111. N.J. Stat. Ann. § 39:5H-20a (2020).
112. 220 Mass. Code Regs. § 274.21 (2020).
113. 66 Pa. Cons. Stat. § 2604.1(b)(5) (2019).
114. Ala. Code § 32-7C-29(b) (2020).
115. Ky. Rev. Stat. Ann. § 281.6301 (2020).

others demand that the reviews be performed annually,[116] or less frequently, such as every two or three years.[117] Colorado requires that the checks be conducted every five years.[118] By contrast, Massachusetts requires the TNC to conduct background checks not less than once every six months.[119] Also, the MA DPU is required to conduct the background check not less than once annually.[120] Some states, such as Delaware, require annual reviews of driving records.[121]

If the MA DPU learns of and verifies a driver's arrest (not conviction) that would disqualify the driver from operating on the platform, it is required to immediately suspend or revoke the driver's clearance certificate (which is not required by most other states) and notify the relevant TNC(s). The TNC must then immediately deactivate the driver.[122] Under Pennsylvania law, the PA PUC may issue an order to a TNC requiring disqualification of a driver if during any three-year period the driver commits five or more violations of statewide law applicable to TNCs or is convicted of a criminal offense that would have disqualified the driver from operating on the platform.[123] In Missouri, the TNC is required to revoke a driver's ability to accept trip requests upon receipt of information regarding convictions for fraud, a sexual offense, use of a motor vehicle to commit a felony, an offense involving property damage, an act of violence, or an act of terror.[124]

Some states obligate TNC drivers to self-report any changes in their criminal background or driving history records. For instance, in Connecticut, drivers have a duty to inform the TNC within 24 hours of a change that affects their eligibility to operate

116. Vt. Stat. Ann. tit. 23, § 751(b)(2) (2020).
117. Conn. Gen. Stat. Ann. § 13b-119 (2020).
118. Colo. Rev. Stat. § 40-10.1-605(3) (2020).
119. 220 Mass. Code Regs. § 274.06(2) (2020).
120. *Id.* § 274.06(3).
121. Del. Code Ann. § 1913(c) (2020).
122. 220 Mass. Code Regs. § 274.06(3) (2020).
123. 66 Pa. Cons. Stat. § 2609(c) (2019).
124. Mo. Rev. Stat. § 387.436 (2020).

on the platform.[125] Pennsylvania law obligates a driver to notify the TNC immediately upon conviction of any offense that disqualifies the driver from being eligible to provide services.[126] Under Virginia law, a driver must inform the TNC of any event that may disqualify him, including a change in the registration of his or her vehicle; the revocation, suspension, cancellation, or restriction of his or her driver's license; a change in his or her insurance coverage; a motor vehicle moving violation; and a criminal arrest, plea, or conviction.[127]

### 5. Other Driver Requirements

A common practice among the states is to require individuals to possess a valid driver's license, proof of registration for the vehicle that will be used to provide a prearranged ride, and proof of automobile liability insurance for the vehicle.[128] States impose varying requirements for the age of the driver, with some being 18,[129] 19,[130] or 21 years old.[131] Massachusetts has a rule that if an individual is under the age of 23, he or she must have had the driver's license for three years.[132]

In addition to the standard requirements, Colorado law requires the TNCs to provide proof that the person is medically fit to drive.[133] Under Connecticut law, the TNC must have a policy prohibiting the driver from operating on the platform if ability is impaired by illness, fatigue, or some other condition that would likely preclude safe operation of such vehicle.[134]

Some states limit the number of consecutive hours that drivers may provide services. Examples include Colorado law, which prohibits drivers from providing services for more than

---

125. Conn. Gen. Stat. Ann. § 13b-118, 119 (2020).
126. 66 Pa. Cons. Stat. § 2605(b)(6) (2019).
127. Va. Code Ann. § 46.2-2099.49.F. (2020).
128. Kan. Stat. Ann. § 8-2720(6)–(8) (2020).
129. *See, e.g.*, Tex. Occ. Code Ann. § 2402.104 (West 2020).
130. *See, e.g.*, Kan. Stat. Ann. § 8-2720(9) (2020).
131. *See, e.g.*, 66 Pa. Cons. Stat. § 2605 (2019).
132. 220 Mass. Code Regs. § 274 (2020).
133. Colo. Rev. Stat. § 40-10.1-605(d)(IV) (2020).
134. Conn. Gen. Stat. Ann. § 13b-119 (2020).

12 consecutive hours.[135] Under Massachusetts law, a TNC is required to ensure that after 12 hours, the driver logs out of the digital network for at least eight consecutive hours. For any driver who violates this requirement, the TNC must bar access to the digital network for at least 24 consecutive hours.[136] Connecticut law prohibits drivers from using the network for more than 14 consecutive hours or more than 16 hours within a 24-hour period.[137]

Pennsylvania obligates TNCs to establish a driver training program and provide, in writing or electronically, materials that are designed to ensure that each driver understands safety and driving requirements while logged on to a digital network or providing a prearranged ride.[138] TNCs operating in Nebraska are also subject to a requirement for a driver training program.[139]

Under Pennsylvania law, a TNC driver may not smoke during a prearranged ride.[140] Florida law prohibits TNC drivers from altering presentation of information on the digital network to an enforcement official for the purpose of interfering with enforcement.[141] Although most states' laws expressly exclude TNC drivers from complying with any requirements to obtain a commercial license, Nevada imposes a mandate for drivers to obtain a state business license within six months after beginning to provide services, and to renew it annually thereafter.[142] Also, the vast majority of states only require the TNC to submit an application to the regulator, and some even specify that the TNC may make filings on behalf of the driver. However, in New Jersey, the driver is required to submit an application, including a Social Security number.[143]

---

135. Colo. Rev. Stat. § 40-10.1-605(e) (2020).
136. 220 Mass. Code Regs. § 274.07 (2020).
137. Conn. Gen. Stat. Ann. § 13b-118 (2020).
138. 66 Pa. Cons. Stat. § 2604.1(7) (2019).
139. Neb. Rev. Stat. § 75-325 (2020).
140. 66 Pa. Cons. Stat. § 2605(b)(9) (2019).
141. Fla. Stat. § 627.748 (12) (2020).
142. Nev. Rev. Stat. Ann. § 706A.160.4 (2020). Alaska also has a requirement for drivers to obtain a business license. Alaska Stat. § 43.70.020 (2020).
143. N.J. Stat. Ann. § 39:5H-16 (2020).

## 6. Identification of Drivers of Vehicles

States generally require TNCs to ensure that passengers receive sufficient information about the driver and vehicle to confirm the prearranged ride. Most jurisdictions require the digital network to display at least a photo of the driver and the license plate number of the vehicle.[144] Some states require the driver's first name and a description of the vehicle, such as the make and model.[145] California requires an image of the make and model of the vehicle.[146] Under North Carolina law, the network must also show the approximate location of the vehicle on a map.[147] Nevada requires the TNC to provide the passenger with a photo of the driver and the license number.[148] In Massachusetts, TNCs are required to issue certificates to drivers that includes their legal name, up-to-date facial image, license plate of vehicle, a statement that a two-part background check has been completed, and a statement or logo to identify the TNC. The certificate must be readily available in the digital network and visible in the vehicle.[149] Colorado law mandates the use of exterior markings that identify the driver's personal vehicle as a vehicle for hire.[150]

Under Alabama law, it is a violation of the law to impersonate a TNC driver, and if this occurs while committing a felony, it is considered an aggravating factor for sentencing purposes.[151] Per Connecticut's statute, a person who wrongfully holds himself out as a TNC driver is guilty of a misdemeanor.[152] The law in New Jersey has a provision obligating TNCs to take steps to prohibit unauthorized individuals from operating on the platform. These measures include (i) assigning a unique network access key to each driver; (ii) requiring each driver to keep it

---

144. *See, e.g.*, IDAHO CODE § 49-3710 (2020); N.H. REV. STAT. ANN § 376-A:6 (2020); ARK. CODE ANN. § 23-13-707 (2020).

145. ALA. CODE § 32-7C-26 (2020); 66 PA. CONS. STAT. § 2604(b)(8) (2019).

146. CAL. PUB. UTIL. CODE § 5445.1 (West 2020).

147. N.C. GEN. STAT. § 20-280.5(b)(4) (2020).

148. NEV. REV. STAT. § 706A.200 (2020).

149. 220 MASS. CODE REGS. § 274.05 (2020).

150. COLO. REV. STAT. § 40-10.1-605(1)(o) (2020).

151. ALA. CODE § 32-7C-29(c) (2020).

152. CONN. GEN. STAT. ANN. § 13b-119(g) (2020).

confidential; and (iii) establishing procedures for responding to complaints from passengers that the picture in the digital network did not match the driver.[153]

Several states impose requirements for the use of placards to assist passengers in identifying TNC drivers. Whereas some jurisdictions, such as Arizona, simply require the use of placards while operating on the platform that identify the TNC,[154] other state laws have established specific criteria that must be followed. For example, in Connecticut, the placard must be removable and adhere to specific requirements, including being displayed on the passenger side if it is illuminated.[155] Massachusetts law requires the placard to be reflective, illuminative, or otherwise visible at night or in a low-light environment.[156] Under Michigan law, the placard must be visible from 50 feet and identify the TNC.[157] Ohio requires that the name of the TNC be prominently displayed on the vehicle,[158] whereas Rhode Island mandates that the placard be in a conspicuous place.[159]

In what appear to be among the more onerous regulatory requirements relating to the placard, New Jersey law imposes very extensive and specific obligations on TNCs. For instance, each vehicle must display two identifying markers and maintain electronic information that allows law enforcement to confirm the driver's identity, including a color photo, the make and model of the vehicle, the license plate number, and record of ride. The markers must be placed on the front windshield and rear window when a driver is logged on to the platform. If they are capable of being illuminated, the driver is required to make them visible during times of darkness. Further, the TNC must issue each driver a two-dimensional barcode or similar image that is unique to that driver and vehicle. The law requires it to

153. N.J. Stat. Ann. § 39:5H-21 (2020).
154. Ariz. Rev. Stat. Ann. § 28-9552 (2020).
155. Conn. Gen. Stat. Ann. § 13b-118(a) (2020).
156. 220 Mass. Code Regs. § 274.03 (2020).
157. Mich. Comp. Laws § 257.2111 (2020).
158. Ohio Rev. Code Ann. § 4925.03 (LexisNexis 2020).
159. 39 R.I. Gen. Laws § 39-14.2-11 (2020).

be capable of being scanned by a rider to confirm the identity of the driver and vehicle. These barcodes must be on the driver and passenger side rear windows while the driver is logged on to the network. If a driver fails to comply with these provisions, the TNC is subject to a $250 fine. Also, the TNC is required to prohibit the driver from operating on the platform if he or she fails to comply with these requirements. When a driver terminates status of using the network, he or she must return the identifying markers to the TNC.[160]

Likewise, Virginia's placard requirements are very specific, prohibiting the use of no more than two removable, illuminated, interior, TNC-issued trade devices. The devices may use a single steady-burning color when the TNC is logged in and may change to a different steady-burning color once the driver accepts a ride and is within 0.4 miles of such passenger. Additional criteria under Virginia's law include that the illuminated display may not exceed 5 candlepower; exceed 20 square inches; utilize red, blue, or amber lights; project a glaring or dazzling light; or attach to the windshield.[161]

### 7. Independent Contractors

While this topic is not germane to driver integrity, many state laws address whether the driver is an independent contractor or an employee of the TNC. One can surmise that the TNCs negotiated these provisions in response to litigation in many jurisdictions over the applicability of employment laws to TNCs and their drivers.

A common approach is for the law to state that the driver is an independent contractor if several conditions are met. For instance, in West Virginia, the law states that drivers are not employees of the TNC if (i) the TNC does not prescribe specific hours when drivers must be logged into the digital network; (ii) the TNC imposes no restrictions on the driver's ability to use digital networks of other TNCs; (iii) the TNC does not assign a driver to a particular territory in which to operate; (iv) the TNC

160. N.J. Stat. Ann. § 39:5H-23 (2020).
161. Va. Code Ann. § 46.2-2099.50.B. (2020).

does not restrict the driver from engaging in any other occupation or business, and (v) the TNC and driver agree in writing that the driver is an independent contractor of the TNC.[162] Other jurisdictions set forth the same or similar conditions as West Virginia without the requirement for the TNC and driver to have a written agreement to this effect.[163] The law in Arkansas expressly excludes TNCs from being required to provide workers' compensation if the requisite conditions are met.[164]

Other states lean more toward the drivers being independent contractors without all of the conditions. For instance, Alaska's law provides that the TNC is not an employer of the driver.[165] Under North Carolina law, it is a rebuttable presumption that the TNC driver is an independent contractor.[166] In Ohio, the law states that the drivers are not employees unless otherwise agreed in a written contract.[167] Per Tennessee law, TNCs shall not be deemed to own, control, operate, or manage the personal vehicles used by TNC drivers.[168]

## E. Vehicle Safety

Many states' laws governing TNCs impose requirements designed to ensure the safety of the vehicles that are used to provide transportation service to the public. Some states simply require the vehicles to comply with the jurisdiction's requirements for all vehicles that are operated in the state. Examples of these states include Indiana, Kansas, Maine, South Dakota, and Texas.[169] Texas also mandates that the vehicles have four doors,

---

162. W. Va. Code § 17-29-11 (2020).

163. *See, e.g.*, N.H. Rev. Stat. Ann § 376-A:20; Ind. Code § 8-2.1-19.1-4 (2020).

164. Ark. Code Ann. § 23-13-719. (2020).

165. Alaska Stat. § 28.23.080 (2020).

166. N.C. Gen. Stat. § 20-280.8 (2020).

167. Ohio Rev. Code Ann. § 4925.10 (LexisNexis 2020).

168. Tenn. Code Ann. § 65-15-302 (2020).

169. Ind. Code § 8-2.1-19.1-7 (2020); Kan. Stat. Ann. § 8-2713 (2020); Me. Stat. tit. 29-A, § 1675.4 (2020), S.D. Codified Laws § 32-40-6 (2020); Tex. Occ. Code Ann. § 2402.111 (West 2020).

which is also a requirement in other states, including Nevada and Connecticut.[170]

Some jurisdictions go further and require the vehicles to be subject to inspection by either a certified mechanic or the TNC itself. For example, in Nebraska and Alaska, TNCs are obligated to either conduct an initial safety inspection or have one performed by a licensed mechanic.[171] Other states require that the inspections be ongoing. Colorado mandates annual safety inspections by a certified mechanic, as do Michigan and New Jersey.[172] In addition to requiring annual inspections by certified mechanics, Pennsylvania's law also requires TNCs to ensure that the vehicles remain in continuous compliance with the inspection requirements, and notes that they are always subject to inspection by PA PUC enforcement officers. Under the law of the District of Columbia, the TNC must verify that the vehicle is inspected within 90 days of beginning service and be determined to be safe by a licensed mechanic in the District of Columbia or at an inspection station in Maryland or Virginia.[173]

Some jurisdictions impose standards regarding the age of the vehicles that are used. For instance, Rhode Island bars vehicles that are older than 15 years, whereas Connecticut and Alaska bar vehicles more than 12 years old.[174] In Pennsylvania, vehicles over ten model years old may not be used, unless they are alternative fuel vehicles, in which case they may not be more than 12 model years old. Additionally, Pennsylvania law imposes a limit of 350,000 miles on the odometer of vehicles used to provide TNC services.[175]

---

170. Tex. Occ. Code Ann. § 2402.111 (West 2020); Nev. Rev. Stat. § 706A.180.1 (2020); Conn. Gen. Stat. Ann. § 13b-119(h) (2020).

171. Neb. Rev. Stat. § 75-328 (2020); Alaska Stat. § 28.23.110 (2020).

172. Colo. Rev. Stat. § 40-10.1-605(g) (2020); Mich. Comp. Laws § 257.2109 (2020); N.J. Stat. Ann. § 39:5H-22 (2020).

173. D.C. Code § 50-301.29a(4) (2020).

174. 39 R.I. Gen. Laws § 39-14.2-9 (2020); Conn. Gen. Stat. Ann. § 13b-119(h) (2020); Alaska Stat. § 28.23.110 (2020).

175. 66 Pa. Cons. Stat. § 2606 (2019).

## F. Insurance

### 1. Coverage Amounts

Insurance requirements are typically the most complex and comprehensive provisions of the statewide laws. They are also very similar across the states, with the main variable being the amount of coverage that must be maintained. Other differences are in the disclosures that TNCs must make to drivers and in the protections for insurance companies issuing policies to the drivers.

New York is representative of a common model followed throughout the country. Either the TNC, the driver, or a combination of both, must maintain primary automobile insurance, which recognizes that the driver is a TNC driver and using the vehicle to transport passengers for compensation, when (i) the driver is logged on to the digital network and (ii) while the driver is engaged in a prearranged trip. As is customary across the states, different amounts apply to these two different situations.[176]

Under New York law, when the TNC driver is logged on to the network but has not yet accepted a ride, the coverage must be at least $75,000 for death and bodily injury per person, at least $150,000 for death or bodily injury per accident, and at least $25,000 for property damage per accident. Once the TNC driver has accepted and is engaged in a prearranged trip, the required amounts are at least $1,250,000 for death, bodily injury, and property damage.[177]

New York's coverage amounts are among the higher levels required by state laws. For instance, in Pennsylvania, the required amounts for being logged on are $50,000 for death and bodily injury per person, $100,000 per accident, and $25,000 for property damage, and the minimum amount during a prearranged trip is $500,000.[178] Pennsylvania's required levels for when the driver is logged on to the network are followed by

176. N.Y. VEH. & TRAF. LAW § 1693 (McKinney 2020).
177. *Id.*
178. 66 PA. CONS. STAT. § 2603.1 (2019).

many other states.[179] Frequently, however, states require a minimum of $1,000,000 during trips.[180] An example of a jurisdiction that exceeds New York's coverage levels is Minnesota, which mandates coverage of $1,500,000 while the driver is on a trip.[181] By contrast, New Hampshire requires only $300,000 during this period.[182] Rather than mandating certain coverage levels, some state laws, including Idaho and Massachusetts, require TNCs to comply with the requirements of the state's insurance laws.[183]

Several jurisdictions specify the need for TNCs to maintain uninsured or underinsured motorist coverage. For instance, New Jersey law requires this coverage from the time the driver is logged on to the network and mandates minimum coverage of $1,500,000 during trips.[184] Under Nebraska law, TNCs are obligated to carry uninsured and underinsured coverage for both drivers and passengers.[185] Missouri law also has underinsured motorist provisions.[186] Another state law with uninsured and underinsured coverage requirements is Illinois, which requires the TNC to carry such coverage in the amount of $50,000 during a prearranged trip.[187]

It is common for state laws to require the TNC's insurance to be primary in the event of a lapse in the driver's insurance or if it does not provide the required coverage. This means that the TNC's insurer is obligated to provide coverage with the first dollar of a claim and has a duty to defend the claim. State laws also often contain provisions making it clear that the TNC's coverage

---

179. *See, e.g.*, Conn. Gen. Stat. Ann. § 13b-120(a) (2020).

180. D.C. Code § 50-301.29c(a) (2020); Colo. Rev. Stat. § 40-10.1-604(2) (2020); Iowa Code § 321N.4 (2020).

181. Minn. Stat. § 65B.472 (2020).

182. N.H. Rev. Stat. Ann. § 376-A:8 (2020).

183. Idaho Code § 49-3708 (2020); 220 Mass. Code Regs. § 274.09 (2020).

184. N.J. Stat. Ann. § 39.5H-10 (2020).

185. Neb. Rev. Stat. § 75-333 (2020).

186. Mo. Rev. Stat. § 379.1703 (2020).

187. 625 Ill. Comp. Stat. 57/10 (2020). As of the writing of this book, the Illinois Transportation Network Providers Act is scheduled for repeal on June 1, 2020. 625 Ill. Comp. Stat. 57/34 (2020).

is not dependent on the denial of the claim by the driver's personal insurance company.[188]

State laws typically require drivers to carry proof of coverage at all times while operating in the digital network. Also, in the event of an accident, drivers are required to provide this proof to interested parties, insurers, and law enforcement officials. The drivers are further obligated to disclose, upon request, whether they were logged on to the network or providing a prearranged trip at the time of the accident.[189]

The laws in some states address limitations on a TNC's liability. For example, in Pennsylvania, the law specifies that the TNC may not require a passenger or driver to sign a waiver of liability and expressly prohibits such a waiver from being in the terms of service during the downloading of the app.[190] In the District of Columbia, the law requires the TNCs' insurance coverages to be published on its website and prohibits the company's terms of service from being used to contradict or evade the insurance requirements.[191] California and Illinois laws make it clear that the insurance requirements do not limit the TNCs' liability.[192]

## G. Driver Disclosures

Many states require the TNCs to disclose the following information in writing to drivers, before the drivers are allowed to accept a request for a prearranged trip on the digital network: (i) the insurance coverage, including the types of coverage and the limits for each coverage, that the TNC provides while the TNC drivers are using the platform; and (ii) that the driver's own automobile insurance policy might not provide any coverage when the TNC driver is logged on to the digital network or engaged in a prearranged trip.[193] Under Massachusetts law, the

---

188. *See, e.g.*, 66 Pa. Cons. Stat. § 2603.1(a)(5) (2019).
189. *See, e.g.*, 66 Pa. Cons. Stat. § 2603.1(a)(9) (2019).
190. 66 Pa. Cons. Stat. § 2603.1 (2019).
191. D.C. Code § 50-301.29c(h) (2020).
192. Cal. Pub. Util. Code § 5434 (West 2020); 625 Ill. Comp. Stat. 57.10 (2020).
193. *See, e.g.*, 66 Pa. Cons. Stat. § 2603.2 (2019).

driver has an obligation to disclose to the insurer, within seven days of receiving a driver certificate, that the vehicle is being used for TNC services.[194] Several states impose an additional obligation on TNCs to disclose to the driver that if the driver's vehicle has a lien against it, the continued use of the vehicle without physical damage coverage might violate the terms of the contract with the lienholder.[195]

Pennsylvania law takes a different approach with lienholders and imposes an obligation on the TNC to also make the required disclosures relating to lessors. A TNC must disclose prominently and with a separate acknowledgement of acceptance by drivers the following terms:

- TNC will provide you notice whether it provides insurance to repair your personal vehicle if you have an accident while driving on the platform;
- If TNC does not provide coverage for damage to your car, your personal policy might not provide the coverage and you may be required to pay all costs to repair the vehicle unless you purchase extra insurance;
- If you financed the purchase or lease of the vehicle, you must notify your lender or lessor that you will use your vehicle to provide transportation network service;
- Your lender or lessor may require you to purchase extra insurance or purchase it on your behalf and bill you for the costs of the policy;
- The failure to notify a lender or lessor or to have insurance to cover the cost of damage may cause your vehicle to be repossessed or your lease revoked; and
- If you have questions, you should contact your insurance agent, your lender or lessor, or the Pennsylvania Insurance Department.[196]

---

194. 220 Mass. Code Regs. § 274.09 (2020).

195. Me. Stat. tit. 24-A, § 7304 (2020); N.Y. Veh. & Traf. Law § 1694 (McKinney 2020); Ohio Rev. Code Ann. § 3942.04 (LexisNexis 2020).

196. 66 Pa. Cons. Stat. § 2604.5 (2019).

Another common protection that states have afforded lienholders is that if the TNC's insurer makes payment for a claim covered under comprehensive and collision coverage, the TNC must cause the insurer to issue payment directly to the business repairing the vehicle or jointly to the owner of the vehicle and the primary lienholder.[197] Delaware law makes clear that nothing limits a lender from requiring the TNC driver to maintain comprehensive collision coverage to cover accidents when logged on but not transporting a passenger.[198]

Hawaii law mandates a different set of disclosures to drivers. Under this state law, which only addresses insurance coverage, either the insurer or the TNC must disclose certain information if the TNC is the only named insured. Those disclosures include the coverages and that all optional coverages available may not have been purchased. The insurer or TNC is also required to obtain written acknowledgement from the drivers of those written disclosures.[199]

## H. Protections for Insurers

A common practice across the state laws is the inclusion of language designed to protect the companies who issue personal automobile insurance policies to drivers operating on a TNC's digital network. For example, the New York law provides that insurers that write motor vehicle insurance may, in the insurance policy, exclude any and all coverage afforded under the policy to an owner or operator of a TNC vehicle for any loss that occurs while the driver is logged on or providing a trip.[200] State laws also have provisions making it clear that insurers are not required to provide coverage under personal insurance policies.[201] These

---

197. Colo. Rev. Stat. § 10-10.1-604 (2020); Ariz. Rev. Stat. Ann. § 28-9558 (2020); 625 Ill. Comp. Stat. 57/10 (2020).

198. Del. Code Ann. tit. 2, § 1910 (2020).

199. Haw. Rev. Stat. § 431:10C-703(g)(3) (2020). As of the writing of this book, this law is scheduled for repeal on September 21, 2021. Haw. Rev. Stat. § 431:10C (2020).

200. N.Y. Veh. & Traf. Law § 1695 (McKinney 2020).

201. *See, e.g.*, Colo. Rev. Stat. § 40-10.1-604 (2020).

laws typically note that the driver's personal insurer has no duty to defend.[202]

## I. Operations

### 1. Trips Arranged through Digital Network

Most of the state laws contain provisions designed at regulating the day-to-day operations of TNCs and their drivers. Common requirements include the need for all rides to be arranged through the digital network, such that no trips may be accepted via street hails or telephone calls.[203] Alabama law makes it a misdemeanor for a driver to arrange a trip outside the digital network.[204]

Similarly, many states ban cash payments.[205] However, in Ohio, cash payments are acceptable if authorized by the TNC. If this occurs, the driver is obligated to notify the TNC through the digital network of the amount of the payment, which must be confirmed by the rider. The law further clarifies that this provision is not to be construed as requiring the TNC to accept cash payments.[206]

### 2. Customer Service

Some state laws impose various customer service requirements on TNCs. For example, as to overall operations, Pennsylvania law requires TNCs to take reasonable steps to ensure that the service provided by each driver is safe, reasonable, and adequate.[207] In Nevada, the law expressly bars drivers from deceiving a passenger, taking a passenger to a different destination, taking a longer route, and failing to comply with reasonable and lawful requests of passengers as to speed of travel and route.[208]

---

202. *See, e.g.*, Ark. Code Ann. § 23-13-709, 710 (2020).

203. *See* Del. Code Ann. tit. 2, § 1915 (2020); Ariz. Rev. Stat. Ann. § 28-9556 (2020); Tex. Occ. Code Ann. § 2402.108 (West 2020).

204. Ala. Code § 32-7C-31 (2020).

205. Idaho Code § 49-3712 (2020); Kan. Stat. Ann. § 8-2715 (2020).

206. Ohio Rev. Code Ann. § 4925.08 (LexisNexis 2020).

207. 66 Pa. Cons. Stat. § 2604.3(a) (2019).

208. Nev. Rev. Stat. Ann. § 706.280 (2020).

Some states require TNCs to maintain websites for sharing specific information with consumers. As an example of a common approach, Nebraska law mandates that the TNC maintain a website that provides a customer service or e-mail address, as well as the telephone number and e-mail address of the Nebraska Public Service Commission.[209] Under Colorado law, a TNC has flexibility to use either its digital network or website to make available a customer support telephone number.[210]

In Pennsylvania, the law requires TNCs to maintain a website that provides consumers with at least two of the following methods for communicating with the TNC: (i) a customer service telephone number, (ii) an e-mail address, (iii) a hyperlink, and (iv) any other communication method that allows a person to communicate directly with the TNC's customer service department. This website must also show the telephone number to file complaints with the PA PUC and the agency's Internet website address.[211] Nevada law obligates TNCs to provide contact information of the Transportation Authority on its website or within the digital network and to create a system to receive and address complaints from consumers during normal business hours.[212]

The information required by Virginia law for inclusion on the website is more extensive than most other states. Virginia mandates that TNCs publish information on their websites about their fare calculation methods, driver screening criteria, description of offenses that are grounds for disqualifying a driver, means for passengers to report reasonable suspicion of the driver being under the influence of alcohol or drugs, information about training and testing policies, standards for vehicles, a customer support telephone number or e-mail address, and instructions regarding any alternative methods for reporting a complaint.[213]

---

209. Neb. Rev. Stat. Ann. § 75-325 (2020).
210. Colo. Rev. Stat. § 40-10.1-605(1)(k) (2020).
211. 66 Pa. Cons. Stat. § 2604.1(b)(10) (2019).
212. Nev. Rev. Stat. § 706A.260 (2020).
213. Va. Code Ann. § 46.2-2099.48.D. (2020).

## J. Privacy of Customer Information

Many states' laws have provisions designed to protect the confidentiality of personally identifiable and financial information of customers. Following a common practice, Indiana law bans disclosure of such information unless the customer knowingly consents or the disclosure is done pursuant to a legal obligation or as part of an investigation into a violation.[214] In Colorado, the law specifies that the limitation on disclosure does not apply to aggregated user data.[215] Several other states, including Texas and Iowa, also allow for the disclosure of passenger identifying information (i.e., name and telephone number) to drivers in order to facilitate communications between the passenger and the driver.[216] The laws in some states, such as North Dakota and Connecticut, require the TNCs to follow the publicly disclosed terms of their privacy policies or obtain passenger consent.[217] On the issue of consent, Pennsylvania law requires the TNC to obtain consent through a separate document from the terms of service. Also, Pennsylvania law expressly bans the sale of personally identifiable or financial information. In Massachusetts, the privacy requirements are applicable to both driver and passenger information.[218]

## K. Discrimination and Accessibility

The vast majority of jurisdictions prohibit TNCs and drivers from discriminating against passengers. For instance, New Mexico's law requires the TNC to adopt a written policy of nondiscrimination on the basis of destination, race, color, national origin, religious belief or affiliation, sex, disability, age, sexual orientation or gender identity with respect to TNC drivers, riders, and potential riders, and further obligates the TNC to notify TNC

---

214. Ind. Code § 8-2.1-19.1-14 (2020).

215. Colo. Rev. Stat. § 40-10.1-605(m) (2020).

216. Tex. Occ. Code Ann. § 2402.153 (West 2020); Iowa Code § 321N.10 (2020).

217. N.D. Cent. Code § 39-34-04 (2020); Conn. Gen. Stat. § 13b-118(f) (2020).

218. 220 Mass. Code Regs. § 274.10 (2020).

drivers of the policy. This law also mandates that TNC drivers comply with all applicable laws regarding nondiscrimination.[219]

Under Pennsylvania law, the ban on discrimination includes refusing to provide service to a certain class of passengers or certain localities.[220] Missouri law has a similar provision that prohibits the TNC from using geographic location to exclude certain areas based on income, race, and ethnicity, and a violation of this provision is punishable by a one-month suspension of the TNC's license.[221] In Illinois, if local government has a requirement for licensed chauffeurs not to avoid underserved areas, TNC drivers are subject to the same requirement.[222]

The District of Columbia's law gives specific examples of discriminatory conduct, such as refusal of service on the basis of a protected characteristic, using derogatory or harassing language on the basis of a protected characteristic, refusal of service based on the pickup or drop off location of the passenger, or rating a passenger on the basis of a protected characteristic.[223] The law in the District of Columbia, however, also explains that it does not constitute discrimination for a driver to refuse to provide service to an individual with disabilities due to violent, seriously disruptive, or illegal conduct by the individual. At the same time, the driver may not refuse to provide service because the individual's disability results in the appearance of involuntary behavior that may offend, annoy, or inconvenience the driver.[224] When a passenger makes a reasonable allegation of discriminatory conduct in the District of Columbia, the TNC must immediately suspend the driver and conduct an investigation.[225]

Other state laws also describe situations where a driver is not obligated to transport a person. For example, under Colorado law, a driver may refuse to transport a person who is acting in

219. N.M. Stat. Ann § 65-7-16 (2020).
220. 66 Pa. Cons. Stat. § 2604.3(a) (2019).
221. Mo. Rev. Stat. § 387.439 (2020).
222. 625 Ill. Comp. Stat. 57-20(f) (2020).
223. D.C. Code § 50-301.29a(10)(A) (2020).
224. *Id.* § 50-301.29a(10)(B) (2020).
225. *Id.* § 50-301.29a(10)(C)–(D) (2020).

an unlawful, disorderly, or endangering manner; a person who is unable to care for himself and is not in the charge of a responsible companion; or the driver has already committed to providing a ride.[226] Similarly, in Texas and South Carolina, a driver may refuse to transport a passenger acting in an unlawful, disorderly, or endangering manner.[227] Virginia law contains a nearly identical provision, except that when this occurs, the driver is obligated to report the refusal to the TNC.[228]

Accessibility to TNC services by the disabled population is a high priority for most jurisdictions. Many state laws require TNCs to transport service animals and to refrain from imposing additional charges to transport persons with disabilities.[229] With respect to service animals, Rhode Island specifies that they must be in the passenger compartment, provided they do not impede the safe operation of the vehicle.[230] In Pennsylvania, drivers are required to permit service animals in the passenger compartment, unless the driver has a medical allergy on file.[231] Also, Pennsylvania law obligates TNCs to make the digital network accessible to hearing- and visually impaired passengers.[232]

As to wheelchair-accessible vehicles (WAVs), two primary models exist among the state laws. One approach is to require the TNC to provide passengers with the opportunity to request a WAV if one is available.[233] A second model requires the TNC to provide passengers with the opportunity to request a WAV and that if the TNC does not offer this service to direct the passenger to an alternative provider, if available.[234] Nearly all states

---

226. Colo. Rev. Stat. § 40-10.1-605 (2020).

227. Tex. Occ. Code Ann. § 2402.109 (West 2020); S.C. Code Ann. § 58-23-1660(A)(11) (2020).

228. Va. Code Ann. § 46.2-2099.48.K. (2020).

229. Idaho Code § 49-3713 (2020); Ala. Code § 32-7C-32 (2020).

230. 39 R.I. Gen. Laws § 39-14.2-21 (2020).

231. 66 Pa. Cons. Stat. § 2604.3(b)(3) (2019).

232. *Id.* § 2604.3(b)(2) (2019).

233. Ohio Rev. Code Ann. § 4925.06 (LexisNexis 2020).

234. Kan. Stat. Ann. § 8-2716 (2020).

ban TNCs from imposing additional charges to serve individuals with disabilities.[235]

California has a particularly aggressive program designed to enhance the accessibility of WAVs. Per the TNC law, the CA PUC must conduct workshops with stakeholders in order to determine community WAV demand and supply. The agency is obligated to provide recommendations regarding the establishment of geographic areas, criteria for expenditures, and educational outreach objectives for programs for on-demand services. Topics of discussion include vehicle specifications, subsidies for wheelchair pickups, maintenance and fuel costs, designated pickup locations where door-to-door service is not feasible, standards for trip requests, response times, rider-initiated cancellation, limiting of stranded users, integration of service into city and county transportation plans, or any necessary training or additional incentives for WAV drivers that results in a measurable impact on service availability, efficiency, and efficacy.[236]

Since July 1, 2019, TNCs operating in California have been required to pay the CA PUC, on a quarterly basis, a minimum of five cents for each completed trip, with the CA PUC having the ability to adjust the fee in each geographic area as necessary based on the cost of providing adequate WAV service within a particular area.[237] The CA PUC distributes the fees to access providers, on a competitive basis, which establish on-demand transportation programs or partnerships to meet the needs of persons with disabilities, including wheelchair users who need a WAV.[238]

TNCs are exempt from paying the charge if they are accessible to persons with disabilities. To obtain this exemption, the TNC must meet the CA PUC's designated level of available WAV service in each geographic area via the digital network. Also, the TNC must have response times for 80 percent of WAV trips requested within a time established by the agency for the particular area. The exemption is only valid for one year and is

---

235. *See, e.g.*, 66 Pa. Cons. Stat. § 2604.3(b)(4) (2019).
236. Cal. Pub. Util. Code § 5440.5(1)(A) (West 2020).
237. *Id.* § 5440.5(1)(B).
238. *Id.* § 5440.5(1)(C).

applicable only to the geographic areas that meet the CA PUC's standards.[239]

Alternatively, a TNC is entitled to offset the fee by the amount it spends during a quarter to improve WAV service on its platform. To obtain approval for the offset, the TNC must demonstrate (i) the presence and availability of drivers with WAVs on its platform; (ii) improved level of service, including reasonable response times, compared to the prior quarter; (iii) efforts undertaken to publicize and promote available WAV services to disability communities; and (iv) a full accounting of funds expended.[240]

TNCs may qualify for the exemption or offset by contracting with a transportation provider.[241] Within 30 days after the end of a quarter beginning after July 1, 2020, a TNC that receives an offset must file a report that contains the following information: (i) number of WAV rides requested, (ii) number of WAV rides fulfilled, (iii) response times, (iv) educational outreach to disability communities, and (v) detailed descriptions of expenditures.[242]

Under the law, the CA PUC must establish yearly benchmarks for TNCs to meet to ensure that WAV users receive continuously improved, reliable, and available service. The benchmarks must include response times, percentage of trips fulfilled versus trips requested, and the number of users requesting rides versus community WAV demand for each geographic area.[243] The CA PUC also has an obligation to submit a report to the legislature by January 1, 2024, that includes a study on the demand for WAVs, the availability of funds, an analysis of the current program capabilities and deficiencies, and recommendations to improve accessibility for persons with disabilities.[244]

---

239. *Id.* § 5440.5(1)(G).
240. *Id.* § 5440.5(1)(B).
241. *Id.* § 5440.5(1)(H).
242. *Id.* § 5440.5(1)(I).
243. *Id.* § 5440.5(1)(J).
244. *Id.* § 5440.5(2)(A).

## L. Fares

The statewide laws in most jurisdictions have taken a hands-off approach regarding the fares that TNCs impose on passengers. Rather than attempting to control the prices that TNCs charge, the state laws focus on disclosure of the fare calculation method and applicable rate, coupled with the provision of an estimated price upon request by the passenger. Wisconsin and Wyoming are examples of this standard approach.[245] One exception to the standard language is Georgia's law, which requires that fares be based on distance, flat fee, base fee, waiting time, cancellation fee, stop fee, event pricing, demand pricing, or time. A violation of this requirement is considered a misdemeanor.[246] Although the language varies from the norm, it provides so many different factors that a TNC could use, such as demand pricing, that effectively it is not truly a deviation from the other jurisdictions. Given the number of criteria that a TNC may consider, it is difficult to fathom a scenario where a violation of the law's requirement could be shown.

A few states address dynamic pricing, which takes place when users request a trip in the same area at the same time, such as during a downpour or sporting event. The purpose of a surge in the TNC's price is to help ensure that riders receive a quick response because it encourages more drivers to get on the road and to the area where demand is higher than normal.[247]

Pennsylvania law requires TNCs to notify a potential passenger prior to accepting a ride through its digital network any time dynamic pricing is in effect.[248] Additionally, TNCs operating in Pennsylvania are limited during a time when the governor has declared a state of disaster or emergency to using a multiplier that is reflective of multipliers used during the past 60 days. The

245. Wis. Stat. § 440.425 (2020); Wyo. Stat. Ann. § 31-20-103 (West 2020).

246. Ga. Code Ann § 40-1-196 (2020).

247. *Why Are Prices Higher Than Normal?*, Uber, https://help.uber.com/riders/article/why-are-prices-higher-than-normal---?nodeId=34212e8b-d69a-4d8a-a923-095d3075b487 (last visited Mar. 6, 2020).

248. 66 Pa. Cons. Stat. § 2607(d) (2019).

law specifies that for a TNC to exceed these limits constitutes a violation of the state's Price Gouging Act.[249]

In Connecticut, TNCs must disclose that dynamic pricing is in effect, provide an estimate of the fare, and include a feature requiring confirmation of acceptance by the passenger.[250] Connecticut law also limits the increase to no more than two and one half times the usual price during a state of disaster or emergency.[251] Under Nebraska law, the TNC is obligated to disclose that dynamic pricing is in effect and confirm the passenger's understanding. During a state of emergency, Nebraska law bans TNCs from putting dynamic pricing into effect.[252]

Most states require TNCs to provide electronic receipts upon completion of trips. A common approach across the country is for the transmittal of an electronic receipt to the passenger's e-mail address or account on the digital network that documents the (i) origination, destination, mileage, and time estimated on the trip; (ii) driver's first name; and (iii) total amount paid, if any.[253] In Virginia, the receipt must include a map of the route taken, dates and times when the trip began and ended, and contact information for additional support.[254] Arkansas law requires an itemization of the total fare paid, if any.[255]

## M. Enforcement

### 1. Inspections and Audits

Many of the state laws address the ability of the regulator to conduct inspections or audits of records. The frequency and extent to which this can occur vary widely, suggesting that these provisions of the law were negotiated during the enactment of the legislation. For example, Alabama law specifies that the Alabama Public Service Commission (AL PSC) may inspect a random

249. *Id.* § 2607(e).
250. Conn. Gen. Stat. § 13b-118(4)(B) (2020).
251. *Id.* § 13b-118(4)(C).
252. Neb. Rev. Stat. § 75-329 (2020).
253. *See, e.g.*, 66 Pa. Cons. Stat. § 2607(a) (2019).
254. Va. Code Ann. § 46.2-2099.48.J. (2020).
255. Ark. Code Ann. § 23-13-708 (2020).

sample of records no more than once per year, but also recognizes that the AL PSC may review records anytime to investigate a specific complaint against a driver or TNC.[256] By contrast, under Connecticut law, the Commissioner of Transportation (CT COT) may not audit records more than four times per year.[257]

Whereas some state laws provide for these audits to occur at mutually agreed upon locations and to entail only a review of the records, Delaware law permits the Division of Motor Vehicles (DE DMV) to request records.[258] The TNCs operating in Delaware must provide the records within ten days, and the law specifies that the DE DMV may not retain criminal background checks. Further, the DE DMV is obligated to destroy records within 180 days. As with several other state laws, Delaware's statute also expressly exempts disclosure of this information under the applicable freedom of information or right to know law.[259] Under Nebraska law, this protection from disclosure is not applicable if the records are used as evidence in a civil penalty or criminal proceeding.[260] In New Jersey, the Motor Vehicle Commission (NJ MVC) may also request that the TNC provide records. The TNC has 14 business days to do so and can request an additional 14 days. Also, the TNC may exclude information identifying the driver.[261]

Under Montana law, the Public Service Commission (MT PSC) may request up to 1,000 unique identification numbers, each of which has been assigned to a driver, and may request copies of records for up to ten of the TNC's drivers who may be identified only by the identification number. The TNC is required to comply in electronic format within one business day and may redact records to protect the privacy of drivers. Unless required

256. Ala. Code § 32-7-33 (2020).
257. Conn. Gen. Stat. § 13b-118 (2020).
258. Del. Code Ann. tit. 2, § 1919 (2020).
259. *Id.* Maine also has a provision requiring a TNC to transmit records within 10 business days. Me. Stat. tit. 24-A, § 274.13 (2020).
260. Neb. Rev. Stat. § 75-329 (2020).
261. N.J. Stat. Ann. § 39.5H-25 (2020).

by the Montana state constitution, the MT PSC may not publicly disclose this information.[262]

The Department of Insurance in Mississippi has the right to inspect a sample of records, up to 50 drivers, and can do a supplemental audit.[263] In Utah, the Division of Consumer Protection may audit random samples of records no more than twice per year or specific records anytime to investigate a complaint.[264] Under Vermont law, the Commission of Motor Vehicles is authorized, not more than once per year, to visually inspect a random sample of up to 25 drivers' records per TNC, which has an ongoing duty to make such records available for inspection.[265]

## 2. Fines and Penalties

State laws vary widely on how enforcement and the imposition of fines, penalties, or other remedial measures are handled. Whereas some states only authorize the assessment of penalties against the TNCs, others permit the regulator to take action against, or require the TNC to take action involving, the driver.

Many state regulators are empowered to suspend, revoke, or alter a permit that has been issued; refuse to renew a permit; and impose civil penalties for violations of the law.[266] State laws that permit action against or involving the driver include Nebraska, where the NE PSC may suspend the driver,[267] and Pennsylvania, where the PA PUC may issue an order directing disqualification of the driver.[268] In Virginia, a TNC with knowledge of a driver violating the law is obligated to remove the driver from the platform for at least a year.[269]

Under Nevada law, the Transportation Authority (NV TA) may suspend or revoke a TNC's permit and impose a fine not to exceed $100,000 per violation if it was willful and endangered

262. Mont. Code Ann. § 69-12-407 (West 2015).
263. Miss Code Ann. § 77-8-35 (2020).
264. Utah Code Ann. § 13-51-104 (West 2015).
265. Vt. Stat. Ann. tit. 23, § 752 (2020).
266. *See, e.g.*, Colo. Rev. Stat. § 40-10.1-605(7), 606 (2020).
267. Neb. Rev. Stat. § 75-325(3) (2020).
268. 66 Pa. Cons. Stat. § 2609(c) (2019).
269. Va. Code Ann. § 46.2-2099.48.C. (2020).

public safety. When deciding on the amount of the fine, the NV TA is required to consider the size of the TNC, the severity of the violation, good faith efforts to rectify the violation, and the TNC's compliance history.[270]

In Arkansas, the Department of Transportation (AR DOT) is required to consider the same factors as the NV TA in determining the amount of the fine, but the caps on the fines are much lower. The AR DOT may impose fines that do not exceed $1,000 per violation, unless the violation was knowing, in which case it may not exceed $5,000.[271] New Hampshire law is similar but the penalty may not exceed $500 for the first offense and $1,000 for subsequent offenses, with repeated violations possibly resulting in suspension or revocation.[272] Rhode Island law authorizes somewhat higher civil penalties of $5,000 for the first violation, $7,500 for the second violation, and $10,000 for the third violation. The TNC is thereafter required to develop a remediation plan.[273]

The law in Delaware vests jurisdiction over contested violations with the Court of Common Pleas and subjects the TNC and the TNC driver to fines up to $100 for the first violation, $500 for a second violation, and $1,000 for a third violation. A TNC is not subject to financial penalties, however, if it takes corrective steps within a reasonable time period. The DE DMV may suspend or revoke a permit if a pattern of violations evidence the TNC's intentional disregard of public safety. Under Georgia law, violations of the TNC law are misdemeanors.[274]

In Michigan, a TNC that knowingly allows a driver to operate in violation of the rules is guilty of a misdemeanor punishable by a fine of not more than $1,000 per violation or imprisonment for not more than 90 days, or both. The Department of Licensing and Regulatory Affairs (MI DLRA) may also assess a fine to cover

---

270. Nev. Rev. Stat. Ann. § 706A.300 (2020).
271. Ark. Code Ann. § 23-13-721. (2020).
272. N.H. Rev. Stat. Ann. § 376-A:18 (2020).
273. 39 R.I. Gen. Laws § 39-14.2-22 (2020).
274. Del. Code Ann. § 1921 (2020).

the actual cost of the investigation, including attorneys' fees.[275] Further, under Michigan law, the attorney general can institute appropriate criminal proceedings, and the MI DLRA can bring an action in a circuit court, which may award damages.[276]

Several states specify certain violations that warrant the imposition of a fine or penalty. For instance, in Colorado, the Public Service Commission may fine a TNC up to $500 for failure to serve a passenger, but the TNC is not liable unless the driver's violation has been previously reported to the TNC in writing and the TNC has failed to reasonably address the violation.[277] In Arizona, if a driver is found soliciting rides or accepting street hails, the regulator can impose a civil penalty on the TNC of up to $1,500 per violation.[278] Failure of the driver to display a placard in Maine subjects the TNC to a $500 monetary penalty,[279] while in Pennsylvania such violations have typically generated the payment by TNCs of $50 civil penalties.[280]

Under Missouri law, the TNC may not deny or manipulate access to the digital network to evade law enforcement. A first violation is subject to a fine of $50,000, with a second violation punishable by a fine of $150,000 and a third violation punishable by a fine of $300,000.[281]

The law in South Carolina provides that a person who misrepresents himself as a TNC driver is guilty of a misdemeanor and shall be fined not more than $500, imprisoned not more than 30 days, or both. Further, a person who uses the trade dress or network in furtherance of criminal activity is guilty of a misdemeanor and shall be fined not more than $100,000, imprisoned for not more than two years, or both.[282]

---

275. Mich. Comp. Laws § 257.2149 (2020).

276. *Id.* § 257.2151.

277. Colo. Rev. Stat. § 40-10.1-605(7) (2020).

278. Ariz. Rev. Stat. Ann. § 28-9556 (2020).

279. Me. Stat. tit. 24-A, § 274.13 (2020).

280. *See, e.g.*, Pa. Pub. Util. Commission v. Rasier-Pa LLC, Pa Puc Docket No. c-2018-3003049.

281. Mo. Rev. Stat. § 387.439 (2020).

282. S.C. Code Ann. § 58-23-1640 (2020).

In Maine, operating without a permit or failing to maintain the required insurance is considered a Class D crime.[283] Other states authorize fines for operating without a permit, with Connecticut law capping the fine at $50,000 and New Jersey and Maryland laws capping the fine at $500.[284]

## N. Recordkeeping and Reporting

Most jurisdictions require TNCs to maintain records, although the retention periods vary, and some states obligate TNCs to submit reports to the regulator. Several states require TNCs to retain records of trips and drivers for one year.[285] New Mexico law requires TNCs to retain records of trips, drivers, and alcohol/substance abuse complaints for four years.[286] Some states require the TNC to maintain all of these records for two years[287] or three years.[288]

Several states require TNCs to maintain additional types of records for varying time periods. For instance, Colorado mandates the retention of vehicle inspection records for 14 months, criminal background checks for five years and driver history checks for three years.[289] Under Massachusetts law, driver records only need to be retained for one year, while the TNC must maintain trip and vehicle information for three years, along with records of prices and accessibility. As to the suspension or revocation of driver certificates, incidents reported, and criminal background results, Massachusetts law obligates TNC to retain these records for seven years.[290] Under Texas law, the TNC must

283. ME. STAT. tit. 29-A, § 1672 (2020).

284. CONN. GEN. STAT. ANN. § 13b-117 (2020); N.J. STAT. ANN. § 39.5H-4 (2020); MD. CODE ANN., PUB. UTIL. § 10502 (2020).

285. MICH. COMP. LAWS § 257.2113(a) (2020); MISS CODE ANN. § 77-8-33 (2020); N.C. GEN. STAT. § 2-280.5(c)(1) (2020).

286. N.M. STAT. ANN. § 65-7-17 (West 2016).

287. *See, e.g.*, OHIO REV. CODE ANN. § 4925.07 (2020).

288. *See, e.g.*, CONN. GEN. STAT. ANN. § 13b-118(e)(1) (2020).

289. COLO. REV. STAT. § 40-10.1-605(2) (2020).

290. 220 MASS. CODE REGS. § 274.11 (2020).

maintain records evidencing compliance with legal requirements for two years and driver records for five years.[291]

Pennsylvania law has a three-year record retention requirement for all records that it requires the TNC to maintain. In Pennsylvania, the law identifies specific records, including insurance, background checks, driver history reports, licenses, vehicle registration, complaints, suspension of drivers, insurance disclosures, vehicle information, and accidents.[292] Under Rhode Island law, the driver records need to include the "log into" and "logs out of" data, the number of trips the driver performed, the total miles driven, and fares collected. Also, TNCs operating in Rhode Island must maintain records that show the number of passenger complaints and the results of any investigations.[293] Similarly, South Carolina law requires TNCs to maintain records for three years, including trip data (specified as time of log on, time and place service commenced, address of destination, amount of fare, and any inquiry or complaint and how it was resolved), vehicle inspections, and initial and annual verifications of drivers.[294]

Virginia's law contains specific recordkeeping requirements for TNCs. At a minimum, they must include results of criminal history records check for each driver; results of driving history research report for each driver; driver's license records; results of sex offender screening; proof of compliance with vehicle ownership, registration, and inspection requirements; driver insurance; proof of compliance with notice and disclosure requirements relating to operational requirements for drivers; insurance and driver screening; proof that the TNC obtained certification from the driver of securing consent of each owner, lessor, and lessee of the vehicle; data regarding driver activity while logged in to the platform; records regarding any actions taken against a driver; contracts or agreements between TNC and drivers; information identifying each driver, including name, date of birth, driver's license number, and the state issuing the license; and information

291. Tex. Occ. Code Ann. § 2402.151 (West 2020).
292. 66 Pa. Cons. Stat. § 2604.1(b)(2) (2019).
293. 39 R.I. Gen. Laws § 39-14.2-20 (2020).
294. S.C. Code Ann. § 58-23-1670 (2020).

identifying each vehicle, including the make, model, model year, vehicle identification number, license plate number, and state issuing the license plate.[295]

Most state laws obligate TNCs to produce these records to the regulator in response to a request associated with a complaint and investigation.[296] Under the District of Columbia's law, the mayor may request information from a TNC for any trip referenced in a Metropolitan Police Department report that references an alleged crime occurring during a trip using the digital network.[297]

A few state laws impose periodic reporting requirements on TNCs. For instance, North Dakota's law contains a semi-annual reporting requirement that includes information as to where the TNC operates, the number of accidents, and the number and types of violations. Failure to report can result in a civil penalty of up to $500, and with two more violations, the Department of Transportation can prohibit the TNC from operating.[298] New Jersey's law contains a provision for the TNC to enter into a memorandum of understanding with the Department of Transportation for the submission of trip data.[299] Under South Carolina law, the TNCs must submit trip information on a quarterly basis to the Public Service Commission.[300]

In the District of Columbia, TNCs are required to submit data on a quarterly basis to the Department of For Hire Vehicles (DFHV) and the District Department of Transportation that shows the total number of drivers; a log of anonymized data relating to the trips (including the latitude and longitude for the points at which each ride originated and terminated, the date and time of request, pickup and drop-off, and whether a private or shared service was requested); the total miles driven; the average fare; and the average distance for shared service trips and

295. VA. CODE ANN. § 46.2-2099.53 (2020).
296. *See, e.g.*, S.C. CODE ANN. § 58-23-1670 (2020).
297. D.C. CODE ANN. § 50-301.29a(13)(B) (2020).
298. N.D. CENT. CODE § 39-34-05 (2020).
299. N.J. STAT. ANN. § 39.5H-6 (2020).
300. S.C. CODE ANN. § 58-23-1700 (2020).

private service trips.[301] The law expressly prohibits the DFHV from requiring the TNC to provide a list of drivers or vehicles.[302]

In some states, a reporting requirement is triggered when an accident occurs. For example, in Missouri, when a TNC receives information that a driver has been involved in a traffic accident that results in serious bodily injury or a fatality, the TNC is obligated to notify the Department of Revenue of the driver's name, license number, and license plate number.[303] In Pennsylvania, the law requires TNCs to comply with its regulations and orders regarding the reporting of any accidents involving personal vehicles.[304] The requirements in Pennsylvania that are applicable to common carriers mandate a telephonic notification to PA PUC staff within 24 hours of an accident involving the death of a person.[305]

301. D.C. Code Ann. § 50-301.29a(13) (2020).
302. *Id.* § 50-301.29g.
303. Mo. Ann. Stat. § 387.436 (2020).
304. 66 Pa. Cons. Stat. § 2604.1(b)(11) (2019).
305. 52 Pa. Code § 29.44.

CHAPTER THREE

# Liability Issues in Ridesharing Cases

## I. Introduction

In 2014, there were approximately 160,000 active Uber drivers in the United States.[306] By 2019 there were more than 3,500,000 Uber drivers worldwide.[307] With more ridesharing drivers on the road, it is safe to assume that the number of motor vehicle accidents involving ridesharing drivers will increase. In 2018, it was reported that there had been a 2 percent to 3 percent increase in the number of fatal motor vehicle accidents that can be attributed to an increase in the use of ridesharing services.[308] As accidents involving ridesharing drivers become more common, finding the correct way to allocate liability between drivers and ridesharing companies for injuries caused in car accidents becomes a pressing necessity. Defining the relationship between a ridesharing driver and ridesharing company, like Uber or Lyft, will have a significant impact on the ultimate allocation of liability for injuries that occur in the ridesharing context. However, there are legal theories that could result in a ridesharing company being held liable for injuries caused by a driver, regardless of how the relationship between the driver and coordinator is defined. Legal theories exist that could impose liability directly on the company,

306. Iqbal, *supra* note 4.
307. *Id.*
308. Charlotte Jee, *Uber and Lyft Are Behind a Sharp Rise in US Traffic Deaths*, MIT TECH. REV. (Oct. 25, 2018), https://www.technologyreview.com/f/612346/uber-and-lyft-are-behind-a-sharp-rise-in-us-traffic-deaths/.

but the legal status of the relationship between drivers and companies is still of primary importance.

This chapter explores how the relationship between the ridesharing driver and ridesharing company can impact allocation of liability in the event of any injury. Furthermore, this chapter outlines the principles that may support holding a ridesharing company responsible for the torts committed by associated drivers. Lastly, this chapter explores a variety of legal theories that could be used to assert claims directly against ridesharing companies in the event one of their drivers harms a ridesharing customer or a third party.

## II. The Phases of the Ride, and Their Effect on Liability Generally

Ridesharing is associated with a 3 percent rise in fatalities for pedestrians and motor vehicle occupants.[309] This rise in the number of ridesharing accidents is coupled with the unfamiliar landscape of people-to-people technology and allocating liability and responsibility of insurance coverage. For the purpose of identifying who bears the risk of loss, four phases of the ridesharing experience have been identified:

> Phase 0: The app is closed, and driver mode is off. The car is being used for personal use.
>
> Phase 1: The app is open, and the driver is waiting for a rider.
>
> Phase 2: A fare has been accepted, and the driver is on the way to the rider's location.
>
> Phase 3: This phase begins when the rider is in the vehicle and ends when the rider reaches his destination.

An understanding of these phases is a necessary precursor to understanding when the insurance policies of the ridesharing driver or ridesharing company may apply in the event of an accident.

309. Barrios et al., *supra* note 6.

While in Phase 0, neither Lyft nor Uber provides insurance for the driver. Maintaining personal coverage during this phase is the responsibility of the driver. However, when a driver is furnishing a personal vehicle for ridesharing (Phases 1, 2, and 3), their personal insurance might not apply. Many personal automobile insurance policies provide an exclusion for automobiles when they are used with ridesharing apps. Whereas this issue is more fully explored later in this book, suffice it to say that this gap has also created a market for policy riders or endorsements to personal automobile insurance policies.[310] These endorsements provide coverage and attempt to limit or close the gap in coverage that has traditionally been excluded under the ridesharing exclusions to such policies.

Recently, there has been greater regulatory focus on closing the gap in coverage created by ridesharing, which could leave an injured third party[311] without a way to pay for injuries caused by a ridesharing driver. The gap in coverage was highly publicized on New Year's Eve, 2014, after an Uber driver struck and killed a six-year-old child in a crosswalk in San Francisco.[312] Although this is tragic in itself, the accident occurred while in Phase 1 of ridesharing, so the accident was not within the scope of Uber's insurance policy. Following this accident, some state and local governments enacted laws and regulations to require that insurance coverage be available to cover drivers as a prerequisite to allowing the company and its drivers to operate in their jurisdiction.[313]

By way of example, in 2015, Ohio's legislature carved out new regulations regarding ridesharing companies or, in the language of the statute, "transportation network companies." The new regulations are subject to enforcement by the state's Public Utilities Commission and attempt to bridge the coverage gap between a driver's personal coverage and the ridesharing

---

310. *See infra* Chapter 3, Section III.

311. Third party in this context refers to someone other than the driver or any passengers in the driver's vehicle.

312. Yanelys Crespo, *Uber v. Regulation: "Ride-Sharing" Creates a Legal Gray Area*, 25 U. Miami Bus. L. Rev. 79 (2016).

313. *See supra* Chapter 2, Section III.F.

company's coverage.[314] For insurance purposes, the relevant portion of the legislation provides that ridesharing companies shall not permit a driver to operate the ridesharing platform unless the driver has (i) his own automobile insurance or (ii) the company's insurance, with both policies meeting the requirements of section 3942.02 of the Ohio Revised Code.[315] Section 3942.02 requires that each company's driver be covered by a policy that recognizes him as a driver for a ridesharing company and recognizes the fact that the driver uses his vehicle to transport passengers for compensation while the driver is logged in to the company's platform and engaged in the company's services.[316] Put more simply, ridesharing companies are required to provide insurance for a driver when the driver is engaged in those companies' services. Ridesharing companies also list insurance requirements, broken down by city of service, on their websites, as local and state standards vary across the country, although Uber requires drivers to sign in to access those requirements.[317]

To comply with the new laws,[318] both Uber and Lyft introduced insurance to cover third-party injuries during Phases 1, 2, and 3 of ridesharing. In Phase 1, when the driver has the app open and is driving around while waiting for a rider, both Uber and Lyft have added contingent liability as part of their services to the drivers. Coverage for Phase 1 is of great importance because drivers are spending a significant amount of time on the road without passengers—only having passengers in the car 59 percent of the time they are active on the app.[319]

During Phase 1, Lyft and Uber provide contingent liability coverage assuming the driver does not have personal coverage,

---

314. Andrew L. Smith, Ridesharing Regulations Arrive in the Buckeye State (2016) https://rolfeshenry.com/Uploads/files/Ridesharing%20Regulations%20Arrive%20in%20the%20Buckeye%20State%20-%20CBA%20Report%20%20March%202016.pdf.

315. Ohio Rev. Code Ann. § 4925.04(B) (LexisNexis 2020).

316. *Id.* § 3942.02(A)(1)(a)–(b).

317. *See Insurance Requirements*, Uber, https://help.uber.com/driving-and-delivering/article/insurance-requirements?nodeId=6e7ac56f-a12b-440a-9e6e-83acea284b55 (last viewed Mar. 5, 2020).

318. *See supra* Chapter 2.

319. Barrios et al., *supra* note 6.

or the personal coverage does not apply. This contingent liability insurance insures the driver's liability with respect to a third party if the driver is at fault in an accident with the following limits:

- $50,000 in bodily injury per person;
- $100,000 in bodily injury per accident; and
- $25,000 in property damage per accident.[320]

Both Uber and Lyft acknowledge that these coverage limits are the minimum insurance maintained for the driver, as different states and localities have enacted laws with required minimums in which ridesharing companies must be compliant. The requirement for minimum liability coverage places ridesharing apps on a closer footing to their taxicab counterparts.

Note, however, this coverage only applies if the driver is at fault in an accident. If the other driver is at fault, the ridesharing driver will presumably bear the burden of funding any necessary repairs to his own vehicle or medical expenses the ridesharing driver incurs if the driver-at-fault is uninsured or underinsured. Thus, the gap in coverage may not be completely closed. To convey this gap in coverage to its drivers, Uber has explicitly stated that drivers may make a claim against the third-party's insurance or consult their personal insurance policies for applicable coverage under such circumstances.[321]

During Phases 2 and 3, when the driver either has accepted a passenger on the app or has the passenger in the vehicle, Uber and Lyft provide accident coverage under three circumstances:

1. Third-party liability coverage (Uber) or primary automobile liability (Lyft);
2. Uninsured or underinsured motorist coverage; and
3. Contingent collision and comprehensive coverage.[322]

---

320. *Insurance*, LYFT, https://help.lyft.com/hc/en-us/articles/115013080548-Insurance-Policy (last visited Mar. 5, 2020).

321. *Insurance*, UBER, https://help.uber.com/driving-and-delivering/article/insurance-?nodeId=a4afb2ed-75af-4db6-8fdb-dccecfcc3fd7 (last visited Mar. 5, 2020).

322. *Insurance*, LYFT, *supra* note 320; *Insurance*, UBER, *supra* note 321.

First, Uber and Lyft provide $1,000,000 in liability coverage. As for Lyft, its coverage is designed to be the driver's primary insurance coverage during the second and third phases, offering a policy limit of $1,000,000 per accident.[323] Uber's liability coverage is limited to bodily injury and property damage suffered by third parties.[324]

Next, both Uber and Lyft provide uninsured or underinsured motorist coverage. The ridesharing companies limit this coverage to injuries sustained by the driver and any riders in the driver's vehicle where another driver is at fault and lacks sufficient insurance.[325] Uber's uninsured/underinsured motorist bodily injury coverage limit is at least $250,000 but varies from state to state.[326] Lyft does not publish a threshold limit and instead notes the variance among states.[327] Lyft does not have a deductible for its uninsured or underinsured motorist coverage.[328]

Finally, Uber and Lyft provide contingent comprehensive coverage for their drivers while in Phases 2 or 3. Although the name and concept for this policy is the same, there are distinct differences between Lyft's and Uber's respective policies. For example, for this insurance to apply at all, the drivers must maintain comprehensive and collision coverage as part of their personal auto insurance policies. However, both ridesharing companies offer contingent collision damage. In the event of an accident, both Lyft and Uber will provide coverage for physical damage to the vehicle regardless of whether the ridesharing driver is at fault.[329] The amount payable is up to the actual cash value of the vehicle for both companies, but Lyft specifies it will pay the actual cash value or cost of repair, whichever is less.[330]

Another notable difference between the companies is that Lyft breaks out a distinct contingent comprehensive policy for

323. *Insurance*, LYFT, *supra* note 320.
324. *Insurance*, UBER, *supra* note 321.
325. *Insurance*, LYFT, *supra* note 320; *Insurance*, UBER, *supra* note 321.
326. *Insurance*, UBER, *supra* note 321.
327. *Insurance*, LYFT, *supra* note 320.
328. *Id.*
329. *Insurance*, LYFT, *supra* note 320; *Insurance*, UBER, *supra* note 321.
330. *Insurance*, LYFT, *supra* note 320.

physical damage resulting from a non-collision event to the driver's car up to the lesser of its actual cash value or cost of repair.[331] A non-collision event includes fire, natural disaster, vandalism, or similar event.[332] Nonetheless, the personal insurance that the ridesharing companies allude to in this area of their policy is presumably an extension of the driver's personal insurance policy, since, as just noted, personal insurance policies generally do not cover the driver when he is engaged in commercial use. Also note that in such a case, the driver must pay a $1,000 deductible to Uber or a $2,500 deductible to Lyft before this coverage would apply.[333]

With more and more drivers opting to drive for both Uber and Lyft,[334] a complex overlap regarding which ridesharing app will cover liability arises before we even begin to evaluate the interplay between Uber and Lyft. Because it is acceptable to drive for both Uber and Lyft simultaneously,[335] questions are likely to arise as to which ridesharing company's policy should apply in the event of an accident. Obviously, which app is turned on at the time of the accident or which company the driver is providing services for at the time of accident are the key questions here. However, when a driver is using multiple apps, the waters become significantly murkier.

To understand just how complex the coverage issues may be, consider the following scenario: a driver picks up a Lyft passenger and then sees a request for an Uber ride near the Lyft passenger's destination.[336] If the driver accepts the Uber fare, he will be in Phase 3 with respect to Lyft, Phase 2 with Uber, and Phase 1 with any other ridesharing apps that may be running in the background of his phone. Such a situation may not be an uncommon occurrence as ridesharing services continually

331. *Id.*

332. *Id.*

333. *Id.*

334. Brett Helling, *How to Drive for Uber and Lyft (at the Same Time)*, RIDESTER.COM (July 21, 2020) https://www.ridester.com/drive-for-uber-and-lyft.

335. *Id.*

336. *Id.* Drivers sometimes use multiple phones in order to be able to drive for multiple companies simultaneously.

become more ubiquitous. In the event of an accident, untangling which policies apply will involve very close scrutiny of where the accident occurred relative to the different tasks the driver is simultaneously completing. For instance, if the driver is hit by a third party while dropping off the Uber passenger, there will be a stronger argument that Uber's policy should be primary. Conversely, if the driver is in an accident before the Uber passenger is picked up, Lyft's policy may be looked to first. The permutations of this scenario are virtually endless. In the coming years, courts, litigators, and insurers will be tasked with identifying sound principles to untangle this complicated web of potential liability and overlapping policies.

The principles that will be used for the allocation of liability in accidents involving ridesharing companies is presently being debated. Unfortunately, few, if any, courts have addressed these precise issues.[337] We are left to apply preexisting legal principles to reason that liability would be allocated based on the purpose of the trip, and which company was more directly benefitted by the driver's services at the exact time of the crash. Even when relying on existing legal principles, there are likely to be situations where no clear answer can be reached. In summary, this is an issue on which there will be significant development in the coming years. Interested parties, including attorneys, insurance companies, and claims representatives should be mindful and stay abreast of the developments in this area of law that are sure to come.

## III. Liability and Insurance

The relationship between auto insurance and ridesharing presents many unique challenges, from unraveling which coverage drivers must have in place to which polices may apply at different phases of a ridesharing driver's activities. Regulators at the state and local level have acted to put in place requirements to guard against gaps in coverage that could leave persons injured

337. Smith, *supra* note 10.

by ridesharing drivers without recourse.[338] In turn, the insurance industry has responded with new products to meet the demand brought about by the use of ridesharing. As noted earlier, insurers in many states have also begun selling special ridesharing policies, or policy endorsements, that extended coverage to an insured for use of his or her vehicle for ridesharing. Where available, these policies increase the cost of a driver's car insurance by approximately 20 percent. These personal policies affect the policies ridesharing companies offer to their drivers. If a driver purchases their own commercial driving or special ridesharing insurance policy, then Uber's insurance policies do not apply.[339] Lyft's policies will only apply as excess of the driver's personal policies if the driver has a commercial driving or special ridesharing insurance policy.[340]

In the coming years, lawyers are likely to be confronted with ever-more complex factual scenarios involving ridesharing and insurance coverage.

## A. Personal Auto Policies: What Do They Cover?

A personal auto policy is purchased by a vehicle owner to protect against the financial losses associated with a motor vehicle accident. The most common coverages included in a personal auto policy are liability coverage, collision coverage, and comprehensive coverage.[341]

### 1. Liability Coverage[342]

**Bodily injury liability.** This coverage protects the driver from claims for injuries caused by the driver's negligence.

---

338. *See supra* Chapter 2.

339. *Auto Insurance to Help Protect You*, Uber, https://www.uber.com/us/en/drive/insurance/ (last visited Mar 5, 2020).

340. *Insurance*, Lyft, https://help.lyft.com/hc/en-us/articles/115013080548-Insurance-Policy (last visited Mar. 5, 2020).

341. *A Consumer's Guide to Auto Insurance*, Nat'l Ass'n Ins. Comm'rs, https://www.naic.org/documents/prod_serv_consumer_guide_auto.pdf (last visited July 25, 2020).

342. *Id.*

Covered damages include medical expenses, lost wages, and pain and suffering.

**Property damage liability.** This coverage protects the driver from claims of damage to other's property caused by the driver's negligence. This may include damage to another driver's car, a fence, a tree, or a structure.

**Uninsured motorist coverage.** This coverage is designed to protect the driver. If the driver is injured by another driver who does not have insurance, or a hit and run driver, this coverage takes the place of the other driver's insurance.

**Underinsured motorists coverage.** This coverage also protects the driver. If an at fault driver's insurance does not cover the driver's damages, this coverage will pay the difference up to the driver's policy limits.

### 2. Coverage for the Driver's Car[343]

**Collison coverage.** This coverage pays for physical damage to the policyholder's vehicle thst resulted from hitting another car or object.

**Comprehensive coverage.** This coverage pays for other physical damage that does not result from a collision. Some examples include fire, theft, hail damage, vandalism, or animal damage.

## B. Livery Exclusions

Traditional ridesharing, that is, carpooling, is usually covered by an individual's personal auto policy.[344] However, once an individual begins transporting passengers for a fee, they have likely exceeded the terms of their personal auto policy. Most personal auto policies contain a livery exclusion. Typical livery exclusions exclude coverage for any "liability arising out of the ownership or operation of a vehicle while it is being used as a public or livery conveyance." A policy may also exclude coverage when the

---

343. *Id.*

344. Nat'l Ass'n of Ins. Comm'rs, Transportation Network Company Insurance Principles for Legislators and Regulators 2 (2015).

insured's vehicle is used "to carry persons for a charge," "for commercial purposes," "for compensation," "for a fee," or "for hire." Any of these phrases are indicative of a livery exclusion that may affect coverage for drivers participating in ridesharing.[345] However, the subtle difference in terminology can make determining which ridesharing activities are excluded quite difficult.

Personal auto policies exclude livery services for two primary reasons: (i) the exposures are beyond the scope of a typical policy or (ii) the type of activity would be more appropriately covered by a different product offered by the insurer.[346] Many insurers consider the exposures related to ridesharing to be higher risk than those associated with more traditional uses of a personal automobile. For example, individuals performing ridesharing services are more likely to travel in urban or congested areas. These areas may pose a greater risk for accidents and therefore entitle the insurer to higher premiums. Traditional, noncommercial drivers usually travel fewer miles, whereas rideshare drivers are more likely to drive more miles while looking for customers, again exposing the insurer to greater risk of loss.[347]

Insurers are also concerned that drivers are more likely to use their phones while driving for a ridesharing company, as they must interact with a smartphone app to accept customers and manipulate GPS to determine approved routes. This use of smartphones exposes the insurer to greater losses due to higher incidences of accidents because of distracted driving. Finally, insurers are concerned that vehicles involved in ridesharing are likely to have more passengers than the typical vehicle, which may result in greater losses.[348]

Due to the increased risks of loss, many insurers consider participation in ridesharing services to be a "material change to the insurance contract."[349] As such, the insurer may cancel the policy, refuse to renew it, or deny coverage if there is a loss on the policy related to a driver being involved in an accident. Of

---

345. *Id.* at 7.
346. *Id.*
347. *Id.*
348. *Id.* at 8.
349. *Id.*

course, determining whether an insured is using their vehicle for ridesharing is difficult and can increase costs following an accident. Many insurers now also offer add-on products to provide coverage for individuals performing ridesharing services. These are commonly referred to as "riders" or "endorsements."

## C. What Is a Rider?

"A rider is an insurance policy provision that adds benefits to or amends the terms of a basic insurance policy."[350] Individuals can purchase a rider to add specific types of coverage to an existing policy without buying an entirely new policy. This allows consumers to customize their policies to their specific needs. This can lead to additional savings for the purchaser and allows them the option of buying different coverage at a later time, as their needs change.[351]

Ridesharing riders are most applicable to Phase 1. This is when the ridesharing app is "on" and the driver is waiting for a ride request. During this phase, the driver is not typically covered by the rideshare company's insurance. A personal auto policy may not provide coverage during this period. As such, a driver can purchase a rider to fill this gap.[352]

Several companies now sell riders for this purpose. However, coverage may not be available in every state. For example, as of 2019, Allstate offers rideshare coverage almost nationwide,[353] while Progressive offers coverage in approximately 70 percent of states. Presently, these riders are relatively affordable, with many companies charging between $6 and $20 per month. However, one prominent insurer estimates the cost of ridesharing insurance to be 15 percent to 20 percent above its traditional

---

350. Julia Kagan, *Rider* (Apr. 16, 2019) https://www.investopedia.com/terms/r/rider.asp.

351. *Id.*

352. Kayda Norman, *Rideshare Insurance for Drivers: Where to Buy It, What It Covers*, NERDWALLET (June 1, 2020), https://www.nerdwallet.com/blog/insurance/best-ridesharing-insurance/.

353. *Allstate Ride for Hire*, ALLSTATE, https://www.allstate.com/auto-insurance/ride-for-hire.aspx (last visited Mar. 5, 2020).

premium.[354] With the low cost of ridesharing riders, they are an affordable and effective option to ensure drivers have sufficient insurance coverage during the phase when they are awaiting a passenger.

## D. Commercial General Liability (CGL) Policies

A commercial general liability (CGL) policy covers damages related to bodily injury, property damage, personal injury, and advertising injury to a third party or employee during the course of business. The policy also covers the compensatory and general damages that may result from a lawsuit. Further, a CGL policy covers the associated legal costs incurred when defending against such an action.[355] In the ridesharing context, CGL policies are oftentimes held by the ridesharing companies themselves. In some situations, these policies may also provide coverage for the drivers as well. A CGL policy has a maximum amount that the insurer will pay out during the policy period. Additionally, the policy usually has a maximum the insurer will pay per each occurrence. In the ridesharing context, most companies provide general liability insurance only after the driver has accepted a request.

## E. Parties in a Ridesharing Accident

Following a typical auto accident, discerning the parties and their respective insurers is usually straightforward. For example, if Car A rear-ends Car B, typically each driver carries a single auto insurance policy. The drivers exchange their information, and all the parties and their insurers have been identified. However, in a ridesharing situation, discerning the parties and their insurers can be considerably more complicated.

If Car A is engaged in ridesharing at the time of the accident, there may be multiple parties and policies in play. The first hurdle is determining whether a driver is engaged in ridesharing.

---

354. *Id.*

355. *Understanding General Liability Insurance*, AllBusiness, https://www.allbusiness.com/understanding-general-liability-insurance-2-389-1.html (last visited Mar. 5, 2020).

Further complicating this issue is the fact that a driver may be using more than one ridesharing app at the same time. When a driver is waiting for a ride request, she may have several apps turned on to increase the chances of receiving a request. If a driver is involved in an accident during this phase, it may be difficult to determine whether a ridesharing company's contingent policy is in effect.

Once a driver has accepted a ride, she may be covered by her own personal auto policy, the ridesharing company's commercial policy, as well as a contingent policy. The driver's personal policy may or may not have a rider for ridesharing. In some instances, if the driver has not disclosed to his insurer that he is using his vehicle for ridesharing, the personal auto policy may deny all coverage. Whether the driver is at fault is also likely to be a factor in determining which policies are in effect. Even where the ridesharing company's policy is in effect, the policy limits may depend on the coverage limits of the driver's personal auto policy. Unraveling which polices are in effect and the policy limits in a particular case is a fact-dependent determination.

## F. Insurers of Ridesharing Companies and the Coverages in Place

Following is a chart that sets out some of the general information related to the insurance coverage offered by the largest ridesharing companies. Importantly, this information may vary in individual states or municipalities due to unique regulations on insurance requirements. Regulatory changes drove both Uber and Lyft to provide some degree of insurance coverage for their drivers.[356] Both companies, however, expressed concern in their IPO filings that their insurance policies may prove insufficient to

356. Uber Techs., Inc., Registration Statement (Form S-1) 64 (Apr. 11, 2019), https://www.sec.gov/Archives/edgar/data/1543151/000119312519103850/d647752ds1.htm#toc; Lyft, Inc., Registration Statement (Form S-1) 24 (Mar. 1, 2019), https://www.sec.gov/Archives/edgar/data/1759509/000119312519059849/d633517ds1.htm.

protect them financially.[357] This uncertainty, and the companies' shared desire to mitigate risk and protect their financial interests, could explain why Uber and Lyft require drivers to maintain personal coverage. Furthermore, requiring drivers to maintain their own insurance policies demonstrates less control by the companies, which would likely be important in a court's analysis of whether a ridesharing driver is an employee or independent contractor for purposes of evaluating tort liability. Notably, the different ways ridesharing drivers are insured has so far had no practical impact on claims against ridesharing companies.

| Company | Coverage Provided |
|---|---|
| **Uber**[358] | • Commercial auto liability<br>• Uninsured/underinsured motorist<br>• $1 million per occurrence<br>• Contingent collision and comprehensive equal to the policy limits of the driver's personal policy ($1,000 deductible) |
| **Lyft**[359] | • Commercial auto liability<br>• Uninsured/underinsured motorist<br>• $1 million per occurrence<br>• Contingent collision and comprehensive with $50,000 limit per accident ($2,500 deductible) |

# IV. Liability and Employment Status

## A. Introduction

Defining the relationship between a ridesharing driver and a ridesharing company like Uber or Lyft will have a significant impact on the ultimate allocation of liability for injuries that occur in the ridesharing context. This section explores the relationship between ridesharing drivers, the respective companies, and how liability is allocated in the event of an injury based on the classification of that relationship. Further, this section addresses the standards that courts may use to determine a

357. Uber Registration Statement, *supra* note 356, at 63–64; Lyft Registration Statement, *supra* note 356, at 24–25.

358. *Insurance*, UBER, *supra* note 321.

359. *Insurance*, LYFT, *supra* note 320.

driver's employment status and what positions drivers and ridesharing companies have taken on this issue. Finally, this section outlines the current statutory scheme in each state as it relates to defining this relationship, and the statutory language that each state has adopted, if any.

As briefly mentioned earlier, the classification of ridesharing drivers is of primary importance to the question of the apportionment of liability between drivers and ridesharing companies. The answer to how ridesharing drivers are classified is important, though not wholly determinative of the issue of whether ridesharing companies can be held liable for torts committed by their drivers. If ridesharing drivers are routinely held to be employees for the purposes of tort law, it will be significantly easier to establish that the ridesharing operator is vicariously liable for injuries caused by its drivers.[360] Typically, the third party held accountable for someone else's tort is a company that employs the tortfeasor. The tort theory supporting this use of vicarious liability is that it allows for better allocation of risk and cost of injuries between companies, employees, and injured third parties. To better understand the contours of the debate surrounding the apportionment of liability in the ridesharing context, it is necessary to look at the general principles surrounding vicarious liability and worker classification. This examination will begin with an explanation of the differences between employees and independent contractors, followed by a brief overview of the tests employed by courts when tasked with making this distinction.

In a traditional car accident context, apportionment of liability is fairly simple. Take the following example:

> Driver A and Driver B are both driving their own vehicles on their personal time. Driver A runs a red light and collides with Driver B, causing damage to both vehicles. Driver A has liability insurance that covers the damage to Driver B's vehicle. Driver B was also physically injured

360. Vicarious liability is the legal concept that permits third parties to be held liable for the tortious acts of others.

> beyond the scope of Driver A's liability insurance coverage. Driver B sues Driver A for negligence and recovers the excess amount in medical bills, which were not covered by Driver A's insurance policy. Driver A is able to satisfy this judgment in full.

Now let's take a more involved example. Instead of driving on his personal time, Driver A is a traveling salesman in route to a client, driving his own vehicle:

> Driver A and Driver B are both driving their own vehicles. Driver A is an employee of a medical device sales company and is on his way to visit a client. Driver B is driving on his personal time. Driver A runs a red light and collides with Driver B, causing damage to both vehicles. Driver A has liability insurance that covers the damage to Driver B's vehicle. Driver B was also physically injured beyond the scope of Driver A's liability insurance coverage. Driver B sues Driver A for negligence and also sues Driver A's employer because Driver A was working on the company's behalf when the accident happened. Driver B recovers the excess amount in medical bills, which were not covered by Driver A's insurance policy from both Driver A and Driver A's employer.

However, if Driver A was not an employee of the medical device sales company and instead was contracted to sell the devices independently, the liability would be apportioned differently. In this case, the scenario would play out exactly as in the first scenario where Driver A and Driver B were both driving their own vehicles on their personal time. This is where the theory of vicarious liability comes into play. Vicarious liability allows an injured party to sue both the tortfeasor and his or her employer, if the employee was working within the scope of his or her employment at the time of the accident. The general underlying principle of this theory is that because the employer was deriving a benefit from the employee's activities, the employer should also share in the burden of costs stemming from torts caused by the employee's actions.

This scenario grows even more complicated when viewed in the context of ridesharing drivers. This is largely because the parties involved take different stances on who is benefiting from a driver's actions at any particular time. Moreover, the matter of which person or entity is deriving a benefit from an action is but one aspect of consideration of whether drivers are employees or independent contractors.

## B. Vicarious Liability for Injuries Caused by Ridesharing Drivers

Unsurprisingly, the various parties involved in ridesharing take different positions on defining and describing the interplay between ridesharing company and driver. For instance, Uber refers to its drivers as "partners," emphasizes the flexibility provided to its "partners," and insists drivers are independent contractors.[361] Conversely, drivers seek the enhanced protections that come with being classified as an employee. Likewise, injured parties, hoping to establish a ridesharing company's liability for an injury caused by a driver, focus heavily on the control ridesharing companies exercise over drivers.

The issue of defining the relationship between drivers and companies in the employment law context has been frequently litigated and presents its own host of issues. For example, workers labeled as independent contractors struggle with enforcement of their employment rights, as they are unable to rely on the Department of Labor or collective bargaining for protection.[362] Independent contractors are also unable to seek unemployment benefits or workers' compensation, among many other limitations that come with the label of independent contractor.[363]

The positions taken by ridesharing operators in prior legal disputes over how drivers should be classified for the purposes of employment law give insight into the arguments that

361. McPeak, *supra* note 9, at 364.

362. Ashley L. Crank, *O'Connor v. Uber Technologies, Inc.: The Dispute Lingers—Are Workers in the On-Demand Economy Employees or Independent Contractors?* 39 Am. J. Trial Advoc. 609, 611 (2016).

363. *Id.*

ridesharing companies and injured parties are likely to make in the tort context. When these employment questions have been litigated, the companies typically seek to distance themselves from the transportation aspect of their operations.[364] Companies like Uber and Lyft have argued that they are merely "technology companies" and not employers of their drivers.[365] These companies take the position that they provide a technological service, which connects independent drivers to people in their areas who need a ride. Some operators go so far as to describe the service they provide as being more like that of a phone book than a transportation service.[366] Uber's contract with its drivers stresses that it "does not provide transportation services" and "is not a transportation carrier."[367]

By casting themselves as mere facilitators, ridesharing companies aim to avoid the legal liabilities attached to operating as a transportation company, including liability for injuries caused by ridesharing drivers. Although ridesharing has often been considered by courts in an employment context, few rulings have been issued on this question as a matter of tort law.[368] As ridesharing has moved from a novel, disruptive technology to a commonplace fact of life, we have seen these questions arise more frequently.

Arguments from ridesharing companies aimed at persuading courts that their companies are more like a technology company, such as eBay, than a traditional taxi or transportation service have not been well received. Two courts in the Northern District of California that considered the issue of the employment classification of rideshare drivers found Uber's and Lyft's mere

364. *See* Cotter v. Lyft, Inc., 60 F. Supp. 3d 1067, 1078 (N.D. Cal. 2015); O'Connor v. Uber Techs., Inc., 82 F. Supp. 3d 1133,1137 (N.D. Cal. 2015).

365. *See* Cotter v. Lyft, Inc., 60 F. Supp. 3d 1067, 1078 (N.D. Cal. 2015); O'Connor v. Uber Techs., Inc., 82 F. Supp. 3d 1133,1137 (N.D. Cal. 2015).

366. Emily Badger, *The Strange Tale of an Uber Car Crash and What It Means for the Future of Auto Insurance*, CityLab (Sept. 10, 2013), https://www.citylab.com/transportation/2013/09/real-future-ride-sharing-may-all-come-down-insurance/6832/.

367. *See id.*

368. Crank, *supra* note 362, at 611.

"technology company" arguments to be "fatally flawed" and "obviously wrong."[369] In reaching the conclusion that rideshare drivers are entitled to the protections afforded to employees, these courts relied on many of the same factors that prospective plaintiffs are likely to point to in a tort context. These factors include the detailed instructions ridesharing companies provide to drivers on how to conduct themselves and the fact that drivers are essential to ridesharing companies generating revenue.[370]

The California Labor Department found that Uber drivers are employees under a California labor statute.[371] The agency made this determination based on the fact that Uber provides the app drivers use to match with riders, mandates vehicle specifications, requires insurance coverage, sets all prices, and performs pre-employment screening such as background checks.[372]

### 1. Common Law: Employee versus Independent Contractor

In broad terms, what distinguishes an employee from an independent contractor is the level of control the hiring party exerts over the worker. For an employer/employee relationship to exist, the purported employer typically must have a right to directly control the manner and means by which an employee accomplishes the tasks assigned by the employer.[373] If a company exercises sufficient control to justify imposing the employee classification on workers, then the company will be responsible for injuries caused by the employee in the course and scope of the execution of the employee's duties. Conversely, if the purported employer does not control the manner and means of the employee's work, then the relationship is that of an independent contractor. An independent contractor is a person who is assigned a job to complete, but who is not specifically instructed on *how* to

369. *See Cotter* 60 F. Supp. 3d at 1077; *O'Connor* 82 F. Supp. 3d at 1141.

370. *Cotter*, 60 F. Supp. 3d at 1077; *O'Connor*, 82 F. Supp. 3d at 1141.

371. *See* Berwick v. Uber Techs., Inc., No. 11-46739 EK, 2015 WL 4153765, at *6 (Cal. Dep't of Labor June 2, 2015).

372. *Id.*

373. Restatement (Third) of Agency § 2.04 (Am. Law. Inst. 2006).

do the job. Contractors are merely provided with what needs to be accomplished and the payment for completing the task.

Ostensibly, hiring parties have less control over the actions of an independent contractor than over the actions of an employee. As such, there is less reason to hold hiring parties responsible for the actions of a contractor. In the context of an employer/employee relationship, the employer is recognized as having the authority to control the employee's actions. Conversely, a contractor is subject only to the terms of the agreement with the hiring party, and not the hiring party's whims over how to complete the agreed upon tasks.[374]

### a. The "Control Factors" Test

Although control is the primary consideration in worker classification disputes, stating that control is the determinative issue provides little guidance on how to analyze specific relationships. In an effort to clarify what we mean by "control," the Supreme Court has analyzed 12 factors relevant to this inquiry.[375] These factors are:

- The skill required to complete the task
- Which party provides the tools necessary to complete the work
- Where the work is done
- How long the relationship between the parties will continue
- Which party has discretion over when and how long the hired party works
- Whether the hiring party is permitted to assign additional tasks to the worker
- The method used to issue payment
- The hiring party's role in providing assistance to the hired party

374. It is important to point out that a contractor's actions can be used as a basis for establishing vicarious liability to the same extent as an employee if the tortious actions of the contractor were controlled by the hiring party.

375. Nationwide Mutual Ins. Co. v. Darden, 503 U.S. 318, 323–24 (1992).

- Whether the task accomplished by the worker is part of the hiring party's regular business
- Whether the hiring party is a company or business, as opposed to an individual
- Whether the worker receives benefits
- The tax implications related to the hired party[376]

These factors can be useful to determine whether sufficient control exists to establish an employer/employee relationship, but they are not the only relevant factors. Other facts that courts may consider are the understanding between the parties and whether the worker is held out to the public in a way that makes them appear to be associated with the hiring party.[377]

*i. Skill Required to Complete the Task*

In examining the factors employed by the Supreme Court, there are factors that place ridesharing drivers on different sides of the analysis. For example, drivers for Uber or Lyft need not "try out" for employment by way of showcasing their superior driving talents to company representatives. This would indicate that there is no special skill set necessary to qualify to become a driver. However, both Uber and Lyft perform Department of Motor Vehicles (DMV) background checks to ensure that the prospective driver does not have an accident history, which lends itself to the argument that because drivers must have some minimally positive track record with the DMV, special skill is required.[378]

Those hoping to establish that driving is a specialized skill will point to cases like *FedEx Home Delivery*.[379] In *FedEx Home Delivery*, the D.C. Circuit held that FedEx drivers who had to take a brief course in delivery driving could qualify as specially

---

376. *Id.*

377. *See* Restatement (Second) of Agency § 220(h) (Am. Law. Inst. 1958).

378. *See, e.g., Driver Requirements: DMV Check,* Lyft, https://help.lyft.com/hc/en-us/articles/115012925687-Driver-requirements#dmv (last visited June 7, 2019).

379. *See* FedEx Home Delivery v. NLRB, 563 F.3d 492, 500–01 (D.C. Cir. 2009).

skilled employees.[380] Conversely, others have pointed out that driving is not a unique skill. For instance, as one commentator on the subject has noted "if an activity as common as driving a car qualifies as a special skill, it is difficult to imagine what would not. . . . Accordingly, driving for Uber should not require a particularly special skill."[381] Moreover, the *FedEx Home Delivery* case can likely be distinguished simply by the types of vehicles involved. The drivers in *FedEx Home Delivery* were driving trucks that are not common personal vehicles. This is not the case with ridesharing drivers who generally drive their own vehicles to perform their work.

*ii. Which Party Provides the Tools Necessary*

When a hiring party provides the tools to the worker that are necessary to perform the job, it is more likely that the relationship is that of employer–employee. Conversely, a worker who supplies and maintains her own set of tools to perform her work is more likely to be found to be a contractor. In the standard ridesharing model, drivers for Uber and Lyft generally provide their own vehicles. Thus, at first glance it would seem clear that this factor would weigh heavily towards drivers being considered contractors with ridesharing companies. However, some programs offered by ridesharing companies complicate this issue. Moreover, the other essential tool necessary for a ridesharing transaction to take place—the ridesharing mobile app—is supplied entirely by the ridesharing company. Without use of the mobile apps developed, published, and operated by companies like Uber and Lyft it is unlikely that any particular driver would engage with any particular rider.

---

380. *Id.*

381. Henry Ross, *Ridesharing's House of Cards: O'Connor v. Uber Technologies, Inc. and the Viability of Uber's Labor Model in Washington*, 90 WASH. L. REV. 1431, 1466 (2015).

## C. Ridesharing Mobile Apps as a Tool Necessary to Provide Ridesharing Service

While ridesharing companies are correct in their position that their technology acts as a facilitating mechanism to pair drivers with riders, this mechanism can also be characterized as a "tool" that is critical to the job of ridesharing. Without these mobile apps supplied by ridesharing companies, it is certain that far fewer persons would engage in hiring strangers for rides. The apps supplied by companies are relied on by users to connect them with available drivers who are able to meet riders' needs in terms of how far they are going, the size of vehicle they require, and/or whether they prefer to pay a premium to ride in a luxury vehicle. In this way, a rider's use of a company's app, which is provided wholly by a ridesharing company, is a key component of the work to be accomplished—pairing the rider with their desired ride.

As for drivers, the mobile apps they are provided by ridesharing companies function not only as a means of notifying a driver that someone is "hailing" a ride, but the apps also provide directions to pick-up and drop-off locations and allow a direct, specialized line of communication between a driver and a ridesharing company. In short, without the ridesharing mobile apps, ridesharing in its current iteration would not exist. Parties hoping to establish an employment relationship may argue ridesharing companies are providing a tool necessary to carry out the task performed by ridesharing drivers simply by operating the mobile apps that brought about ridesharing as it exists presently.

Conversely, ridesharing companies are likely to argue that simply having created a technology that pairs drivers with riders is not a "tool" necessary to perform the work of rides for hire. This type of transaction, individuals hiring others to provide transportation services, has existed for thousands of years. A ridesharing company would be correct to assert that its technology is not "essential" to the job of providing transportation to individual riders. The mobile apps published by these companies serve only to streamline a transaction that could exist absent the involvement of the third-party ridesharing operator. In short, the tool necessary to provide a car ride for hire is a car.

## D. Ridesharing Companies May Directly Provide Tools and Maintenance Services to Drivers

Notably, Uber and Lyft offer an option to become a driver even if you do not provide your own vehicle. Uber partners with companies such as Fair, Getaround, and Hertz so drivers who either do not have, or do not want to use, their own vehicles can rent one by an hourly, weekly, or longer basis. Uber includes a footnote on its website about this service, which states, "Uber is not responsible for the products or services offered by other companies."[382] Lyft offers a similar Express Drive program, which allows drivers to rent a car to complete trips and return it when they are done. As of March 2019, "more than 180,000 people" had rented a car through the Express Drive program.[383] To facilitate ease of rental, Lyft deducts the price of the rental from the earnings of the driver.[384]

It would be reasonable to assume that when a driver is using a personal vehicle for ridesharing work, that driver is responsible for the maintenance and upkeep of the vehicle he or she uses to complete rides. This, again, suggests that ridesharing drivers who do not use a ridesharing company to obtain a vehicle provide the "tools" needed to perform their work. However, even this line can be blurred by some of the programs offered by ridesharing companies. For instance, in the past, Lyft has provided a "driver rewards program," which has offered drivers discounts on fuel, maintenance, and additional costs of operation.[385] Similarly, Lyft has, at times, offered phone mounts, which drivers use to have easy access to their phones while driving, as part of a "welcome package" for new drivers.[386]

---

382. *Vehicle Solutions*, Uber, https://www.uber.com/us/en/drive/vehicle-solutions/ (last visited June 4, 2019).

383. Johana Bhuiyan, *Lower Pay and Higher Costs; The Downside of Lyft's Car Rental Program*, LA Times (May 20, 2019), https://www.latimes.com/business/technology/la-fi-tn-lyft-express-drive-20190520-story.html.

384. *Express Drive*, Lyft, https://www.lyft.com/expressdrive (last visited June 4, 2019).

385. *Driver Bonus*, Lyft, https://www.lyft.com/driver-bonus (last visited June 5, 2019).

386. Helling, *supra* note 334.

Lyft has taken this a step further and is debuting "driver centers," where Lyft drivers can get their cars serviced for 50 percent off "on most frequently needed car maintenance . . . 50% faster than traditional repair shops."[387] For areas without these driver centers, Lyft is also providing mobile service maintenance, where local technicians provide on-demand service to Lyft drivers.[388] Those hoping to establish that drivers are employees would lean on programs like this to establish that Lyft is providing the tools necessary to complete the job. Although obviously not quite the same as providing the car, providing a discounted rate and platform for maintenance inches Lyft closer to providing the materials necessary to perform the work of rideshare driving. Conversely, Lyft would likely argue this is an optional benefit given only to its loyal drivers and cannot amount to supplying the tools necessary to perform a task. After all, a phone mount and vehicle maintenance are only useful after the driver has already supplied the primary pieces of equipment—the car and phone. However, this type of interdependence indicates a closer relationship between the driver and the company than the "mere technology company" or "facilitator" argument asserted by ridesharing companies.

Lyft also provides insurance coverage on the Express Drive vehicles used by drivers and $1,000,000 of liability insurance for drivers in the Express Drive program.[389] Similarly, Uber maintains liability insurance when a driver is online with the driver app, which ranges from $25,000 to $100,000 depending on what is damaged.[390] When a passenger is on board for a ride, Uber maintains $1,000,000 of liability insurance, $1,000,000 of uninsured or underinsured motorist injury coverage, and contingent

---

387. Jon McNeill, *Introducing Lyft Driver Services*, A MEDIUM CORPORATION (Mar. 26, 2019), https://medium.com/@jmaclyft/introducing-lyft-driver-services-ac1ab9488ac6.

388. *Id.*

389. Bhuiyan, *supra* note 383.

390. *Driving With Uber*, UBER, https://www.uber.com/a/us/ (last visited July 25, 2020).

collision and comprehensive coverage up to the cash value of the vehicle.[391]

Although the most obvious tool required to work as a ride-sharing driver—the vehicle—is typically provided by the drivers themselves, programs such as rental vehicles offered through ridesharing companies, subsidized maintenance, and insurance coverage ensure the analysis is less than clear cut. As ridesharing companies' demand increases, they will be looking to implement more of these programs to entice drivers into contracting with them. As these programs grow in breadth and scope, the pendulum may begin to swing even further toward a determination that ridesharing companies employ their drivers.

*i. Where the Work Is Done*

Ridesharing companies have some level of control over the route drivers take to complete their rides. For example, Uber drivers are free to choose their preferred navigation provider, but Uber has an in-app navigation system that caters specifically to drivers.[392] Lyft debuted a similar in-app navigation system shortly after Uber, where Lyft partnered with Google Maps.[393] Drivers are not required to use either provided navigation system, but if they do, drivers are able to que up their next ride immediately after dropping off a passenger.[394] Many ridesharing drivers prefer to opt into using Waze because of its real-time traffic route altering that is permitted by the ridesharing companies.[395] Ultimately, companies like Uber and Lyft suggest an optimized route, but they do not actually control the routes their drivers

391. *Id.*

392. Maya Choksi, *A New Navigation Experience for Drivers*, UBER NEWSROOM (Mar. 15, 2017), https://www.uber.com/newsroom/a-new-navigation-experience-for-drivers/.

393. Johana Bhuiyan, *Lyft's New In-app Navigation for Drivers Knocks Out One More Previous Uber Advantage*, VOX MEDIA (Oct. 12, 2017), https://www.vox.com/2017/10/12/16462006/lyft-drivers-in-app-navigation-google-maps.

394. Choksi, *supra* note 392.

395. James A. Martin, *The GPS Navigation Apps Lyft Drivers Love—and Why*, CIO (May 31, 2016), https://www.cio.com/article/3075831/the-gps-navigation-apps-lyft-drivers-love-and-why.html.

take. This is more indicative of drivers being an independent contractors than employees.

Conversely, in some situations where large numbers of riders are anticipated, like airports or entertainment venues, specialized pick-up and/or drop-off locations are utilized.[396] However, use of specified locations is sometimes mandated to ridesharing companies and passengers by government authorities attempting to better regulate the flow of traffic.[397] Ridesharing companies have also experimented with vehicles that traverse the same route in a given area—much like a bus line.[398] In the event a crash were to occur while a ridesharing driver were traversing one of these routes that was predetermined by the ridesharing company, the calculus on this factor would change dramatically. With the result most likely being that the hiring ridesharing company would be held to have controlled where the work occurred. Given that control is the lynchpin determination, a collision in such a circumstance would likely result in the ridesharing company being vicariously liable for injuries caused by a hired driver.

*ii. How Long the Relationship between the Parties Will Continue*

Uber's driving contracts specify that the relationship between Uber and its drivers is terminable at will, as are the vast majority of jobs in America.[399] Under the language of the contracts, there is no guaranteed employment period, and drivers are free to stop driving whenever they choose.[400] Although the relationship between Uber and its drivers is immediately severable, the fact that the arrangement is for an indefinite period makes the

396. Maya Kaufman, *LaGuardia Airport Changes How Uber-Lyft Pick Passengers*, Patch (Oct. 23, 2019) https://patch.com/new-york/jackson-heights-elmhurst/laguardia-airport-changes-how-uber-lyft-pick-passengers.

397. *See id.*

398. Carmel DeAmicis, *Lyft Kills Off HotSpots as Uber Launches Copycat "Smart Routes" Service*, Vox (Aug 25, 2015), https://www.vox.com/2015/8/25/11618002/lyft-kills-off-hotspots-as-uber-launches-copycat-smart-routes-service.

399. Ross, *supra* note 381, at 1466.

400. *Id.* at 1476–77.

resolution of this factor likely to be a draw.[401] Conversely, the fact that a ridesharing company retains the right to terminate a driver at will could be relied on to suggest that the ridesharing company has reserved the right to control how the job is performed. The underlying rational for such an argument would be that there is no greater control mechanism than a hiring party's ability to terminate a worker for not complying with the hiring party's wishes.

*iii. Which Party Has Discretion over When and How Long the Hired Party Works*

Uber and Lyft both market the flexibility of their drivers' schedules to entice drivers and absolve themselves of liability for injuries. Drivers can launch the app and decide when they are willing to accept fares. Lyft advertises on its website, "you choose what to wear and listen to, and when you get paid" and "with Lyft, you'll drive (and earn) whenever you want, 24/7."[402] Similarly, Uber advertises that an individual can drive with Uber "when you want" and emphasizes there is no schedule imposed on drivers by Uber.[403]

However, Uber and Lyft both implement checks and balances on their drivers that support the argument that drivers do not have full autonomy to take rides if and when they want. For example, both Uber and Lyft limit the amount of time a driver can drive for a given company. Uber shuts its most active drivers out of the app for a required six-hour break after they have driven for 12 hours straight.[404] Although this rule impacts less than half of drivers who drive for Uber, it creates limitations similar to the federal regulations for truck drivers, which limits truckers to 11 hours of daily driving and requires at least a

401. *Id.* at 1477.

402. *Is Driving with Lyft Right for You?*, Lyft, https://www.lyft.com/driving-jobs (last visited June 4, 2019).

403. *Driving With Uber*, Uber, https://www.uber.com/a/us/ (last visited July 25, 2020).

404. Kirsten Korosec, *Uber Is Setting New Limits to Help Prevent Accidents from Drowsy Driving*, Fortune (Feb. 12, 2018), http://fortune.com/2018/02/12/uber-app-limits-driver-shifts-drowsy-driving/.

30-minute break for every eight hours driven.[405] Similarly, the Uber app reminds drivers that they are to drive within the posted speed limit and to take breaks so they are alert behind the wheel.[406] As a safety precaution, Lyft requires drivers to take a "full, uninterrupted 6-hour break for every 14 hours [they are] in driver mode."[407] This standard is more flexible than the federal regulations controlling truck drivers, which may have negative effects on overall safety.

The drive time "ceilings" are not the only way that ridesharing companies exert control over how and when drivers accept rides. For instance, Lyft drivers taking advantage of the Express Drive program, discussed earlier, are required to give at least 20 rides every seven days to be able to rent a vehicle from Lyft.[408] Additionally, as a general rule, ridesharing drivers are provided limited information when they are notified a person has requested a ride.[409] Specifically, drivers are not told the rider's specific location or destination until a ride has been accepted.[410] Thus, drivers are asked to decide whether to accept a ride without having complete information about the task they are being hired to perform. Ridesharing companies on the other hand, have a complete set of information about the rider and proposed trip that is not shared with the ridesharing driver.[411] The imbalance

405. *Id.*

406. *Safety*, UBER, https://www.uber.com/us/en/drive/safety/ (last visited July 5, 2020).

407. *Taking Breaks and Time Limits in Driver Mode*, LYFT, https://help.lyft.com/hc/en-us/articles/115012926787-Taking-breaks-and-time-limits-in-driver-mode (last visited June 4, 2019).

408. *Express Drive*, LYFT, https://www.lyft.com/expressdrive (last visited June 4, 2019).

409. *Receiving Trip Requests*, UBER, https://help.uber.com/driving-and-delivering/section/receiving-trip-requests?nodeId=5fcd4670-532a-4347-a099-d826e1d6f6e4 (last visited Dec. 31, 2019).

410. *See id.* Drivers are notified if a requested ride is considered a "long trip" and are typically provided with the expected trip length prior to accepting the fare. Some options also exist to allow drivers to receive ride requests for riders going to certain general areas.

411. It should be noted that withholding rider and destination information until after a fare is accepted by a driver may be an effective tool at combatting racial bias. In fact, some local laws prohibit "destination

of information between the driver and the ridesharing company before an individual ride is accepted is an additional facet of how ridesharing companies operate that could be relied on to support an argument that ridesharing companies exert "control" over drivers. Although some level of control lies with the drivers themselves, drive time ceilings and acceptance rate floors suggest a greater degree of control is being exerted by the ridesharing company. These factors could convince a court that the ridesharing company does control the manner and means of the hours worked by the drivers. This factor would likely be significant to any determination that an employer/employee relationship existed. At a minimum, limitations imposed by ridesharing companies are likely to create questions of fact, which would likely need to be resolved by factfinders on a case-by-case basis.

*iv. Whether the Hiring Party Is Permitted to Assign Additional Tasks*

Ridesharing companies do not force their drivers to take another ride after one has been completed. Uber says, "if you're . . . a driver and you don't want to accept . . . trip requests, you can just log off."[412] However, if you consistently and consecutively decline trip requests, then you may be temporarily logged out of the account and will be unable to complete new trips.[413] For Uber, each city has a maximum cancellation rate based on the average cancellation rate of drivers in that area.[414] If a driver's cancellation rate continually exceeds the maximum limit, his or her account may be deactivated.[415]

Ultimately, ridesharing companies do not have the power to require their drivers to accept and complete rides above any minimum that may be required to keep the driver's account active. This characteristic of the ridesharing company's relationship to its driver is more indicative of an independent contractor than an

---

discrimination," which occurs when drivers are unwilling to accept riders going to certain communities. *Id.*

412. *Community Guidelines*, UBER, https://www.uber.com/legal/community-guidelines/us-can-en/ (last visited June 7, 2019).

413. *Id.*

414. *Id.*

415. *Id.*

employee–employer relationship. However, both the minimum requirements placed on drivers and the policy of deactivating drivers who refuse too many fares undercut the notion that drivers are absolutely free to accept rides at their own whim.

*v. The Method Used to Issue Payment*

Ridesharing drivers are typically not paid a salary or an hourly rate.[416] Instead, they are paid a percentage of the fares that passengers pay when they take a ride.[417] Additionally, drivers for Lyft keep all of the tips they receive form passengers, as well as the occasional cash bonus that Lyft offers as an incentive to complete rides during peak times.[418] Uber drivers also keep the entirety of their tips, with no overhead charges from Uber.[419]

The data on how much money rideshare drivers are making is inconsistent. In January 2019, Ridester reported the data from its 2018 Independent Drivers' Earning Survey. Ridester surveyed more than 2,600 drivers and determined that Lyft drivers made an average of $17.50 per hour.[420] Ridester also reported that Uber drivers made approximately $2.00 less per hour than Lyft drivers.[421] However, these findings conflicted with a study conducted by NerdWallet indicating that, in 2019, Uber drivers averaged $15.97 per ride and Lyft drivers only $11.48.[422] Further, after paying all expenses, the NerdWallet survey indicated that drivers for Uber and Lyft average between $8.55 and $11.77 per

---

416. While this statement is true as a general proposition, there are some exceptions. For instance, Uber offers some programs that allow drivers to secure a guaranteed hourly rate. *See Uber Hourly Rate Guarantee,* aliva, (Feb. 19, 2019), http://www.alvia.com/uber-hourly-rate-guarantee/ (last visited July 25, 2020).

417. Ellie Martin, *How Much Do Lyft Drivers Make, Really? Factors that Eat into Lyft Driver Salary*, RIDESTER, (Jan. 21, 2019), https://www.ridester.com/how-much-do-lyft-drivers-make/.

418. *Id.*

419. *Tipping, How It Works*, UBER, https://www.uber.com/drive/partner-app/how-tips-work/ (last visited June 5, 2019).

420. Martin, *supra* note 417.

421. *Id.*

422. Eric Reed, *How Much Do Uber and Lyft Drivers Make in 2018?*, STREET (Dec. 11, 2018), https://www.thestreet.com/personal-finance/education/how-much-do-uber-lyft-drivers-make-14804869.

hour.[423] These figures vary widely according to the source of the data. Variations in average pay are likely a result of factors such as surge pricing, location, hours worked, tipping, and expenses. For example, Uber drivers in New York City average $29.34 per trip, compared to only $10.99 in Chicago.[424] In 2017, the Federal Trade Commission required Uber to pay out $20,000,000 to settle charges that it "misled prospective drivers with exaggerated earning claims."[425] In turn, Uber was permanently restrained from making any misrepresentations regarding the income a driver is likely to earn,[426] which may be the reason for Uber's lack of data on the income of its drivers.

Ridesharing companies promote ease of payment to their drivers. On Lyft's website, it advertises that its drivers "can cash out any day of the week . . . instantly—as long as you've earned at least $5."[427] In March 2019, Lyft debuted "Lyft Driver Services" which included "Lyft Direct," a no-fee bank account and debit card to save drivers money on gas, groceries, and other purchases.[428] The Lyft Direct debit card allows drivers to instantly access their earnings after each ride.[429] Uber has a similar debit card program through GoBank, which provides cash back on purchases at places like Walmart, Advance Auto Parts, Jiffy Lube, and general fuel purchases at any location.[430]

---

423. *Id.*

424. *Id.*

425. Erik Sherman, *FTC Says Uber Misled Drivers, Company to Pay $20M Settlement*, Forbes (Jan. 19, 2017), https://www.forbes.com/sites/eriksherman/2017/01/19/ftc-says-uber-misled-drivers-company-to-pay-20m-settlement/#7ae3adab1c78.

426. *See* FTC v. Uber Technologies, Inc., Stipulated Order for Permanent Injunction and Monetary Judgment, (N.D.C.A.) (Jan. 19, 2017).

427. *Pay*, Lyft, https://www.lyft.com/driver/pay (last visited June 5, 2019).

428. McNeill, *supra* note 387.

429. *Id.*

430. *Debit Details*, Uber, https://www.uber.com/legal/payments/uber-debit/uberdebitdetails/ (last visited June 5, 2019).

*vi. The Hiring Party's Role in Providing Assistants to the Hired Party*
This factor is the least applicable to the ridesharing context. Drivers could make the argument that by providing services like "maintenance hubs," ridesharing companies are providing drivers with "assistants." However, this is probably a stretch. Many cases that considered this factor of the analysis found that it pointed to the existence of an employer–employee relationship when the hiring party actually hired assistants for the hired party.[431]

*vii. Whether the Task Accomplished by the Worker Is Part of the Hiring Party's Regular Business*
Courts considering this factor in the ridesharing context have often focused on the fact that ridesharing companies depend entirely on drivers for the business model to succeed. Without drivers willing to participate in the ridesharing programs, there is no business. This factor would almost certainly feature prominently in a determination that an employee/employer relationship exists between a given driver and ridesharing company. Although ridesharing companies may argue they are technology companies, courts will likely find it difficult to overlook the reality that ridesharing companies derive income from transportation.[432]

*viii. Whether the Hiring Party Is a Company or Business, as Opposed to an Individual*
This is the most straightforward of the factors. Clearly, ridesharing companies, the hiring parties, are legitimate incorporated businesses and not individuals who are hiring drivers to complete rides. Uber and Lyft are American multinational transportation network companies, commonly referred to as TNCs.[433]

---

431. *See* Cosgriff v. Valdese Weavers LLC, 2012 U.S. Dist. LEXIS 46245 (S.D.N.Y. 2012).

432. O'Connor v. Uber Techs., Inc., 82 F. Supp. 3d 1133, 1141 (N.D. Cal. 2015); Cotter v. Lyft, Inc., 60 F. Supp. 3d 1067, 1077 (N.D. Cal. 2015).

433. Dave Kilduff, *The Effect of IPOs on Transportation Network Companies Like Uber and Lyft*, Phocus Wire (Mar. 19, 2019), https://www.phocuswire.com/effect-of-IPOs-on-transportation-network-companies.

These TNCs are delineated from traditional taxi and limousine companies because they are not subject to the same stringent standards regarding commercial insurance, inspections, and special licenses for drivers.[434] Thus, this factor could weigh in favor of the drivers being employees.

*ix. Whether the Worker Receives Benefits*

Uber drivers pay expenses out of pocket, do not have traditional employee benefits, and are not entitled to an hourly wage or a salary.[435] Lyft takes a similar stance, stating, "Drivers and riders are users of the platform and aren't employees of the company. As members of the community platform, drivers and riders aren't entitled to benefits, worker's compensation, or unemployment insurance."[436] However, many drivers involved in the ridesharing industry, and some regulatory officials, would like to see a change.

In May 2019, Uber drivers in New York City went on strike over pay and lack of benefits in advance of the company's $90 billion IPO,[437] which took place on May 9, 2019.[438] Prior to this strike, in October of 2018, Uber had suggested that it would be working toward providing benefits to drivers everywhere in the future.[439] Uber has recently begun providing drivers in the European Union with health care, accident insurance, and maternity

---

434. Commercial Ride-Sharing, Ctr. Ins. Pol'y & Res. Nat'l Ass'n Ins. Commissioners, https://www.naic.org/cipr_topics/topic_commercial_ride_sharing.htm (last updated Mar. 4, 2020).

435. Ross, *supra* note 381, at 1432.

436. *Tax Information for US Drivers*, Lyft https://help.lyft.com/hc/en-us/articles/115012926967-Tax-information-for-US-drivers#classified (last visited June 7, 2019) (emphasis in original).

437. An IPO is an initial public offering, where a private corporation begins offering stock for sale to the public for the first time to raise investment capital.

438. Lauren Feiner, *Uber Ends Its First Day of Trading Down More than 7%*, CNBC (May 10, 2019), https://www.cnbc.com/2019/05/10/uber-ipo-stock-starts-trading-on-the-new-york-stock-exchange.html.

439. Jen Wieczner, *Uber CEO: We Want to Give All Drivers Insurance, Benefits*, Fortune (Oct. 4, 2018), http://fortune.com/2018/10/04/uber-driver-benefits-insurance/.

and paternity leave.[440] Because of the classification of drivers as independent contractors, ridesharing companies are not violating federal law by failing to pay drivers a minimum wage or paid time off.[441]

*x. The Tax Implications Related to the Hired Party*

Lyft states on its website that while some drivers are eligible to receive a 1099-K or 1099-MISC from Lyft, "no matter the type of income you report, you are not considered an employee of Lyft."[442] To qualify to receive a 1099-K from Lyft in 2018, a driver must take at least 200 rides and at least $20,000 in gross ride receipts from passengers in the year, unless the driver is a resident of Vermont or Massachusetts, where they only have to generate $600 in gross ride receipts with no ride minimums.[443] To qualify for a 1099-MISC in 2018, a driver had to receive $6,000 from activities other than driving, like referral bonuses, weekly guarantees, and other bonuses.[444]

Similarly, Uber drivers had to make more than $20,000 in customer payments and provide more than 200 rides or deliveries to qualify for a 1099-K in 2018.[445] A driver who received more than $600 in miscellaneous payments from promotions or referrals would qualify for a 1099-MISC.[446]

*xi. Balancing Factors*

The lists of factors to be analyzed when considering the question of worker classification can be useful in clearly defining the contours of a worker's relationship with a hiring party; the lack of clarity as to how individual factors are weighted makes

---

440. *Id.*

441. Annie Nova, *'The Algorithm is our Boss': Uber Drivers Face Long Hours, no Benefits and Sometimes Danger*, CNBC (June 1, 2019), https://www.cnbc.com/2019/06/01/how-much-do-uber-drivers-really-make-three-drivers-share-the-math.html.

442. *Tax Information*, *supra* note 436 (emphasis in original).

443. *Id.*

444. *Id.*

445. Tax Information, UBER, https://www.uber.com/drive/tax-information/ (last visited June 7, 2019).

446. *Id.*

outcomes difficult to predict. Application of tests of this type have led to inconsistent results, which has in turn led some to the conclusion that the multifactor analysis begs the question of employee status as much as it answers it.[447] Furthermore, many of these factors could go either way depending on the evidence presented in any individual case. As a result, the bar may be set by the first court to make this determination in a tort context.

### b. Ridesharing Drivers' Employment Status in a Tort Context

The lack of case law on this issue in a tort context is likely attributable to quick settlement of tort cases brought by third parties, and the arbitration provisions to which passengers are generally subject. When signing up to be a passenger for Uber, patrons agree to an arbitration clause that says if they have any issues, they must be resolved through arbitration and not in court.[448] Drivers for Uber are held to a similar arbitration clause, unless they have opted out.[449]

An example of quick settlement of a ridesharing personal injury case can be found with relative ease. For example, an Uber driver struck and killed a six-year-old girl in San Francisco, California, while searching for his next fare.[450] In this case, *Ang Liang Liu v. Uber Technologies, Inc.*, Uber maintained that it was not responsible for the girl's death.[451] The case was settled out of court in mid-2015.[452] If that case had gone to trial, the court would have had to determine whether the driver was an employee or independent contractor of Uber at the time of the

447. David Weil, U.S. Dep't of Labor, Wage & Hour Div., Administrator's Interpretation No. 2015-1 2 (2015), https://www.blr.com/html_email/AI2015-1.pdf.

448. *Terms of Use*, Uber, https://www.uber.com/legal/en/document/?name=general-terms-of-use&country=united-states&lang=en (last updated Dec. 25, 2019).

449. *Id.*

450. *Family of Girl Killed in SF Crosswalk Suing Uber for Wrongful Death*, CBS S.F. Bay Area (Jan. 27, 2014), https://sanfrancisco.cbslocal.com/2014/01/27/family-of-girl-killed-in-sf-crosswalk-suing-uber-for-wrongful-death/.

451. Answer, Ang Liang Liu v. Uber Techs., Inc., No. CGC-14-536979, 2015 Cal. Super LEXIS 7172 (S.F. Super. Ct. May 1, 2014).

452. CBS S.F. Bay Area, *supra* note 450.

accident. It is hard to tell how this would have played out, but there are certainly factors that would have been of particular importance in making that determination.

The factors that would have lent themselves to the argument that the driver who struck and killed the six-year-old in San Francisco was an employee include (i) the fact that the driver would have been paid directly by Uber, (ii) the fact that Uber is a company and not an individual and, most importantly, (iii) the fact that drivers are crucial to Uber's business model. Without drivers, Uber would be nothing. The complaint filed in the San Francisco case alleged that Uber bore responsibility for the accident, even though the driver was not actively transporting or traveling to a passenger.[453] The basis for this argument was the claim that Uber derives an economic benefit from having drivers logged in to Uber's app regardless of whether the driver has a rider in the car or is on the way to a rider.[454] The plaintiff in *Liu* claimed that Uber benefits from having more drivers logged into the app because riders using the Uber app are able to see how many active drivers are in their area.[455] A greater density of available drivers could entice a rider to select Uber over a competing company. Presumably, the *Liu* plaintiff planned to argue that Uber was deriving a benefit from the driver's use of its app, and, thus, Uber should share the burden of compensating those injured by the driver's actions. In response, Uber claimed this theory of liability was entirely novel and that well-established legal principles would result in the dismissal of the claim.[456]

Moreover, applying the control factors to the *Liu* case suggests that the driver likely would have been found to have been an independent contractor. Specifically, (i) no special skill was required for the driver to simply have the app open; (ii) the driver could have logged out of the app or stopped driving

453. Complaint, Ang Liang Liu v. Uber Techs., Inc., No. CGC-14-536979, 2015 Cal. Super LEXIS 7172 (S.F. Super. Ct. Jan. 14, 2014).

454. *Id.*

455. *Id.*

456. Answer, Ang Liang Liu v. Uber Techs., Inc., No. CGC-14-536979, 2015 Cal. Super LEXIS 7172 (S.F. Super. Ct. May 1, 2014).

before striking the girl with no interference from Uber; (iii) Uber did not control the route the driver took to find his next fare; (iv) the driver was classified by Uber as an independent contractor; and (v) perhaps most importantly, this driver was between fares, looking for his next rider. Thus, he was not actively receiving any type of instructions from Uber, and any benefit Uber was deriving was, at most, a passive benefit.

Obviously, this case never got to this stage because the parties agreed to an undisclosed settlement prior to the case being decided.[457] If Uber had opted to litigate the case to its conclusion, and had the court applied the factors just set out, the case likely would have come out on the side of holding the driver to be an independent contractor, and, thus, Uber would not have been vicariously liable for any damages caused by the driver's negligence. However, a different outcome would be far more probable had the driver been in Phase 2 or Phase 3 of a ride, rather than in Phase 1, searching for a fare. Even presented with a favorable, albeit tragic, factual situation, Uber did not want to risk leaving this issue to the court. Uber's decision was likely motivated, at least in part, by the fact that a negative precedent could have been set for future cases, which in turn would have a significant impact on the valuation of the company. Plainly, if Uber or other ridesharing companies were responsible for compensating plaintiffs injured by their drivers' acts, it would impose a significant financial cost on those companies.

Although there is little case law in the tort context at present, we can be sure that it is on the horizon. What is uncertain is how courts will ultimately resolve these issues. Rather than settle for this uncertainty, as discussed in the next section, some states have taken the preemptive step of answering the question of whether drivers are independent contractors or employees through legislation.

---

457. Bob Egelko, *Uber Settles Suit with Family over Girl's New Year's Eve Death*, S.F. CHRON. (July 15, 2015), https://www.sfchronicle.com/bayarea/article/Uber-settles-suit-with-family-over-girl-s-New-6385063.php.

## 2. Statutory Law: Employee versus Independent Contractor

In the wake of the ridesharing boom and significant lobbying efforts by ridesharing companies, some states have codified how ridesharing drivers are to be classified.[458] Most states that have made such a determination presume that ridesharing drivers are independent contractors. Colorado, for example, was the first state to pass such legislation.[459] The lobbying firm responsible received more than $80,000 from Uber and gig-work platform, Handy.[460] Regulatory agencies are also the targets of lobbying efforts to cement the status of ridesharing drivers as independent contractors.[461]

Following is a chart that identifies the status of classification of ridesharing drivers in each state, identifies the relevant statute, and provides a brief summary of the pertinent provisions from each state's code. Whereas some states have affirmatively defined the employment status of ridesharing drivers, others have established multifactor tests that courts must rely on when making such a determination. Additionally, some states have passed legislation that addresses only limited aspects of the issue, such as whether ridesharing drivers are entitled to workers' compensation benefits.

---

458. Gali Racabi, *Transportation Network Companies (TNC) and Marketplace Contractors (MC) State Law: Preemption of Local Government Regulations and Treatment of Employment Status of Drivers*, OnLabor (Oct. 19, 2018), https://onlabor.org/state-tnc-and-mc-legislation-preemption-and-employment-status-of-drivers/.

459. Patrick Hoge, *Colorado Becomes First State to Pass Law Embracing Uber, Lyft et al.*, S.F. Bus. Times (June 5, 2014), https://www.bizjournals.com/sanfrancisco/morning_call/2014/06/colorado-uber-lyft.html.

460. Noam Scheiber, *Is Gig Work a Job? Uber and Others Are Maneuvering to Shape the Answer*, N.Y. Times (Mar. 26, 2019), https://www.nytimes.com/2019/03/26/business/economy/gig-economy-lobbying.html.

461. *Id.*

### a. Statutes and Regulations Impacting the Employment Status of Ridesharing Drivers

California recently enacted a new law concerning the employment status of many workers,[462] codifying the California Supreme Court's holding in *Dynamex Operations West v. Superior Court of Los Angeles*.[463] The law creates a rebuttable presumption that workers are employees, unless the employer can satisfy a three-part test:

> **(A)** The person is free from the control and direction of the hiring entity in connection with the performance of the work, both under the contract for the performance of the work and in fact.
>
> **(B)** The person performs work that is outside the usual course of the hiring entity's business.
>
> **(C)** The person is customarily engaged in an independently established trade, occupation, or business of the same nature as that involved in the work performed.[464]

Under this law, Uber and Lyft drivers are now designated employees by law. Uber, Lyft, and other similar companies proposed a ballot initiative in response, seeking to exempt their businesses.[465] Uber and another tech company also sued the state of California, challenging the law as unconstitutional.[466] At the time of this book's writing, New York, New Jersey, and Illinois were investigating similar laws, and a few presidential hopefuls had expressed support for the law.[467]

---

462. CAL. LAB. CODE § 2750.3 (West 2020).

463. 416 P.3d 1, 7 (Cal. 2018).

464. CAL. LAB. CODE § 2750.3(a)(1) (West 2020).

465. Eli Rosenburg, *Can California Rein in Tech's Gig Platforms? A Primer on the Bold State Law That Will Try*, WASH. POST (Jan. 14, 2020), https://www.washingtonpost.com/business/2020/01/14/can-california-reign-techs-gig-platforms-primer-bold-state-law-that-will-try/.

466. Anthony J. Oncidi, *Uber and Postmates File Lawsuit Challenging California's New Independent Contractor Law (AB-5)*, NAT'L L. REV. (Dec. 31, 2019), https://www.natlawreview.com/article/uber-and-postmates-file-lawsuit-challenging-california-s-new-independent-contractor.

467. Rosenburg, *supra* note 465.

Though this area of law continues to evolve, the following table provides a summary of other state statutes addressing the employment status of ridesharing drivers.

| State | Code | Provision[468] |
|---|---|---|
| Alabama | Ala. Code § 32-7C-1 | "A transportation network company that is. A corporation, partnership, sole proprietorship, or other entity licensed and operating in this state that used a digital network to connect a TNC rider to a TNC driver who provides a prearranged ride. A TNC may not control, direct, or manage the personal vehicle or the TNC driver who connects to its digital network, except where agreed to by written contract." |
| Alaska | Alaska Stat. § 28.23.080 | Relies on a four-factor test to establish that a driver is an independent contractor instead of an employee. |
| Arizona | Ariz. Rev. Stat. § 23-1603 | Relies on a multifactor test to establish that a driver is an independent contractor instead of an employee. |
| Arkansas | Ark. Code Ann. § 23-13-719 | Relies on a five-factor test to establish that a driver is an independent contractor instead of an employee. |

468. All of the current statutory information in this table is attributable to Gali Racabi, Transportation Network Companies (TNC) and Marketplace Contractors (MC) State Law: Preemption of Local Government Regulations and Treatment of Employment Status of Drivers, ONLABOR (Oct. 19, 2018), https://onlabor.org/state-tnc-and-mc-legislation-preemption-and-employment-status-of-drivers/.

| State | Code | Provision |
|---|---|---|
| California | Cal. Pub. Util. Code § 5431<br>Cal. Lab. Code § 2750.3 (Deering 2020) | "'Transportation network company' means an organization, including, but not limited to, a corporation, limited liability company, partnership, sole proprietor, or any other entity, operating in California that provides prearranged transportation services for compensation using an online-enabled app or platform to connect passengers with drivers using a personal vehicle." |
| Colorado | Colo. Rev. Stat. § 4010.1602 | "A transportation network company is not deemed to own, control, operate, or manage the personal vehicles used by transportation network company drivers."<br>"A driver need not be an employee of a transportation network company." |
| Connecticut | 2017 Ct. ALS 140, 2017 Ct. P.A. 140, 2017 Ct. HB 7126 | "Transportation network company driver" or "driver" means an individual who is not an employee of a transportation network company, but who uses a transportation network company vehicle to provide prearranged rides. |
| Delaware | Del. Code Ann. tit. 2, § 1911 | Relies on a five-factor test to establish that a driver is an independent contractor instead of an employee. |
| Florida | Fla. Stat. Ann. § 627.748, Sec. 9<br><br>Fla. Stat. Ann. § 451.02 | Relies on a four-factor test to establish that a driver is an independent contractor instead of an employee. |

| State | Code | Provision |
|---|---|---|
| Georgia | Ga. Code Ann. § 33-1-24 (a)(4) | "Transportation network company driver" or "driver" means an individual who uses his or her personal vehicle or permits his or her personal vehicle to be used to provide transportation network company services. Such a driver need not be an employee of a transportation network company. |
| Hawaii | Hawaii HB 10931093 | A transportation network company means "an entity that uses a digital network or software app service to connect passengers to transportation network company drivers; provided that the entity: (1) Does not own, control, direct, or manage the transportation network company vehicles or transportation network company drivers that connect to its digital network, except where agreed to by written contract." |
| Idaho | Idaho Code § 49-3703 | "Transportation network company" or "TNC" shall mean an entity operating in Idaho that meets the requirements of this chapter and uses a digital network or software app service to connect passengers to transportation network company services provided by transportation network company drivers. A TNC is not deemed to own, control, operate, or manage the vehicles used by TNC drivers, and is not a taxicab association or a for-hire vehicle owner. |
| Illinois | 2013 Ill. ALS 1173, 2013 Ill. Laws 1173, 2013 Ill. P.A. 1173, 2013 Ill. SB 2774, § 5 | A TNC is not deemed to own, control, operate, or manage the vehicles used by TNC drivers, and is not a taxicab association or a for-hire vehicle owner. |

| State | Code | Provision |
|---|---|---|
| Indiana | Ind. Code Ann. § 82.119.14<br><br>Ind. Code Ann. § 22163 | Except as otherwise provided in a written contract:<br>(1) a TNC driver who connects to a TNC's digital network is an independent contractor of the TNC; and<br>(2) a TNC is not considered to do either of the following:<br>(A) Control, direct, or manage a TNC driver who connects to the TNC's digital network.<br>(B) Own, control, operate, or manage a personal vehicle used by a TNC driver to provide prearranged rides. |
| Iowa | Iowa Code § 321N.1<br>See also Iowa Code § 93.2 | A transportation network company is not deemed to control, direct, or manage a transportation network company driver that connects to its digital network, or the driver's personal vehicle, except as agreed to by the company and the driver pursuant to a written contract. |
| Kansas | Kan. Stat. Ann. § 8-2702 | A transportation network company shall not be deemed to control, direct, or manage the personal vehicles or transportation network company drivers that connect to its digital network, except where agreed to by written contract. |
| Kentucky | Ky. Rev. Stat. Ann. § 336.137 | Relies on a six-factor test to establish that a driver is an independent contractor instead of an employee. |

| State | Code | Provision |
|---|---|---|
| Louisiana | La. Rev. Stat. Ann. § 45:201.44 | A transportation network company means "a person, whether natural or juridical, that uses a digital network to connect transportation network company riders to transportation network company drivers who provide prearranged rides, or a person, whether natural or juridical, that provides a technology platform to a transportation network company rider that enables the transportation network company rider to schedule a prearranged ride." |
| Maine | Me. Stat. tit. 29-A, § 1676 | This subchapter does not apply to claims or proceedings involving workers' compensation. (Expressly exclude application on workers comp.) |
| Maryland | Md. Code Ann., Pub. Util. § 10101 | Transportation network company means "a company that operates in the State using a digital network to connect passengers to transportation network operators or transportation network partners for transportation network services." |
| Massachusetts | Mass. Ann. Laws ch. 159A½ | A transportation network company means, "a corporation, partnership, sole proprietorship or other entity that uses a digital network to connect riders to drivers to pre-arrange and provide transportation." |
| Michigan | Mich. Comp. Laws Serv. § 257.2137 | Relies on a five-factor test to establish that a driver is an independent contractor instead of an employee. |
| Minnesota | No pending legislation | |

| State | Code | Provision |
|---|---|---|
| Mississippi | Miss. Code Ann. § 77-8-21 | Relies on a five-factor test to establish that a driver is an independent contractor instead of an employee. |
| Missouri | Mo. Rev. Stat. § 387.432 | Transportation network companies shall not be considered employers of transportation network company drivers, except when agreed to by written contract. |
| Montana | Mont. Code Ann. § 69-12-101(20) | A transportation network carrier may not be deemed to control, direct, or manage the personal vehicles or transportation network carrier drivers that connect to its digital network, except where agreed to by written contract. |
| Nebraska | Neb. Rev. Stat. Ann § 75-302 | Transportation network company has the definition found in section 75-323. A transportation network company shall not own, control, operate, or manage drivers' personal vehicles. |
| Nevada | Nev. Rev. Stat. Ann. § 706A.090 | Except as otherwise provided in this chapter and the regulations adopted pursuant thereto or by a written contract between a transportation network company and a driver, a company shall not control, direct or manage a driver or the motor vehicle operated by a driver. |
| New Hampshire | N.H. Rev. Stat. Ann. § 376-A:20 | Relies on a five-factor test to establish that a driver is an independent contractor instead of an employee. |

| State | Code | Provision |
|---|---|---|
| New Jersey | N.J. Stat. 39:5H-22 | Transportation network company means "a corporation, partnership, sole proprietorship, or other entity that is registered as a business in the State or operates in this State, and uses a digital network to connect a transportation network company rider to a transportation network company driver to a prearranged ride." |
| New Mexico | N.M. Stat. Ann. § 65-7-2 | "transportation network company" means a corporation . . . but which shall not:<br>(1) be deemed to control, direct or manage the personal vehicles or transportation network company drivers that connect to its digital network except where agreed to by written contract; or |
| New York | 2016 Bill Text NJ S.B. 2179 failed in the House | If it passed, it would have held that "A transportation network company shall not be deemed to control, direct, or manage a transportation network company driver or the driver's personal vehicle that connects to the company's digital network, except where agreed to by written contract." |
| North Carolina | N.C. Gen. Stat. § 20-280.8 | A rebuttable presumption exists that a TNC driver is an independent contractor and not an employee. The presumption may be rebutted by application of the common law test for determining employment status. |

| State | Code | Provision |
|---|---|---|
| North Dakota | N.D. Cent. Code § 26.140.101(07) | A transportation network company may not be deemed to control, direct, or manage the personal vehicles or participating drivers that connect to the transportation network company's online-enabled app or platform, unless agreed to by written contract. |
| Ohio | Ohio Rev. Code Ann. § 4925.10 | Transportation network company drivers are not employees, except where agreed to by written contract. If the parties agree to the application of one or more of these laws in a written contract, the transportation network company shall notify the appropriate agency of the election to cover the driver. If the parties subsequently change this election, the transportation network company shall notify the appropriate agency of the change. |
| Oklahoma | Okla. Stat. tit. 47, § 1011 | A TNC shall not be deemed to control, direct, or manage the personal vehicles or participating drivers that connect to its digital network, except where agreed to by written contract. |
| Oregon | No statewide legislation, but Roseburg, Oregon Code of Ordinances Sec. 9.08.005 | "Transportation Network" is one or more drivers working as independent contractors and utilizing a digital dispatch system and using personal motor vehicles in the provision of transportation services. |
| Pennsylvania | 53 Pa. Cons. Stat. Ann. 57A01 | A transportation network company is a "person or entity that obtains a license to operate a transportation network service by the authority and uses a digital network to facilitate prearranged rides." |

| State | Code | Provision |
|---|---|---|
| Rhode Island | 39 R.I. Gen. Laws § 14.216 | TNC drivers shall be independent contractors and not employees of the TNC if they are determined to meet federal and state law and regulation relating to independent contractors, and the TNC and TNC driver agree in writing that the TNC driver is an independent contractor of the TNC. |
| South Carolina | S.C. Code Ann. § 58-23-1610 | A transportation network company means "a person, corporation, partnership, sole proprietorship, or other entity operating in this State that uses a digital network, platform, or Internet-enabled app to connect a passenger to a transportation network driver for the purpose of providing transportation for compensation using a vehicle." |
| South Dakota | S.D. Codified Laws § 32-40-1 | Transportation network company drivers who provide prearranged rides and that does not control, direct, or manage the personal vehicles or transportation network company drivers that connect to its digital network, except where agreed to by written contract. |
| Tennessee | Tenn. Code Ann. § 65-15-302(b) | A transportation network company shall not be deemed to own, control, operate, or manage the personal vehicles used by transportation network company drivers and is not deemed to control or manage transportation network company drivers. |
| Texas | Tex. Occ. Code § 2402.114 | Relies on a five-factor test to establish that a driver is an independent contractor instead of an employee. |

| State | Code | Provision |
|---|---|---|
| Utah | Utah Code Ann. § 1351102,103 | A transportation network driver is:<br>(a) an independent contractor of a transportation network company; and<br>(b) not an employee of a transportation network company. |
| Vermont | No pending legislation | |
| Virginia | Va. Code Ann. § 46.22000 | A transportation network company means "a person who provides prearranged rides using a digital platform that connects passengers with TNC partners." |
| Washington | No pending legislation | |
| West Virginia | W. Va. Code § 172911 | Relies on a five-factor test to establish that a driver is an independent contractor instead of an employee. |
| Wisconsin | Wis. Stat. Ann. § 440.41 | A licensed company is not considered to control, direct, or manage a participating driver or that participating driver's personal vehicle used for engaging in transportation network services, except as provided in this subchapter or in a written agreement between the licensed company and the participating driver. |
| Wyoming | Wyo. Stat. Ann. § 3120110 | Relies on a multifactor test to establish that a driver is an independent contractor instead of an employee. |

## 3. Conclusion

When courts finally have the opportunity to make a determination on ridesharing drivers' employment status in a tort context, there are many details to examine. Courts can approach this problem by turning to the common law control factors test and weighing the factors and the evidence supporting them against one another. Courts can look to the determinations that have been made in an employment context to see if the same standard is the appropriate one to apply in a tort context. Lastly, courts can turn to the statutes adopted in each individual state, which may or may not have some bearing on the question. Ultimately, there is no conclusive answer to the question of whether ridesharing drivers are independent contractors or employees for purposes of vicarious tort liability.

## E. Additional Considerations for Vicarious Liability Issues

As discussed previously, the classification of ridesharing drivers is of primary importance to the question of apportioning liability (and insurance coverage) between drivers and ridesharing companies. The answer to the question of how ridesharing drivers are classified is important, though not wholly determinative of the issue of whether ridesharing companies can be held liable for torts committed by associated drivers. This is because if ridesharing drivers are routinely held to be employees for the purposes of tort law, it will be significantly easier to establish that the ridesharing company is vicariously liable for injuries caused by drivers.[469] Typically, the third-party held accountable for someone else's tort is a company that employs, or otherwise controls the actions of, a tortfeasor. Under the doctrine of *respondeat superior,* an employer may be held liable for the negligent actions of an employee that caused a plaintiff's injury, even if the employer does not engage in any conduct related to the plaintiff.[470] The tort theory supporting this use of vicarious liability is that it allows for better allocation of risk and cost of injuries between companies, employees, and injured third parties.

In the event an employment relationship is found, only the first step of establishing vicarious liability through the *respondeat superior* theory has been accomplished. The second element that must be proven to hold a company liable for the tortious

469. Vicarious liability is the legal concept that permits third parties to be held liable for the tortious acts of others.

470. *See* Krueger v. Mammoth Mountain Ski Area, Inc., 873 F.2d 222, 223 (9th Cir. 1989).

acts of an employee is that the employee be within the "course and scope" of his work at the time the injury is caused.[471] The Restatement (Second) of Agency provides that a worker is within the "course and scope" of their job when the task during which the tort occurs (i) is of the kind he or she is employed to perform, (ii) occurs substantially within the authorized time and space limits, and (iii) is actuated, at least in part, by a purpose to serve the employer.[472]

In the ridesharing context, the answers to questions of when a driver is within the "course and scope" of their work is complicated by the different "phases" of a ridesharing transaction. As previously explained, the acts of ridesharing drivers can be split into four phases. The phase in which an incident occurs will have a significant impact on the probable division of liability due to the differing degrees of involvement of the ridesharing company during each phase. For instance, Phase 1 is the period where the driver does not currently have a rider in the vehicle and does not have a ride pending but has her ridesharing app running. Phase 2 is the time when the driver has matched with a rider and is driving to the pickup location. Finally, Phase 3 is the time where the driver is taking her passenger to the passenger's preselected destination. Although a convincing argument can be made that a driver is within the course and scope of the work they are doing on behalf of a ridesharing service during Phases 2 and 3, it is less clear that injuries that occur during Phase 1 can be in any way attributed to the ridesharing coordinator. This is because during Phase 1, drivers are free to go where they like, with no input from the ridesharing company. Although vicarious liability is not always required to hold the ridesharing coordinator responsible, it does increase the probability of such an outcome.

### 1. Standard Negligence Claims

If vicarious liability can be established based on the relationship between a driver and a ridesharing company, the company could be held liable for standard negligence claims for which the driver

---

471. *Id.*

472. Restatement (Second) of Agency § 228 (Am. Law. Inst. 1958).

may be liable. This includes liability arising from simple car accidents that are typically brought under some theory of negligence.

### 2. Joint Enterprise Liability

A joint enterprise is a business form that may exist when two persons are engaged in a common business purpose.[473] Joint enterprise liability is a specific form of vicarious liability.[474] Under joint enterprise liability, one of the participants in the joint enterprise may be liable for the negligence of another participant.[475] Under this theory of liability there does not need to be a formal employee–employer relationship, only a finding of mutual control over the subject matter of the enterprise or over the property involved in the claim. It is a fact-specific inquiry requiring a case by case analysis.[476]

Although joint enterprise liability has not been applied directly to ridesharing, it has been found in a variety of business relationships such as landlord–tenant, a relationship between two oil companies, and even a car owner and the driver.[477] In order to find liability between two parties under this theory, courts look at the arrangement between the parties, including allocation of responsibilities and financial burdens. This theory may be effective in establishing liability of ridesharing companies for the torts committed by drivers. The joint enterprise standard is flexible and evolving. Joint enterprise liability is intended to continue changing with social and economic norms.[478] As such, if it becomes the case that persons injured by ridesharing drivers are routinely left without a way to recover for their injuries, plaintiffs, and courts, may look to the concept of joint enterprise liability to ensure that any societal cost associated with ridesharing is shared with the companies profiting from this enterprise. Conversely, if other traditional legal theories and mechanisms of

---

473. Symposium, *Regulating Ridesharing Platforms Through Tort Law*, 39 U. Haw. L. Rev. 357, 378

474. *Id.*

475. *Id.*

476. *Id.*

477. *Id.*

478. *Id.*

recovery are effective at ensuring innocent injured parties are not left without recourse, there may be little reason to look to join enterprise liability as the basis of a claim against a ridesharing company.

## V. Direct Liability

Even in the event that the determination is made that ridesharing drivers are independent contractors, there are still a number of ways that a ridesharing company can be held liable for injuries caused by a driver. These direct claims against ridesharing companies are discussed in the following sections of this chapter. One of the most obvious methods of imposing liability directly on the ridesharing company, without vicarious liability, is a claim against the ridesharing company for its own negligent acts that can be casually linked to an injury. In other words, these claims depend on identifying an act or omission by a ridesharing company that created an unreasonable risk of injury to passengers or the public.

### A. Direct Liability for Negligent Hiring and Retention

Even in a jurisdiction where ridesharing drivers are deemed independent contractors, ridesharing companies are not wholly immune from liability for injuries caused by drivers. This is because companies have a duty to exercise reasonable care in their hiring and retention practices, even where independent contractors are involved. Under a theory of negligent hiring, supervision, and retention, a plaintiff may be able to hold a ridesharing company directly liable if they can prove that an unfit worker caused an injury and the hiring party was negligent in the hiring, training, supervision, or retaining of the tortfeasor. The plaintiff asserting such a claim also has the burden of proving that the hiring party knew or had reason to know of a specific risk of harm or hazard and that specific risk of harm resulted in an injury.[479]

479. *See* Restatement (Second) of Agency § 213 (Am. Law. Inst. 1958).

Ridesharing companies have encountered legal problems with respect to their public representations regarding hiring practices. Importantly, these issues related to the "safety" of a company's hiring practices are wholly independent from the employee/independent contractor question. In the past, Uber and Lyft frequently touted their "industry leading background checks" for drivers, but ultimately these claims created problems when it was revealed that the safety checks performed on drivers were not as thorough as advertised.[480] Specifically, Uber paid $28,500,000 to settle claims related to its practice of charging drivers "safe rides fees" in response to allegations that the charge was misleading.[481] Uber also agreed to stop its use of the phrase "the safest ride on the road" and to stop referring to its background check process as "the gold standard."[482]

Additionally, Lyft settled a suit for $500,000 that required it to no longer describe its background check process as "industry leading."[483] Both Uber and Lyft have used Sterling Talent Solutions to perform their background checks.[484] Sterling prides itself on the advanced technology it uses, citing its accuracy and speed.[485] However, Sterling's practices have been questioned based on its high volume of files and reoccurring employee errors.[486] Numerous lawsuits have been brought against Sterling for failure to protect victims from criminal acts of cleared drivers.[487] These lawsuits include a claim that Lyft failed to detect a prior conviction of a Lyft driver who was charged with assault, kidnapping, robbery, and unlawful restraint of one of his

480. Ellen Huet & Joel Rosenblatt, *Uber to Pay $28M to Settle Claims over Its 'Safe Rides Fee'*, INS. J. (Feb. 12, 2016), https://www.insurancejournal.com/news/west/2016/02/12/398528.htm.

481. *Id.*

482. *Id.*

483. Rosalind Adams, *A Lyft Driver with a Criminal Record Was Charged with Rape. So Why Was He Even Behind the Wheel?*, BUZZFEED (May 30, 2019), https://www.buzzfeednews.com/article/rosalindadams/lyft-sterling-background-checks.

484. *Id.*

485. *Id.*

486. *Id.*

487. *Id.*

passengers in 2018.[488] Since then Sterling lost its contract with Lyft, but it is presumed that they still do some business with one another.[489]

Background checks, when done correctly, are an effective preventative measure. However, when the background checks fail or disqualifying problems arise after the driver is already working for the ridesharing company, victims may establish liability through negligent hiring or retention claims.

### 1. Negligent Hiring Claims Based on Criminal Acts Committed by Ridesharing Drivers

Negligent hiring claims can be linked to accusations of sexual assault, rape, and kidnapping by ridesharing drivers. In the past four years, more than 120 Uber and Lyft drivers have been accused of these criminal activities.[490] *Newsweek* reported that 31 drivers have been convicted of these types of crimes and there are dozens of cases still pending.[491] Beyond criminal prosecution, a victim may also attempt to hold the ridesharing company accountable under claims of negligent hiring and retention.

A negligent hiring/retention claim requires a plaintiff to prove (i) the employer knew or should have known that the employee had a particular unfitness for the position so as to create a danger of harm to third persons, (ii) such particular unfitness was known or should have been known at the time of the employee's hiring or retention, and (iii) this particular unfitness proximately caused the plaintiff's injury.[492]

In perhaps the most high-profile example of a negligent hiring claim brought against a ridesharing company, two women

---

488. *Id.*

489. *Id.*

490. Ewan Palmer, *Uber and Lyft Drivers Accused of More than 120 Rapes and Sexual Assaults: Report*, Newsweek (May 1, 2018) https://www.newsweek.com/uber-and-lyft-drivers-accused-more-120-rapes-and-sexual-assaults-report-906544.

491. *Id.*

492. *Cox v. Indian Head Indus., Inc.*, 123 F. Supp. 2d 892, 905 (W.D.N.C. 1999).

sued Uber after being sexually assaulted by rideshare drivers.[493] In *Doe v. Uber Techs., Inc.*, the court held that both Jane Doe plaintiffs sufficiently pled claims against Uber for fraud arising from the claim that the women relied on Uber's statements regarding driver safety when they accepted rides from the two Uber drivers involved.[494] However, the court dismissed one plaintiff's negligent hiring, supervision, and retention claims based on the fact that the driver who allegedly committed the assault on that plaintiff had been in the United States for fewer than three years, and there was no information available to Uber to put them on notice of a specific risk of the driver committing a criminal act.[495]

The other claim of negligent hiring survived the motion to dismiss. Doe alleged that the Uber driver had been arrested for domestic assault and ultimately convicted in 2003.[496] However, the background check conducted in 2015 failed to capture this conviction. The court found that Uber should have known about the driver's criminal history, even with the potential that this conviction could have been expunged, such that Uber may be liable for negligent hiring, supervision, and retention. Ultimately this case was settled for an undisclosed amount after the majority of the plaintiffs' claims remained intact after Uber's 12(b)(6) motion.[497] This case established a precedent that a negligent hiring claim against Uber can proceed past the pleading stage.

The *Doe v. Uber* case displays the risks ridesharing companies must deal with and the challenges plaintiffs will face regarding negligent hiring and retention claims. One of the major appeals of the ridesharing model is that it is quick and easy to become a driver. This aspect of ridesharing companies' business plans could quickly be placed in jeopardy if the background checks required to become a driver became more expansive and expensive. Companies like Uber have long resisted calls to

---

493. *Doe v. Uber Techs., Inc.*, 184 F. Supp. 3d 774 (N.D. Cal. 2016).
494. *Id.*
495. *Id.*
496. *Id.*
497. *Id.*

impose a background check that includes fingerprinting prospective drivers, in part because it would place a hurdle into the simple process of becoming a driver.[498] Some states have acted to require that ridesharing drivers are more thoroughly vetted. For instance, Massachusetts recently passed legislation requiring potential drivers to submit to an additional state-run background check.[499] Despite the success of this new legislation, disqualifying numerous drivers due to a history of violent crimes and sexual offenses, this process has not been adopted by Uber and Lyft in every state. Additional background checks with more stringent requirements would make the application process longer and would effectively force ridesharing companies to exert more control over drivers. As this book discussed in previous chapters, ridesharing companies want to limit their control over drivers in order to maintain the independent contractor status of their drivers.

However, the current hiring model continues to pose a significant risk because limiting background checks to a name-based search increases the likelihood that prior crimes or other red flags will be missed.[500] Because applicants could provide inaccurate or incomplete information, background checks are not as effective as they could be.[501]

Conversely, given that ridesharing operators do take some precautions to ensure the safety of their drivers, plaintiffs asserting negligent hiring claims will often face an uphill battle in establishing that the employer knew, or should have known, of specific risks posed by a driver. This is because if the risk posed by a potential driver's criminal history or driving record is sufficiently well concealed, the plaintiff will be unable to establish that the information was reasonably available to the ridesharing

498. Robert Burnson, *Uber Tells Judge Not to Trust Cab Companies in Battle Over Safety*, Ins. J. (May 13, 2016), https://www.insurancejournal.com/news/west/2016/05/13/408431.htm.

499. Adams, *supra* note 483.

500. *Id.*

501. *Id.*

operator. This defense is essentially how Uber was able to have one of the negligent hiring claims asserted against it dismissed in the *Doe* case.[502]

Another case against Uber was filed in D.C. after a passenger was allegedly sexually assaulted by a driver.[503] After the perpetrator pled guilty to criminal charges, the plaintiff brought suit against Uber for $10 million in damages.[504] She claimed both physical and emotional injuries from the assault.[505] This is similar to a case brought in 2017 where the sexual assault victim claimed not only that the driver was a convicted felon, but also that Uber had received prior complaints about the driver and failed to take any action against him.[506]

The increase of these claims has forced Uber and other ridesharing companies to change their approach to addressing these problems. The increased attention from the media forced Uber to change its liability relationship with customers. Previously, Uber held both drivers and users to mandatory arbitration agreements for any and all claims against them.[507] However, in May of 2018, they choose to drop these mandatory agreements for sexual assault and harassment claims. This move will allow courts to create a controlling body of law in this area, which in turn will create more predictability for the victims and the ridesharing corporations. Uber has even made a new commitment to transparency with respect to data related to sexual assaults.[508] In 2019, Uber released data regarding the number of sexual assault and

---

502. *See Doe v. Uber Techs., Inc.*, 184 F. Supp. 3d 774 (N.D. Cal. 2016).

503. Andres Hawkins, *Uber Sued for $10 Million by Woman Who Was Sexually Assaulted by her Driver*, Verge (Apr. 1, 2019) https://www.theverge.com/2019/4/1/18290630/uber-sued-sexual-assault-driver-dc-lawsuit.

504. *Id.*

505. *Id.*

506. *Id.*

507. Daisuke Wakabayashi, *Uber Eliminates Forced Arbitration for Sexual Misconduct Claims*, N.Y. Times (May 15, 2018) https://www.nytimes.com/2018/05/15/technology/uber-sex-misconduct.html.

508. Dara Kerr, *Uber's Data Report on Sexual Assaults to be Released in 2019*, CNET (Nov. 12, 2018) https://www.cnet.com/news/ubers-data-report-on-sexual-assaults-to-come-in-2019-after-ending-arbitration/.

other incidents reported through its app. This is part of Uber's new push "to reduce the sexual violence so prevalent in our society."[509]

There have been suggestions that ridesharing companies should take a proactive approach to combat this problem. This includes ideas such as allowing passengers to select the gender of their driver. A smaller ridesharing app has attempted to fill this void in the market by offering an option not provided by the major competitors. Safr is a ridesharing app that is only available to women.[510] Safr connects female drivers and female passengers in order to prevent potential sexual assaults.[511] Uber has not addressed why it has not provided this option on its platform. However, it may be an inability to meet the demand, because only 27 percent of the drivers for UberX are female.[512] If these types of assaults and allegations continue to rise, ridesharing companies will have a difficult time proving they do not share liability for these incidents.

### 2. Negligent Hiring, Training, or Retention Claims Based on Bad Driving, Mechanical Issues, or Intoxicated Driving

Criminal assaults by drivers are a rare, albeit very serious, occurrence. A more common factual scenario that may allow for imposing direct liability against a ridesharing coordinator arises from car accidents that could be attributable to predictably bad driving, or avoidable mechanical failure. The vehicle eligibility requirements for most ridesharing companies are typically quite minimal, though some cities have imposed stricter inspections

509. Ruth Reader, *Uber Just Promised to Make Sexual Assault Reports Public* (Apr. 11, 2019), https://www.fastcompany.com/90334028/uber-just-promised-to-make-sexual-assault-reports-public; Kate Conger, *Uber Says 3,045 Sexual Assaults Were Reported in U.S. Rides Last Year*, N.Y. Times (Dec. 5, 2019), https://www.nytimes.com/2019/12/05/technology/uber-sexual-assaults-murders-deaths-safety.html.

510. Safr, https://www.gosafr.com/riders/ (last visited Mar. 6, 2020).

511. *Id.*

512. Iqbal, *supra* note 4.

to ensure that vehicles are safe for the road.[513] Generally, a prospective driver's vehicle must pass a cursory inspection, which is aimed at making sure all safety features on the vehicle, such as taillights and seatbelts, are functioning properly.[514] Similarly, ridesharing companies generally do not require that their drivers show they possess advanced ability behind the wheel. Rather, they merely require that those signing up do not have an extensive or recent history of bad driving. Given the relatively relaxed benchmarks to become a ridesharing driver, there is an opportunity for plaintiffs injured in accidents with ridesharing drivers to argue that the ridesharing companies should be responsible for some portion of the cost of those injuries, specifically when the injuries can be tied to an obvious mechanical problem, or the recurrence of a known bad driving habit.

Mechanical problems may not only be a result of Uber's loose car standards but also a part of its actual leasing program. In Singapore, it was reported that Uber knowingly leased drivers defective and recalled cars.[515] It was alleged that Uber was aware of repairs that needed to be made to the cars but allowed their continued use on the road.[516] This resulted in the dashboards of the cars combusting with both drivers and passengers in the vehicle.[517] Although this is an extreme example, it demonstrates the need for safe vehicles and the potentially intentional

---

513. *Does My Vehicle Need to Get Inspected?*, UBER, https://help.uber.com/h/373c9b72-b09d-4604-876b-d8ce203a9b49. Also, it should be noted that Uber now uses different quality classifications for vehicles and drivers, which correspond to the price of a given trip. UberX is the easiest level to qualify a vehicle for. While UberBlack has a demanding vehicle qualification standard. UberBlack also uses professional drivers who have commercial licenses. Jonathan V. Hall & Alan B. Krueger, *An Analysis of the Labor Market for Uber's Driver-Partners in the United States* 16–17 (Princeton Univ., Indus. Relations Section, Working Paper No. 587, 2015).

514. *Vehicle and Document Requirements*, UBER, https://www.uber.com/drive/columbus/vehicle-requirements/ (last visited Mar. 6, 2020).

515. Laurel Wamsley, *Uber Knowingly Leased Unsafe Cars to its Drivers in Singapore, Report Says*, NAT'L PUB. RADIO (Aug. 4, 2017), https://www.npr.org/sections/thetwo-way/2017/08/04/541692151/uber-knowingly-leased-unsafe-cars-to-its-drivers-in-singapore-report-says.

516. *Id.*

517. *Id.*

lack of control Uber exercises over the transportation aspects of its operation.

Additionally, there is some indication that ridesharing companies have struggled to adequately combat risks associated with intoxicated or impaired driving. One of the main accomplishments of ridesharing is the decrease in drunk drivers on the roads. However, last year Uber reportedly faced over $1,000,000 in fines imposed by California state regulators related to the failure to adequately investigate reports of drunk driving that came from Uber customers.[518] An investigation by the California Public Utilities Commission, which is responsible for regulating ridesharing companies, found that out of 154 customer complaints related to intoxicated drivers, Uber had failed to adequately investigate or suspend the driver quickly enough in 151 instances.[519] In the event a person is injured by a driver that a ridesharing company has reason to know is currently intoxicated, or who has been reported for that problem in the past, that injured person would have a strong negligent retention claim that could be asserted against the company.

Whether the driver is considered to be an employee or an independent contractor, if the ridesharing company allows a driver to continue transporting customers while intoxicated, that company will bear some liability for injuries caused by such a driver. Currently, ridesharing companies place the responsibility of reporting intoxicated driving on customers. Such a report requires an immediate suspension of the driver and follow-up investigation of the report. Uber's zero tolerance policy instructs the customer, upon suspicion that their driver may be under the influence, to ask the driver to end the trip immediately and then exit the car and call 911.[520] However, as revealed by the investigation of the California Public Utilities Commission,

518. Steven M. Sweat, *Legal Ramifications of Uber Ignoring Drunk Driver Complaints*, NAT'L L. REV. (Apr. 20, 2017), https://www.natlawreview.com/article/legal-ramifications-uber-ignoring-drunk-driver-complaints.

519. *Id.*

520. *Uber Community Guidelines*, UBER, https://www.uber.com/legal/community-guidelines/us-can-en/ (last updated Jan. 23, 2020).

these mandatory suspensions and investigations do not always occur.[521] There appears to be an alternate "strike system" that the company operates instead of enforcing zero tolerance.[522]

## B. Common Carrier Liability

While ridesharing companies have taken steps to create circumstances that will make it more difficult for injured parties to hold ridesharing companies liable under vicarious liability theories, other available theories could support recovery even where vicarious liability is not available. Specifically, injured parties could argue that ridesharing platforms are essentially modern-day common carriers and therefore owe a heightened, nondelegable duty of care to ensure the safety of passengers. Generally, a common carrier is a company who offers transportation services to the general public.[523] Although some states have done away with the common carrier distinction, in other jurisdictions, this theory can, and has been, used to effectively argue that ridesharing companies owe a heightened duty to customers.

Common carriers differ from taxi companies because of the difference in ride operations and scope. Maryland recently classified Uber's Uber Black Car and SUV services as "for hire carriers."[524] For hire carries cannot stop for customers hailing on the street and can operate throughout the state.[525] This distinction as a for hire carrier will affect the way Uber can operate within the state. They must apply for a motor carrier permit and will no longer be able to use the surge pricing feature.[526]

In the *Doe v. Uber* case, the California Court held that the plaintiffs had alleged sufficient facts to proceed with their claims

---

521. *Id.*

522. Priya Anand, *Here's What Happens When Your Uber Driver Gets a DUI*, BUZZFEED (June 30, 2016), https://www.buzzfeednews.com/article/priya/what-happens-when-your-uber-driver-gets-a-dui.

523. *See* Doe v. Uber Techs., Inc., 184 F. Supp. 3d 774 (N.D. Cal. 2016).

524. Kevin Rector, *Md. Commission Rules Uber Is "Common Carrier," Will Face Regulations*, BALT. SUN (Aug. 6, 2014) https://www.baltimoresun.com/business/bs-bz-uber-common-carrier-20140806-story.html.

525. *Id.*

526. *Id.*

alleging that Uber was a common carrier at the time they sustained their injuries.[527] The *Doe* court also noted that Uber's liability under this theory was unrelated to the question of whether the driver was an employee or a contractor, because liability arose from the company's alleged failure to meet its duty to protect passengers from harm.[528] Thus, plaintiffs in jurisdictions where common carrier claims are still available may be able to establish liability far more easily than in jurisdictions where this theory has been abolished.

Uber argues it does not fall under the common carrier definition because a technology service that connects independent drives with passengers is exempt from the oversight under the Telecommunications Act of 1996.[529] Additionally, it should be noted that some states, namely Florida, have specifically excluded ridesharing companies from the definition of a common carrier, foreclosing this approach to pursue recovery directly from a ridesharing company.[530] This trend has been followed by other states that statutorily define a ridesharing company as a "transportation network company," or "TNC" and excludes TNCs from being considered a common carrier.[531] Other than Maryland's Public Service Commission ruling, no states have statutorily recognized ridesharing companies as common carriers.

## C. Conclusion

Attorneys who plan to incorporate ridesharing cases into their practice have a plethora of legal theories that will need to be considered. Given that there is little case law to provide guidance on how courts are likely to analyze cases involving ridesharing, it will be incumbent on the attorneys working on cases in this field to pursue all available legal theories. Whether from effective arguments against imposing vicarious liability on ridesharing

527. Doe v. Uber Techs., Inc., 184 F. Supp. 3d 774 (N.D. Cal. 2016).

528. *Id.*

529. Adams, *supra* note 483.

530. Fla. Stat. § 627.748 (2020).

531. *See, e.g.*, 66 Pa. Cons. Stat. § 102(3)(i)(x) ("The term [common carrier] does not include . . . A transportation network company. . . .").

operators or the establishment of a novel theory of recovery in ridesharing cases, there will be a tremendous amount of precedent set in this field in the coming years. Attorneys who make it a point to stay informed on developments in this area of the law will be well positioned to handle the eventual influx of cases that will correspond to the increased use of ridesharing services.

## VI. Liability Theories Premised on Trademark Ownership and Licensing

The liability of trademark licensors for the actions of their licensees has been the subject of both discussion[532] and case law[533] for decades, primarily regarding products sold under a licensed

---

532. *See, e.g.*, Kenneth B. Germain, *Tort Liability of Trademark Licensors in an Era of "Accountability": A Tale of Three Cases*, 69 Trademark Rep. 128 (1979); Tara K. Gorman, *Limitations on Licensor's Liability: Can a Licensor Get Away with Capping Trademark Liability?*, Hotel Executive (May 1, 2011), https://www.hotelexecutive.com/business_review/2505/limitations-on-licensors-liability-can-a-licensor-get-away-with-capping-trademark-liability; Lee J. Eulgen, *New Concerns over Product Liability Risk for Trademark Licensors*, Nat'l L. Rev. (Dec. 11, 2012), https://www.natlawreview.com/article/new-concerns-over-product-liability-risk-trademark-licensors; J. Carter Thompson Jr. & Ceejaye Peters, *Litigation: Trademark Licensor Liability in Product Liability Cases*, Law (Oct. 18, 2012), https://www.law.com/insidecounsel/sites/insidecounsel/2012/10/18/litigation-trademark-licensor-liability-in-product-liability-cases/; Erin K. Higgins, *Trademark Licensors Potentially Subject to Strict Liability*, New England In-House (Oct. 7, 2011), https://newenglandinhouse.com/2011/10/07/trademark-licensors-potentially-subject-to-strict-liability/; John W. Behringer & Monica A. Otte, *Liability and the Trademark Licensor: Advice for the Franchisor of Goods or Services*, 19 Am. Bus. L.J. 109 (1981); Margaret Frenkel Goldstein, *Products Liability and the Trademark Owner: When a Trademark Is a Warranty*, 67 Trademark Rep. 587 (1977). *See also* J. Thomas McCarthy, McCarthy on Trademarks and Unfair Competition § 18:74, at 18–189 (2019) ("As Professor Kenneth B. Germain perceptively observed, there exists an 'emerging, probably unstoppable trend in favor of holding trademark licensors liable for the tortious conduct of their licensees. . . .'"

533. *See, e.g.*, Lou v. Otis Elevator Co., 933 N.E.2d 140 (Mass. App. Ct. 2010); Lopez v. El Palmar Taxi, Inc., 676 S.E.2d 460 (Ga. Ct. App. 2009); Kennedy v. Guess, Inc., 806 N.E.2d 776 (Ind. 2004); Patterson v. Central Mills, Inc., 112 F. Supp. 2d 681 (N.D. Ohio 2000); Yoder v. Honeywell, Inc., 104 F.3d 1215 (10th Cir. 1997), *cert denied*, 522 U.S. 812 (1997); Mobil Oil Corp. v. Bransford, 648 So. 2d 119 (Fla. 1995).

trademark. However, the development of the sharing economy generally, and the ridesharing industry specifically, has created new context for the argument in favor of extending "service liability" to licensor companies under whose marks services are advertised, offered, and provided.[534]

By way of a hypothetical, an individual, Rita Rider, has seen advertisements about the efforts a new ridesharing service, CARSHARE, makes in vetting its drivers. Rider downloads the CARSHARE app, signs up for a CARSHARE account, and requests ridesharing services. She is connected with Don Driver, who is offering such services as an accountholder and licensee of CARSHARE through the same branded platform. The car arrives, possibly bearing a CARSHARE sticker or lighted sign in the window to help customers identify it, and Driver asks Rider for her name and if she requested a CARSHARE ride. During the trip, which would not be occurring but for the arrangement through the CARSHARE platform, the car becomes involved in an accident for which Driver is at fault, injuring Rider and possibly others. Not surprisingly, throughout the process, the CARSHARE mark serves not only to identify the source of the services, but also as an assurance of the quality of those services.

There would be little argument that the driver would be liable. However, it may be argued that the ridesharing platform should also shoulder the burden of liability. Ridesharing platforms have consistently argued that they merely facilitate transactions between private individuals and should not be subject to liability when injury occurs as a result of those transactions. However, some fundamental tort law principles suggest the ridesharing platform itself is both deserving of some degree of liability (due, in part, to its profiting from the licensed use of its marks and the services provided thereunder) and is in the best position to bear and redistribute the costs of that liability and any related insurance.

---

534. *See, e.g.*, Molly Cohen & Corey Zehngebot, *Heads Up: What's Old Becomes New: Regulating the Sharing Economy*, Bos. B.J. (Apr. 1, 2014), https://bostonbarjournal.com/2014/04/01/whats-old-becomes-new-regulating-the-sharing-economy/.

In 1979, well before the modern sharing economy had developed, Ken Germain (one of the co-authors of this section) argued just that point in response to license-related product liability cases.[535] In 2015, this section's co-authors updated Ken's work in response to the rise of the sharing economy generally.[536] Since that time, the need for clarification of ridesharing liability has only grown more urgent as these services continue to grow and brands associated with such services continue to become more viable and valuable.

This section provides a brief overview of trademark and trademark licensing law, a summary of policy rationales that have been put forward in support of extending liability to trademark licensors, a summary of relevant case law in the field, and finally arguments that could be raised to support the claim that this type of liability should apply in the ridesharing context.

## A. A Brief Primer on Trademarks and Trademark Licensing

A trademark (often referred to simply as a "mark") can be any word, symbol (or "logo"), slogan, color, design element, or a combination of these that indicates the source of a product or service.[537] Trademark rights are based on, and develop automatically through, use of a trademark in commerce in connection with specific products and/or services. Though registration (with either the U.S. Patent and Trademark Office or individual states) is often available, use of a mark in commerce is all that is necessary to develop "common law" rights, which are enforceable in the geographic region where the goods or services are being provided under the mark.

535. Germain, *supra* note 532.

536. Kenneth B. Germain & Sean K. Owens, *Torts Uber Trademarks or Trademarks Uber Torts: That Is the Question*, 90 Bloomberg BNA Pat. Trademark & Copyright J. 3211 (2015), https://www.whe-law.com/blog/images/BBNA%2009-2015_Torts%20Uber%20Trademark_SEG%20SKO.pdf.

537. While the phrase "service mark" is more specifically used when referring to marks used with services, and the phrase "trade dress" applies to packaging or the appearance of products, the umbrella terms "trademark" and "mark" will be used throughout for the sake of simplicity.

There are, however, several important limitations on what words or elements can receive trademark protection. First, a mark must be sufficiently "distinctive" for consumers to differentiate one source from another. Distinctiveness falls along the following spectrum, with the degree of protectability and examples provided:

| Generic | Descriptive | Suggestive | Arbitrary | Fanciful |
|---|---|---|---|---|
| Never Protectable | Can Become Protectable | Always/Automatically Protectable | | |
| APPLE[538] Apples | AMERICAN Airlines | PROPEL Energy Drink | APPLE Computers | KODAK Cameras |

Generic terms cannot receive trademark protection under any circumstances. They are merely the names for the product or service being offered, and all providers of those products or services must be allowed to inform consumers of such basic information without restraint. Thus, in the ridesharing context, "ridesharing" is the generic term for the service in which no one party can claim exclusive rights. Similarly, descriptive terms "describe" a characteristic of the products or services. While descriptive terms do not receive trademark protection upon initial use in commerce, descriptive terms can "acquire" distinctiveness (otherwise known as "secondary meaning") if, as a result of extensive use in commerce, consumers identify such terms with a single source. By way of example, when consumers hear the phrase "American Airlines," they do not think of all U.S.-based air carriers. Rather, they think of just one: American Airlines. Acquired distinctiveness can be proven through length of use, amount of sales and advertising, consumer surveys or affidavits, third-party media, and so on.

Moving up the spectrum, the remaining categories of marks are considered to be "inherently" distinctive, and thus automatically receive protection without a showing of acquired

538. Third-party trademarks are referenced for illustrative purposes only and are the property of their respective owners.

distinctiveness. Suggestive marks do not merely describe the product or service but convey some bit of information that requires the consumer's imagination to make the connection (e.g. PROPEL energy drink). Arbitrary marks are English-language terms that are used with entirely unrelated products or services (hence, Apple computers). And finally, fanciful (or "coined") terms are nonsense terms (KODAK, IKEA, etc.) and typically receive the highest degree of protection.

Other limitations on what elements can constitute trademarks include that marks cannot be functional (e.g., the color white for bleach; a visible design feature that is also the subject of a utility patent; etc.), deceptive to consumers, a seal of the U.S. government, or several other limitations that (for various policy reasons) preclude the recognition of trademark rights. If, however, a mark is adopted and used in commerce, that use is properly maintained and policed by the owner, the mark is distinctive (or acquires distinctiveness), and does not otherwise run afoul of limitations on what can constitute a mark, the owner of that mark will possess the right to prevent others from using the same or similar marks with related products or services that are directed to overlapping groups of consumers. The purpose of this right, and indeed the fundamental purpose of trademark law generally, is to (i) protect the "trade" of the trademark owner, and (ii) prevent consumers from suffering confusion as to the source (or sponsorship, endorsement, etc.) of a particular product or service.

But trademarks serve purposes other than merely identifying the source of a product and allowing an owner to take action to halt consumer confusion. Through the development of consumer good will, trademarks serve as guarantees about the quality of products or services offered under the marks. They also act as advertising elements that make communication to consumers, and the effort consumers undertake when evaluating different sources, easier and more efficient. Ultimately, then, trademarks serve at least three functions: (i) to identify the party/source responsible for the goods or services bearing the mark; (ii) to guarantee the quality of the goods or services bearing the mark;

and (iii) to serve as an effective advertising device linking consumer demand with the marked goods or services.

The identification function serves both to reward mark owners whose goods or services are satisfactory to the consuming public while discouraging mark owners whose goods or services are viewed as unsatisfactory, whereas the guarantee function is oriented toward the well-being of the consumer. One might also say that the right to make use of the advertising function (purely a matter of interest to trademark owners) carries with it the responsibility to abide by the guarantee function rather strictly. In other terms, one might say that the basic goals of legal recognition of trademarks (and principles of the greater law of unfair competition) have always acknowledged a symbiotic relationship between trademark owners (seeking to protect their honestly obtained and fairly held trade) and consumers (seeking to receive sound goods and services from reputable sources).

Trademark licensing occurs when the owner of a trademark permits another to use a mark in connection with specific goods or services, and with benefits flowing to both the licensor and licensee.[539] The licensee avoids the expense of developing its own brand, and instead is able to sell its products or services under marks with good will and customer loyalty already established, potentially driving sales. The licensor, on the other hand, might receive monetary compensation with little effort or risk. The licensor also retains the right and accepts the duty to exert control over the quality of the products or services being offered under the licensed mark. Further, to the extent the licensee's use

539. Trademark licensing can be contrasted with franchising primarily through the degree of control and interdependence. In a trademark license, the relationship between the parties is typically limited to the granting of the right to use the mark, while the licensor retains the right to exert control over the general quality of the products or services offered under the mark. In a franchise context, which is often heavily regulated at the state level, the franchisor exerts far more control than just monitoring of the overall quality of the goods or services. Rather, the franchisor might control or influence the franchisee's entire business plan and operations, architecture, supply of product, marketing plans and materials, and so on.

of the mark increases the good will, consumer recognition, and market value of the brand, those benefits inure to the owner of the mark, the licensor.

Ultimately, it is through a licensing arrangement that ridesharing platforms operate. Drivers operate as licensees of the ridesharing platforms not just as users (and thus licensees) of the mobile apps that facilitate the transactions, but also effectively as trademark licensees providing transportation services under the mark of the ridesharing platform (indeed, with many drivers displaying the ridesharing platform's marks in their windows). A portion of customer payments flow to the ridesharing platform—as does all the good will, consumer loyalty, and increased brand value that accrues through consumers' use of the services by the "independent" drivers.

## B. Policy Rationales for Extending Liability to Trademark Licensors

Historically, various policy rationales have been advanced to justify the extension of liability to trademark licensors, including honoring justifiable reliance, preventing preventable losses, and spreading of unprevented losses.[540] What follows are some of the underlying theories that could be relied on by litigators seeking to recover from a ridesharing company whose driver has been involved in an accident.

In brief, honoring justifiable reliance simply is a recognition that one who relies on a representation by another—here the assertion in the guise of a licensed trademark that the other stands behind ("guarantees") the goods or services offered to the public—should be held liable for any misrepresentations involved, including a tacit misrepresentation that the business will be conducted safely.[541] The preventing preventable losses theory is the familiar concept that by threatening a party with legal liability for tortious acts, that party will try harder to avoid committing such tortious acts (or allowing such acts to occur by

540. *See* Comment, *Liability of a Franchisor for Acts of the Franchisee*, 41 S. Cal. L. Rev. 143, 153–56 (1968).

541. Germain, *supra* note 532, at 130.

its licensees).[542] In context, this means that by holding ridesharing companies legally responsible for their drivers' torts, the former will be more inclined to carefully choose and supervise the latter, thereby reducing the incidence of tortious conduct.[543] The spreading of unprevented losses, the third theory, involves the equally familiar concept of "enterprise liability," that is, that those who operate the enterprise—the ridesharing companies—are the most able and "deserving" parties to be held responsible for the costs of doing business.[544] This, of course, also offers the injured party the deepest pocket into which to reach. As one commentator long ago put it in the franchising context:

> The franchisee puts his money, time and future on the line and the franchisor makes the profit. Since the franchisor is the one primarily benefited by the franchise, he is the one who is in a better position to absorb the cost of liability insurance. Moreover, he can better distribute the loss because of his superior business position. Imposing liability on the franchisor would theoretically be a strong incentive to induce him to take greater care in his selection of franchisees.[545]

Thus, we see that the very practices that lead to effective trademark licensing—careful quality control, widespread advertising of the licensed trademark, and close supervision of the licensee's actions—may lead courts to conclude, via one legal theory or another,[546] that licensors must share the financial responsibility for the torts of their licensees. Thus, while trademark law principles instruct licensors to keep close tabs on their licensees' uses of their marks, tort law principles warn that supervision that is "too close" may beget liability for damages caused by these licensees' tortious acts, as has been recognized by courts.

---

542. *Id.*

543. *Id.*

544. *Id.*

545. John F. Stuart, Comment, A *Franchisor's Liability for the Torts of His Franchisee*, 5 U.S. FLA. L. REV. 118, 122 (1970).

546. As has been discussed throughout this chapter, courts have variously based their analyses in negligence/warranty, strict liability, vicarious liability, and so on.

## C. Overview of Trademark Licensor Liability Case Law and Theories of Liability

When considering whether to extend liability to licensors in product liability cases, courts have viewed the problem through several different lenses, namely, the direct theories of liability of negligence, warranty, and strict liability versus the indirect theory of agency. Within these various theories, courts typically consider the degree to which the licensor was involved in the design, manufacture, and distribution of the product.[547] Where a licensor is purely passive, liability will often remain with the licensee/manufacturer.[548] Conversely, where the licensor is heavily involved in the design, manufacturing, and so on, of the products bearing the licensed marks, courts have held that both the licensee and licensor are liable for damage caused by the defective branded products.[549] Difficult cases (and potential inconsistencies in the case law) arise when considering how much involvement is enough to create the extension of liability, and whether or how these principles should be extended to the service liability context.

547. *See, e.g.*, Kennedy v. Guess, Inc., 806 N.E.2d 776, 786 (Ind. 2004) (applying a negligence analysis, the court held that trademark licensors should be responsible for "defective products placed in the stream of commerce bearing their marks, but only so much of the liability for those defects as their relative role in the larger scheme of design, advertising, manufacturing and distribution warrants" and that the process of assigning that comparative fault should be left the jury).

548. *See, e.g.*, Dzhunaydov v. Emerson Elec. Co., No. 12-CV-2188 (FB) (RER), 2013 U.S. Dist. LEXIS 179875 (E.D.N.Y. 2016) (declining to extend liability to the licensor of a trademark applied to table saws where the licensor's only involvement in the products' design, manufacture, sale, distribution, or marketing was in graphic design choices related to the instruction manual, labels, etc.).

549. *See, e.g.*, Kasel v. Remington Arms Co., 24 Cal. App. 3d 711 (Cal. Ct. App. 1972) (defendant/licensor held liable under law of warranties for defective firearm shell manufactured by a licensee company that had been formed by defendant, had overlapping directors and officers, and was 40% owned by defendant).

### 1. Negligence

In *Kosters v. The Seven-Up Co.*, the plaintiff suffered injury after a glass bottle fell from an allegedly defective carrying carton approved by defendant franchisor Seven-Up.[550] The Sixth Circuit stated the matter plainly: "a franchisor [or licensor], like a manufacturer or supplier, may be liable to the consumer for its own negligence, without regard to privity."[551] Although Seven-Up argued that it had merely reviewed the defective cartons for their graphics, the court held that Seven-Up's inspection and approval of the cartons, coupled with its control over their "type, style, size, and design" could be sufficient for liability.[552] Thus, where a licensor has the ability to control the quality of products bearing its marks, exercises that control, but does so negligently and without regard to potentially dangerous defects, liability for injury to consumers may extend beyond the licensee.

Conversely, and as exemplified by *Patterson v. Central Mills, Inc.*, cases in which the licensor is a merely passive participant typically do not extend liability to the licensor for negligence.[553] In *Patterson*, a shirt bearing Looney Tunes artwork and branding caught fire, causing injury to its owner.[554] The artwork and trademarks had been licensed by Warner Bros. to the shirt's manufacturer, Central Mills.[555] Though the court acknowledged that Warner Bros. had the right to exercise quality control over the products, it recognized this right was a standard element of any trademark license, it imposed no duty on Warner Bros. to exercise that right, and there was no evidence that Warner Bros. had done so, or that it had participated in the design, manufacture, or distribution of the shirt.[556]

---

550. 595 F.2d 347, 348 (6th Cir. 1979).

551. *Id.* at 352.

552. *Id.* at 352–53 (the case was ultimately remanded for a new trial for other reasons). *See also Kennedy*, 806 N.E.2d. *But see Dzhunaydov*, 2013 U.S. Dist. LEXIS 179875.

553. 112 F. Supp. 2d 681 (N.D. Ohio 2000).

554. *Id.* at 684.

555. *Id.*

556. *Id.* at 692–93.

## 2. Warranty

The warranty theory of liability can also arise when the licensor retains control over the products that bear the licensed marks and consents to their distribution into commerce. It typically arises in manufacturing and distributing franchises, such as was seen in the *Kosters* decision. There, the court further opined that:

> When a franchisor consents to the distribution of a defective product bearing its name, the obligation of the franchisor to compensate the injured consumer for breach of implied warranty, we think, arises from several factors in combination: (1) the risk created by approving for distribution an unsafe product likely to cause injury, (2) the franchisor's ability and opportunity to eliminate the unsafe character of the product and prevent the loss, (3) the consumer's lack of knowledge of the danger, and (4) the consumer's reliance on the trade name which gives the intended impression that the franchisor is responsible for and stands behind the product. *Liability is based on the franchisor's control and the public's assumption, induced by the franchisor's conduct, that it does in fact control and vouch for the product.*[557]

In another example demonstrating the high degree of control that can arise between licensors and licensees, a licensor firearms manufacturer was held liable under principles of warranty for defective shells manufactured by its licensee that had been formed by defendant, had overlapping directors and officers, and was 40 percent owned by the defendant.[558]

## 3. Strict Liability

Some courts (often taking guidance in varying degrees from the Second or Third Restatement of Torts) have also found licensors to be strictly liable where they have supplied ingredients to their

557. 595 F.2d at 353 (emphasis added).

558. Kasel v. Remington Arms Co., 24 Cal. App. 3d 711 (Cal. Ct. App. 1972).

licensees or otherwise exercised a high degree of control over the design, manufacture, or distribution of the goods sold under the licensor's mark. "In these circumstances they are treated as sellers of the products bearing their trademarks" and are thus subject to strict liability.[559]

For example, in *Hartford v. Associated Constr. Co.*, the defendant licensed its nationally advertised trademark for a roofing insulation product under an agreement that gave it considerable quality control over the product's formulation, instructions for installation, and so on.[560] The defendant also supplied a necessary ingredient of the product to its franchisees and was sued when the plaintiff's home suffered damage from the product.[561] Upholding the plaintiff's complaint, the court held that

> as long as the franchisor or trademark licensor can be said to be a link in the marketing enterprise which placed a defective product within the stream of commerce, there is no reason in logic for refusing to apply strict liability in tort to such an entity.[562]

Conversely, where the licensors' involvement in the production of the goods is minimal, entirely passive, or otherwise outside of the chain of distribution, strict liability will not apply. For example, in *Dzhunaydov v. Emerson Electric Co.*, the court declined to extend liability to the licensor of a trademark applied to table saws where the licensor's only involvement in the products' design, manufacture, sale, distribution, or marketing was in certain graphic design choices related to the instruction manual,

---

559. Restatement (Third) of Torts § 14 (Am. Law. Inst. 2005).

560. 384 A.2d 390 (Conn. Super. Ct. 1978).

561. *Id.*

562. *Id.* at 216 (quoting *Kasel*, 24 Cal. App. 3d at 725); *see also* Torres v. Goodyear Tire & Rubber Co., Inc., 786 P.2d 939 (Ariz. 1990), *later proceedings*, 901 F.2d 750 (9th Cir. 1990) (Licensor Goodyear had significant control over the production and overall process by which the faulty GOODYEAR branded tires manufactured by a licensee were manufactured and reached plaintiff); Lou v. Otis Elevator Co., 933 N.E.2d 140 (Mass. App. Ct. 2010) (affirming liability of licensor due to its provision not only of a trademark license but also significant technical and managerial know-how for the production of the faulty escalator).

labels, and so on, and explicitly distinguished such facts against cases in which the imposition of strict liability was appropriate.[563] Similarly, the Ninth Circuit declined to hold Du Pont strictly liable where its TEFLON-branded products were used and advertised as an ingredient in a defective product with which Du Pont otherwise was not involved.[564]

### 4. Agency

Finally, indirect liability can extend to trademark licensors where the licensee is found to have acted as the agent (or apparent agent) of the licensor. Again, the primary inquiry comes down to how much control the licensor exerted over the licensee. For example, in *Drexel v. Union Prescription Ctrs.*, a drugstore franchisor was sued for wrongful death over the misfiling of a prescription by a franchisee pharmacist.[565] As detailed in the franchise agreement,[566] the franchisor maintained significant control over the franchisee, including store location, the right to inspect the premises to ensure it "conform[ed] strictly" to "national standards," the hiring of union members for construction work, inventory requirements, record keeping, and equipment designations.[567] Reversing and remanding the lower court's grant of summary judgment for the franchisor, the court found that the high degree of control raised genuine issues of material fact as to whether there was actual agency. Similarly, evidence that

---

563. Dzhunaydov v. Emerson Elec. Co., No. 12-CV-2188 (FB) (RER), 2013 U.S. Dist. LEXIS 179875 (E.D.N.Y. 2016) (distinguishing Automobile Ins. Co. of Hartford Connecticut v. Murray, Inc., 574 F. Supp. 2d 408, 434 (W.D.N.Y. 2008)) ("[A] trademark licensor may be subject to strict products liability claims where it has 'significant involvement in [the] distribution or is capable of exercising control over [the] quality [of the product] . . . or where evidence shows the licensor to have 'sold, distributed or marketed' the defective product.").

564. Kealoha v. E.I. du Pont de Nemours & Co., 82 F.3d 894 (9th Cir. 1996); *see also* Yoder v. Honeywell, Inc., 104 F.3d 1215 (10th Cir. 1997), *cert. denied*, 522 U.S. 812 (1997).

565. 582 F.2d 781 (3d Cir. 1978).

566. See the appendix to the opinion, *id.* at 797–810, for a copy of this document.

567. *Id.* at 787.

customers of the franchisee believed that they were dealing with the franchisor raised genuine issues as to apparent agency.[568]

A Georgia case involving taxis provides an example of the application of service liability in an apparent agency context.[569] In *Lopez*, the licensor taxi company entered into an agreement with an individual as an independent contractor taxi driver.[570] The licensor required the driver's car to bear the company mark along with other fairly minor controls (a policy of not smoking in the car, asking passengers to wear seatbelts, etc.), but the driver was otherwise permitted to work when he chose.[571] The dispute arose when the plaintiff called the licensor taxi company for a ride, which in turn instructed the driver to carry out the services for the plaintiff.[572] The taxi was involved in an accident, the plaintiff was injured, and the taxi company's insurance refused to compensate the plaintiff for her injuries.[573] The court held that the licensor's advertisements and provision of branded business cards to drivers, coupled with the fact that after the plaintiff called the licensor for a taxi, the licensor responded by providing a taxi displaying its own branding to provide such services, were sufficient to create questions of fact that precluded summary judgment in favor of the licensor.[574] Accordingly, the lower court's dismissal was reversed.[575]

---

568. *Id.* at 795. *Accord* Billops v. Magness Construction Co., 391 A.2d 196 (Del. 1978) (franchise agreement required franchisee to solely display franchisor's sign, logo, and color scheme); Gizzi v. Texaco, Inc., 437 F.2d 308 (3d Cir. 1971). *Contra* Ditri v. Coldwell Banker Residential Affiliates, 954 F.2d 869 (3d Cir. 2002) (franchisor's national advertising regarding ethical business practices did not create liability for the false advertising of an affiliate agency); Mobil Oil Corp. v. Bransford, 648 So. 2d 119 (Fla. 1995); B.P. Oil Corp. v. Mabe, 370 A.2d 554 (Ct. App. Md. 1977).

569. Lopez v. El Palmar Taxi, Inc., 676 S.E.2d 460 (Ga. Ct. App. 2009).

570. *Id.* at 462.

571. *Id.*

572. *Id.* at 463.

573. *Id.*

574. *Id.* at 465.

575. *Id.*

The opposite result was found in *Emery v. Visa International Service Ass'n*, where the licensor, Visa, was sued for unfair business practices arising from mailed solicitations for illegal foreign lottery tickets that could be purchased with VISA credit cards, and where advertised as such.[576] The solicitations were sent by the lottery operators, who were licensed merchants of Visa (and were therefore licensed to display the VISA logo).[577] Dismissing the suit, the court held that "[a] trademark owner's grant of permission to another to use the owner's mark, combined with efforts to 'police' such use, do not make the user agent or intermediary of the owner."[578]

## D. Arguments for and against Extension of Liability to Ridesharing Companies

No court has yet ruled, based on trademark principles alone, that liability should extend to ridesharing platforms (nor, to the authors' knowledge, has a court been presented with the opportunity to do so, as suits typically settle). However, it could be argued that a critical function of a trademark is to "guarantee" the quality of the products or services offered under the mark. As more ridesharing cases are litigated, practitioners dealing with matters involving ridesharing vehicle accidents should be aware of this possible basis for direct liability claims.

As postulated by one group of authors:

> [F]ew trademarks today function primarily as indicia of origin. Even where the maker is still known, a strong brand, today, is more a set of strong, favorable and unique associations, assuring an experience, than it is a reflection of a producer. A strong brand is a promise, an invisible contract with consumers, and a modern trademark is foremost a *trustmark*, not as to source but as to sensation.[579]

---

576. 95 Cal. App. 4th 952, 954 (Cal. Ct. App. 2002).

577. *Id.*

578. *Id.* at 961.

579. Jerre B. Swann, Sr., David A. Aaker & Matt Reback, *Trademarks and Marketing*, 91 Trademark Rep. 787, 807 (2001) (emphasis in the original) (footnote omitted).

To put this view in context, and to allude back to the hypothetical presented at the beginning of this section and the realities of ridesharing, it can be argued there is a significant degree of active involvement by ridesharing platforms in the provision of the transportation services. This involvement could be found to be sufficient control to allow for application of the principle of *respondeat superior*, joint enterprise liability, or one of the other theories of vicarious liability. Trademark liability stands as a parallel, yet alternative, theory that could permit recovery from ridesharing operators—potentially irrespective of the level of involvement or control exerted over the hired party. Of course, only one of the many available theories of liability is needed to allow injured plaintiffs to recover substantial damages.[580] That being said, the way in which the public interacts with ridesharing companies may support an argument that trademark liability can be relied on to establish the direct liability of ridesharing companies, or other sharing economy platforms, whose workers are involved in causing injuries.

Consider the following fact pattern: after a consumer hears about a branded ridesharing service that is touted as more convenient and user-friendly than traditional taxi cabs, the consumer downloads the branded app onto his or her smartphone. The consumer may have also heard that the ridesharing platforms require their drivers to undergo background and driving record checks along with any necessary vehicle inspections to ensure a reasonably safe ride. The consumer then creates an account, agrees to the platform's license terms, submits credit or debit card information to the ridesharing platform, opens the app to see branded cars circling the block in real time, and then requests a privately owned car operated by a licensee of the platform. Upon arrival of the licensee, possibly in a vehicle bearing the ridesharing platform's mark, the consumer enters the car and is driven to the desired destination. The branded app then

580. As one commentator has opined, "[o]n a policy level, courts who search for the 'deepest pocket' will often find a theory of tort liability to fit the facts." McCarthy, *supra* note 532, at 18–193.

processes the payment, allows the consumer to rate his or her experience, and so on.

From this series of interactions and transactions, the consumer will associate the services being rendered (including the source and quality of those services) with the platform, not just with a private individual who happened to be driving the car and who is, in strict legal parlance, merely a licensee of the platform.[581] Moreover, the rider almost certainly will believe that the ridesharing company has done its work to ensure the driver is competent and the vehicle used for the ride can operate safely. In this way, it is clear that the rider is looking to the platform, rather than solely to the driver for assurance of a reasonably safe ride. Although individual drivers can be rated by customers, the source-identifying function of the licensed trademark means that the platform licensor, not the driver, is ultimately reaping the primary benefits of that goodwill, and a significant share of the profits.

It can be argued that fundamental principles of tort liability related to the allocation of risks and benefits between large corporations, individual independent contractors, and innocent third parties, rather obviously suggest extending trademark liability to ridesharing platforms. Persons taking this position would reject the notion that ridesharing platforms are too far removed, or insufficiently involved, to suffer liability. The argument for extending trademark liability would be based on a claim that the functions of the platforms' marks, along with the benefit being derived from the use of that mark, should be sufficient to impose a portion of the risk. In the event other theories of liability fail, extending trademark liability may be relied on as a mechanism to ensure losses suffered by innocent third parties are shared with the "deepest pocket" involved in the transaction. In a sense, the underlying theory is to "follow the money" and extend liability to the service licensor, which should then

581. It goes without saying that should ridesharing drivers ultimately be deemed employees of the platforms, the analysis would obviously tilt even greater in favor of extending liability.

be ready, willing, and able to provide adequate compensation (directly or indirectly) for those harmed as a result of conduct of individuals providing its trademark-bearing services.

Proponents of this theory of extending liability would likely point out that ridesharing companies are in the best position (financially, administratively, etc.) to sustain liability and provide compensation in an efficient manner. Moreover, in a competitive environment, the goodwill of being a good corporate citizen will inure to the benefit of the platforms/licensors. This would have the added benefit to the licensors of helping to improve their reputation and good will for being good corporate citizens who will stand behind their services.

Ridesharing platforms would presumably argue that their involvement is not sufficient to warrant extension of liability. Proponents of extending liability based on trademark may suggest in response that the position of the ridesharing companies misses the point. Liability based on trademark need not be based on the licensor's level of involvement or control. The thinking being that courts should do away with factual inquiries as to how involved a licensor is in the provision of a product or service. Instead, the proposed analysis would be: a trademark licensor, including sharing economy platforms, should be liable for injuries stemming from products and services bearing the licensor's mark. Rather than splitting hairs over the trademark licensor's level of involvement, the inquiry should focus on the consumer-perceived "source" of the services. The relevant questions being: who is understood to be providing and standing behind those services, and who is in the best position to provide compensation for injuries? It may be claimed that this perspective comports with the basic tort law theories of honoring justifiable reliance, preventing preventable losses, and spreading liability for unpreventable losses. It also would potentially ensure consistency and predictability regarding distribution of risks, costs, and liabilities.

Because the arguments for extending liability to ridesharing platforms based on trademark ownership are rooted in fundamental tort principles, it should be noted that other foundational tenants of tort law can be marshalled to undercut the extension of liability in this situation. Specifically, the use of liability based on trademark in this fashion would undermine the concept that, typically, wrongful conduct of some variety is a necessary precursor to civil liability. In most cases where civil liability is imposed, the liable party has either (i) intentionally acted in a way that caused harm to another or (ii) acted in such a way that others are exposed to an unreasonable risk of harm.[582] Liability that is based solely on a party's status as a licensor of trademark would in effect subject certain trademark owners to a form of strict liability that has typically been reserved for persons involved in abnormally dangerous activities.[583] Moreover, the typical motivations for imposing this type of strict liability are not present with ridesharing companies. Generally, a company that engages in very dangerous work is held to be liable by default when its operations cause injuries. The reasoning behind this theory is that the operator of the dangerous business is deriving a benefit from being able conduct its business, while society at large will bear the costs of predictable, but unavoidable, accidents. Because the social utility associated with the dangerous activity is largely retained by the business, it is reasonable for that business to also be responsible for any losses that occur as a result of the danger associated with the activity. Although there may be dangers associated with ridesharing, it could be argued that this is not the type of business that should be subjected to liability absent wrongdoing.

Conversely, if it is understood that a trademark is a trust mark, and if the goodwill that inures through licensed use of a mark flows to the licensor, so too should the risk and liability. While categorically extending such liability would likely increase the cost of doing business (costs that would likely go towards more robust insurance policies), ridesharing platforms[584] are potentially in the best position to provide coverage that extends to individu-

---

582. *See* RESTATEMENT (SECOND) OF TORTS § 6 (AM. LAW. INST. 1979).

583. *Id.* § 519.

584. And many other platforms that fall into the broad category of the sharing economy.

als injured as a result of their services. Moreover, absorbing those costs can be seen as tradeoff or exchange for the benefits derived through licensing of their marks. Thus, under our original hypothetical of the negligent driver (Don Driver), the injured parties (Rita Rider and possibly others) would be certain of efficient and complete compensation from both the ridesharing platform and Driver if trademark liability was extended. Finally, should the ridesharing platform desire indemnification from Driver, that will be between Driver and his insurance providers.

In summary, proponents of extending trademark liability will assert that, considering the costs that the entire system is currently bearing as a result of the litigation, claims, and disputes arising from injuries caused by ridesharing accidents, streamlining and simplifying the liability analysis by extending trademark liability would result in a net benefit. This position will be challenged by those that believe the burden placed on ridesharing companies by extending this type of liability is unnecessary given the availability of traditional tort remedies, which impose liability on conduct deemed to be unreasonably dangerous, rather than basing liability primarily on the ability to pay for claims. If ridesharing licensors were required to stand behind the quality of their services, and provide compensation for when things go wrong, it could benefit the licensors from a marketing perspective and would only increase consumer good will.

## E. Conclusion

Although the issue of liability based on trademark ownership has not been litigated in the ridesharing context, it is an issue that could be key to effectively balancing the societal and individual benefits and burdens of the new ubiquity of a sharing economy. This issue may be particularly important in states where agency liability for ridesharing companies is not available as a result of a legislative determination on the employment status of ridesharing drivers. In these jurisdictions, injured parties, and courts, may be motivated to find a theory that will ensure adequate resources are available to compensate persons injured in accidents involving ridesharing drivers.

CHAPTER FOUR

# Litigating a Ridesharing Case

In this chapter, a few key steps are outlined that can aid in successfully litigating a ridesharing case. First, we will discuss identifying proper defendants and effectively using evidence preservation letters to begin building a case. Next, the unique facets of discovery in a ridesharing case will be mapped. One such aspect of an accident involving a ridesharing driver is that relevant data are nearly always stored in the ridesharing app. Accessing the information from the relevant ridesharing app, as well as other information from smartphones, may prove essential to effective representation in a ridesharing accident case. Further, we will discuss the discoverable information that may be obtained from ridesharing companies and their apps, crafting successful requests for productions, and, finally, authentication of the data obtained.

## I. Identifying Proper Defendants and Effective Evidence Preservation

When anticipating litigation involving a ridesharing driver, there are important first steps any attorney should take as quickly as possible. Time is especially important for putting parties and ridesharing companies on notice for the preservation of documents and their duty to comply. Thus, it will be important to first identify the proper defendants and provide them with preservation letters. As with discovery in many other cases, ensuring the preservation of data and documents you want to access is an important first step.

## A. Identifying Proper Defendants

With all legal issues, identifying defendants is a fact-intensive analysis. As discussed in Chapter 3, there are various theories to impose liability on the ridesharing companies for the actions of their employees. Assuming the incident involves a ridesharing driver facing liability for the injuries of a passenger or pedestrian, the obvious defendants are the driver and the ridesharing company. The less obvious defendants may include the ridesharing passenger, other ridesharing companies with whom the driver is associated, and subsidiaries of the involved companies.

## B. Using Preservation Letters Effectively

A beginning step in the litigation of a ridesharing case is to send preservation letters to the relevant parties, including the ridesharing driver, passenger, and the ridesharing company. The practice of making sure that an anti-spoliation/preservation letter is sent as early as possible after a client is retained will increase the information available during discovery and make it easier to seek sanctions if the information is subsequently destroyed. This letter should also carefully consider the scope of what should be preserved, including what time period is relevant to the issues in the case. Although much of the information that may be useful is likely stored remotely, there is still a significant likelihood that some data will be stored on the physical smartphone itself. This is why it is crucial to include, in a spoliation letter to the driver, that the smartphone owned at the time of the accident not be destroyed, sold, or otherwise altered.

When sending an anti-spoliation letter to a ridesharing company, it is important to broadly define the scope of information you are requesting that the company retain. Doing this can be useful to rebut any assertion that the company was not on notice of a duty to preserve the information. However, a letter must have some limitations on scope to be meaningful—a letter that asks a company to preserve "everything" could create a basis to argue that the lack of specificity permitted the company to rely on its own limitations for the scope of the litigation hold. Appendix A is a sample anti-spoliation letter directed to a ridesharing company that includes requests to retain the relevant types of information that the ridesharing company may have in its possession following a collision.

Additionally, given that many ridesharing drivers use more than one ridesharing platform, it may be useful to determine if there are any other ridesharing companies for which the driver had recently worked.[585] These other companies could have valuable information related to the driver's recent trips and driving history. Furthermore, both major ridesharing companies, Uber and Lyft, place restrictions on how much a driver is permitted to drive in a 24-hour period.[586] A driver could potentially skirt these restrictions by alternating between using Uber and Lyft. The only way to verify this has occurred is to seek information from both major companies after a collision.

It may also be worth considering the location at issue of the litigation. Are there any nearby businesses that may have closed circuit television or some other form of surveillance cameras? In addition to sending preservation letters to the driver and ridesharing companies, it may be prudent to provide area businesses with preservation letters for any video of the accident in question. A video of the incident could change the outcome of the entire case. However, like the ridesharing data stored on servers or cell phones, any surveillance data may be deleted or overwritten shortly after it is recorded. Thus, early evidence preservation letters could be essential to asserting or defending a ridesharing case.

## II. Discovery in a Ridesharing Case and Obtaining Available Records

One of the most important aspects of conducting effective discovery in a ridesharing case is having a plan. An integral part of putting together a discovery plan and putting that plan into action is a strong understanding of the information available and which entities have access to that information.

585. *See* Helling, *supra* note 334.
586. Korosec, *supra* note 404.

## A. Obtaining Data from Smartphones and Ridesharing Apps

Ridesharing apps store an enormous amount of information for their users. Both Uber and Lyft create profiles for all drivers and passengers.[587] This profile is created from the information provided by the user to the ridesharing company, as well as information collected from the use of the app and the ridesharing services. Although this section focuses on the discovery of ridesharing drivers, it is important to note that the ridesharing passenger records can also be sought during litigation.

Both passenger and driver profiles may contain the following information:

- **Basic personal information.** Name, e-mail, phone number, password, username, address, government identification numbers (Social Security number, driver's license or passport), birthdate, photograph, and signature.
- **Payment or banking information**
- **Facebook information.** Lyft allows users to create accounts by using an existing Facebook account. If the account is created from Facebook, then the user profile will also contain name, gender, profile photo, and Facebook friends.
- **Location information.** Precise location of the user created by GPS, IP address, and Wi-Fi while using the app, as well as any locations entered and designated as "home" or "work."
- **Usage information.** Information obtained from any interaction with the app, such as access dates and times, pages viewed, other system activity, type of browser, and third-party sites or services the driver was using before interacting with the app.
- **Transaction information.** Date and time of the ride, amount charged, distance traveled, and specific payment method.

587. *Uber Privacy Notice*, Uber, https://privacy.uber.com/policy/ (last visited Mar. 6, 2020); *Lyft Privacy Policy*, Lyft, https://www.lyft.com/privacy (last visited Mar. 6, 2020).

- **Communication information.** Call and text information between the drivers and passengers, including the date and time of the call or text, and the content of any messages.
- **Device information.** Hardware models, device IP address, operating systems and versions, software, file names and versions, preferred languages, unique device identifiers, advertising identifiers, serial numbers, device motion information, and mobile network information.

Driver profiles are more extensive and may contain additional information:

- **Vehicle and insurance information**
- **Background check information.** Driving history or criminal record.
- **More extensive banking information.** Routing numbers and tax information.

This is an enormous amount of information, but, depending on the specific facts of an individual case, sifting through the information may reveal relevant data that could be crucial to proving or defending a theory of negligence. For example, gaining access to a driver's trip history for the time prior to a collision can be useful to prove that the driver may have failed to exercise due care by speeding from one location to the next in order to be able to make more money by taking additional fares. Alternatively, a driver's account history could be used to show that the driver had been on the road too long in a given span of time and that the driver's exhaustion played a role in causing a crash. Conversely, when defending a ridesharing driver, this same information can be produced to rebut allegations of distraction or exhaustion.

The ridesharing apps are not the only source of electronically stored information that may be very useful in helping to establish your theory of how an accident occurred. The smartphone and its other apps may provide additional relevant data. For instance, you may be able to present evidence that a driver was using a smartphone at the time an accident occurred. This type of evidence can be used to effectively argue that a crash was caused by the driver being distracted at the time of a collision. Furthermore, if the opposing side learns that you are going to be permitted to discover the information necessary to prove that a driver was distracted, they may be left with no choice but to admit to the distraction and cause of an accident, which could result in a quick and favorable settlement.

## B. Appropriately Limiting the Scope of Formal Discovery

Although smartphones record and store a tremendous amount of information, it is unlikely that the entirety of this information will be relevant to the issues at play in a given case. Recognizing this fact and incorporating it into the discovery plan for a case involving a ridesharing accident can lead to more effective discovery in terms of both outcome and cost-effectiveness. Specifically, a broad request for "all information and application data" stored on a smartphone is likely to produce an unwinnable discovery dispute, particularly, if the case is being litigated in federal court, where the Civil Rules place a premium on specific and well-articulated requests.

Two cases from Florida highlight how different approaches of requesting information can lead to significantly different results when it comes to the discovery of smartphone data. In *Holland v. Barfield*, a wrongful death case arising from an accident, the plaintiff requested production of "any and all computer hard drives" and "all cell phones."[588] The plaintiff claimed the request was necessary to uncover conversations between the co-defendants, including texts, Facebook, and Myspace messages.[589] In her request for a protective order, the defendant argued that such a broad request amounted to a "fishing expedition" and would be an invasion of privacy.[590] The court agreed and found that there were less intrusive ways to obtain the requested information.[591] Furthermore, the court took issue

588. 35 So. 3d 953, 954 (Fla. Ct. App. 2010).
589. *Id.*
590. *Id.*
591. *Id.*

with the fact that the request asked for the hardware rather than "the specific information contained therein."[592]

A different outcome was reached in a very similar case, *Antico v. Sindt Trucking*.[593] *Antico* was also a wrongful death case involving a motor vehicle accident, but, in this instance, there was a specific allegation that the defendant driver was distracted by her phone immediately before the collision.[594] Based on that allegation, and the fact that the plaintiff's request was limited in time to the day of the crash, the court allowed the plaintiff's expert to inspect the defendant driver's phone to review essentially all use of the phone in the time leading up to the collision.[595]

Although it is easy to see a smartphone as a treasure trove of discoverable information, attorneys should use a measured approach in discovery involving this technology and make sure their requests are tailored to information likely to be useful and relevant to the issues at hand. Being able to fully articulate why an inspection of an opposing party's smartphone is necessary will make prevailing in a potential discovery dispute far more likely. Finally, courts have shown they are more willing to grant requests that ask for specific information than requests based on sources or locations of information. As an example of how directing requests at specific information is likely to work in practice, compare a request directed at a ridesharing driver that asks for "all data and information related to ridesharing applications" on the driver's smartphone, with a request that is limited to "all data related to trips or fares in the two weeks before the collision." The second version of this request makes clear what specific information is being requested, which will make it easier to rebut an argument that the request is a mere "fishing expedition."

As a party attempting to prevent broad discovery, employing some of the same principles can lead to positive outcomes. Not only will an objection stated with specificity be received more favorably by a court, but setting out the specific grounds for an

592. *Id.*
593. 148 So. 3d 163, 164 (Fla. Ct. App. 2014).
594. *Id.*
595. *Id.*

objection is now a requirement in federal cases.[596] Additionally, when confronted with a request that is too broad, taking the initiative to narrow the scope of the request and responding to that narrowed request is another helpful tactic that can be used to effectively support an argument against a motion to compel, if one is filed.

## C. Using Requests for Production Effectively

As previously stated, limiting requests for production based on relevancy is critical to effectively obtaining information from the ridesharing companies. Uber has published guidelines for filing legal documents on its website.[597] First, Uber requires all legal documents to be served upon its registered agent for service of process. It is important to name Uber and Lyft by the name that matches the name of the entity registered by the Secretary of State, as well as verify the agent of process, because if either of these are incorrect, the ridesharing companies may refuse to accept or acknowledge service.

Additionally, Uber has the following requirements for data requests:

- A sufficiently narrow/defined time period, and the specific data requested within that time period;
- A specific identifying reference (i.e., you must uniquely identify a user or driver/partner, ideally by more than just a name); and
- Your contact information (i.e., name and e-mail address and/or phone number).[598]

Uber's guidelines are consistent with the notion of appropriately limiting the scope of discovery, and if discovery requests are crafted in such a manner, courts are likely to uphold the

596. *See* Fed. R. Civ. P. 34(b)(2)(C).

597. *Uber Guidelines for Third Party Data Requests and Service of Legal Documents*, Uber, https://www.uber.com/legal/data-requests/guidelines-for-third-party-data-requests/en/ (last updated Jan. 22, 2020).

598. *Id.*

request as valid, too. Appendix C has sample interrogatories and requests for production directed to a ridesharing company.

## D. Authenticating and Admitting Evidence

Smartphones record and store tremendous amounts of data about a user's activities. Even the most mundane details of a smartphone user's daily activities can be recorded in great detail. This plethora of information that is now available presents issues in the civil litigation context. As a result of the novel and rapidly changing nature of these technologies, there is little precedent to guide how this information can or should be used in the litigation of a civil case. At the outset, those seeking to use evidence obtained from a ridesharing app should be mindful of the analysis that comes into play with respect to any piece of evidence. Attorneys should ask themselves, is this relevant? Is it substantially more prejudicial than probative? Is there a hearsay issue, or exception that applies? And finally, is this evidence authentic?[599]

Generally, to authenticate data retrieved from a mobile app, you must be able to show to whom the account associated with the app belongs, and who created or authored the data you are seeking to authenticate. In the ridesharing context, this will likely involve showing who the driver account belongs to, and that the driver in question was using the app at the time of the crash. The ridesharing company, if they are not already subject to discovery by being a party in a suit, may be helpful in providing the proof necessary to establish who owns an account. Although technology companies are generally very reluctant to provide underlying data created from the use of an app in response to a subpoena, on the basis that doing so would violate the Stored Communications Act, these tech companies will provide a certificate of ownership relative to the driver account at issue.[600] The certificate of ownership is analogous to an auto title or property deed and provides a necessary link between the party and the account.

---

599. Fed. R. Evid. 401, 402, 403, 901, 902.

600. *Uber Guidelines for Third Party Data Requests and Service of Legal Documents*, Uber, https://www.uber.com/legal/data-requests/guidelines-for-third-party-data-requests/en/ (last updated Jan. 22, 2020).

The prevailing standard that applies to admitting social media evidence, known as the Texas standard, is likely to be very similar to the authentication standard that will apply with respect to the authentication of data retrieved from a ridesharing app. Under the Texas standard, extrinsic evidence is needed to show that data retrieved from an account is authentic. Most frequently, this will take the form of a certificate of ownership and testimony that either the driver in question was using the app at the time, or even potentially that no other person was known to have access to the app.[601] Thus, the data you are seeking to authenticate must have been created by the person in question.[602] Once the app data in question has been authenticated, it can be admitted similar to any other document.

## III. Conclusion

As with any case, effective use of discovery procedures in the context of a ridesharing matter can make or break a case. To ensure you are using the tools available to put your client in the best possible position for settlement talks or an eventual trial, it is necessary to fully consider how the rules of discovery can be best employed in your case. This analysis should include considering the available sources of information, how that information can be obtained, and how that information can ultimately be used to advance your position in a dispute. Given the mountains of information that smartphones and apps can contain, it is critical that attorneys are able to explain what specific information they are seeking, and why this information is relevant to the issues in a specific case. Keeping these requirements in mind will undercut any arguments from opposing counsel that

---

601. *See* Tienda v. Texas, 358 S.W.3d 633 (Tex. Crim. App. 2012) (discussing standard applicable to question of whether social media evidence may be presented to the jury).

602. *How to Get Social Media Evidence Admitted to Court*, AM. BAR ASS'N (Nov. 2016), https://web.archive.org/web/20180614104911/https://www.americanbar.org/publications/youraba/2016/november-2016/how-to-get-social-media-evidence-admitted-to-court.html.

the request to examine a smartphone of ridesharing account is a mere "fishing expedition." Although the law surrounding ridesharing is currently developing, keeping these general principles in mind as you work through cases in this emerging field, and pairing the use of these principles with an understanding of the underlying technology, will put you and your client in the best possible position.

CHAPTER FIVE

# The Future of Liability Related to the Use of Autonomous Vehicles

## I. Introduction

Autonomous or automated vehicles, broadly defined, are vehicles used to move passengers or freight with some level of automation that aims to assist or replace human control.[603] Autonomous vehicle technology is growing at such a rate that some transportation scholars are predicting that it may happen as soon as 2030.[604] The Boston Consulting Group has forecasted that more than one-quarter of the miles Americans will travel by road in 2030 will rely on electrified, autonomous vehicles operated by ridesharing services like Lyft.[605] States like Arizona, California, Florida, and Nevada are allowing fully autonomous

603. Adam Stocker & Susan Shaheen, Shared Automated Vehicles: Review of Business Models 5 (2017), https://www.itf-oecd.org/sites/default/files/docs/shared-automated-vehicles-business-models.pdf.

604. Max W. Gershweir, *The Future of Liability Insurance in the Age of the Driverless Car: the US Perspective*, Kennedys (Apr. 1, 2019), https://www.kennedyslaw.com/thought-leadership/article/the-future-of-liability-insurance-in-the-age-of-the-driverless-car-the-us-perspective.

605. Paul A. Eisenstein, *How Can Ride-Share Companies Navigate a Future with Driverless Cars?*, NBC News (Mar. 6, 2019), https://www.nbcnews.com/business/autos/how-can-ride-share-companies-navigate-driverless-future-n979646.

vehicles without even a safety driver to circulate on public roads to attract self-driving vehicle developers to their states.[606]

There are many positive aspects to what autonomous vehicles mean for the future. For example, self-driving capabilities will be able to provide transportation for people who are otherwise unable to drive because of age or physical impairment.[607] According to Esurance Insurance Services research, in the best-case scenario, a family that gives up its car in favor of ridesharing could save $4,100 in annual transportation costs.[608] Esurance researchers believe two-car households might be willing to only have one car and some urban one-car households might give up their cars entirely, which could save families more money in transportation costs.[609]

There are also some shortcomings and various issues that autonomous vehicles, whether personally owned or used for ridesharing, cannot fix. For example, many hope that autonomous vehicles may be able to address congestion and traffic issues if they are primarily shared.[610] Numerous academic studies show, however, this is not necessarily the case and that a ridesharing model of autonomous vehicles can increase traffic and congestion.[611]

---

606. Sebastian Blanco, *Florida Will Allow Autonomous Cars with No Safety Drivers on Public Roads Starting July 1*, CAR & DRIVER MAG. (June 18, 2019), https://www.caranddriver.com/news/a28073922/florida-autonomous-cars-driverless/.

607. Nancy Gupton, *The Science of Self-Driving Cars*, FRANKLIN INST. (Aug. 1, 2016), https://www.fi.edu/science-of-selfdriving-cars.

608. *How Much Americans Could Save by Ridesharing Driverless Cars Over Owning*, INS. J. (July 3, 2018), https://www.insurancejournal.com/news/national/2018/07/03/494086.htm.

609. *Id.*

610. Thaddeus Miller & Devon McAslan, *With the Launch of Self-Driving Ride-Share Service "Waymo One," What's Next for Cities?*, GREEN BIZ (Feb. 5, 2019), https://www.greenbiz.com/article/launch-self-driving-ride-share-service-waymo-one-whats-next-cities.

611. *Id.*

## II. Future Use of Autonomous Vehicles in Ridesharing

Shared mobility is the shared use of a vehicle that enables users to have short-term access to transportation modes on an "as-needed" basis and encompasses ridesharing.[612] Widespread use of autonomous vehicles is also expected to dramatically reduce the number of auto accidents that result from human error, which currently accounts for more than 90 percent of vehicle-related accidents in the United States.[613] Some industry professionals think autonomous driving is a key aspect of the auto industry's drive toward creating safer roadways.[614] Researchers estimate autonomous vehicles could reduce accident rates in America, saving more than 30,000 lives each year, and avoiding millions of injuries.[615] After all, as General Motors chairman Bob Lutz said, "[t]he autonomous car doesn't drink, doesn't do drugs, doesn't text while driving, and doesn't get road rage. Autonomous cars don't race other autonomous cars and they don't go to sleep."[616]

However, there is widespread skepticism across America about whether fully autonomous vehicles will catch on at all, let alone during this generation. Some developers anticipate that the first fully autonomous cars will be purchased by businesses and the very wealthy because most Americans will be priced out of the market.[617] As of 2017, experts had estimated that truly autonomous vehicles will cost $10,000 to $50,000 more than the price of an equivalent non-automated vehicle, although the technology is expected to get cheaper with time.[618] Prices may not decline enough for most families and individuals to purchase

---

612. Stocker & Shaheen, *supra* note 603, at 7.
613. Gershweir, *supra* note 604.
614. Gupton, *supra* note 607.
615. Stephani R. Johnston, *Autonomous Vehicles and Emerging Tort Implications*, Nat'l L. Rev. (Apr. 11, 2019), https://www.natlawreview.com/article/autonomous-vehicles-and-emerging-tort-implications.
616. *Id.*
617. Ins. J., *supra* note 608.
618. Stocker & Shaheen, *supra* note 603, at 7.

until 2025.[619] In a 2018 Esurance survey, 83 percent expressed low or no interest in giving up control behind the wheel.[620] Esurance found that there were two primary motivating factors: a general unwillingness to give up control and a fear of the unknown, especially among certain generations.[621]

## A. Various Stages of Autonomy

In September 2016, the National Highway Traffic Safety Administration adopted the levels of automation developed by the Society of Automotive Engineers (SAE) International.[622] SAE International defines six levels of automation to classify automated-driving systems.[623] Levels 0 to 3 are considered driver support features, while Levels 3 to 5 are automated driving features.[624] A vehicle at Level 0 has no automation capabilities; the driver steers, brakes, accelerates, and negotiates traffic.[625]

Level 1 autonomy is the most common on the roads.[626] A Level 1 vehicle has driver assisting capabilities, where under certain conditions, the car controls either the steering or the vehicle speed but not both simultaneously.[627] A feature that would be indicative of a Level 1 vehicle would be adaptive cruise

---

619. Ins. J., *supra* note 608.
620. *Id.*
621. *Id.*
622. Kenneth S. Abraham & Robert L. Rabin, *Automated Vehicles and Manufacturer Responsibility for Accidents: A New Legal Regime for a New Era*, 105 Va. L. Rev. 127, 130 (2019).
623. *Path to Autonomy: Self-Driving Car Levels 0 to 5 Explained*, Car & Driver Mag. (Oct. 3, 2017), https://www.caranddriver.com/features/a15079828/autonomous-self-driving-car-levels-car-levels/.
624. Jennifer Shuttleworth, *SAE Standard News: J3016 Automated-Driving Graphic Update*, SAE Int'l (Jan. 7, 2019), https://www.sae.org/news/2019/01/sae-updates-j3016-automated-driving-graphic.
625. Car & Driver Mag., *supra* note 623.
626. Max Langridge, *Self-Driving Cars: Autonomous Driving Levels Explained*, Pocket Lint (Feb. 4, 2020), https://www.pocket-lint.com/cars/news/143955-sae-autonomous-driving-levels-explained.
627. Car & Driver Mag., *supra* note 623.

control.[628] Parking assist as well as some other safety features are examples of Level 1 autonomy.[629]

At Level 2, the car can partially automate by steering, accelerating, and braking in certain circumstances.[630] However, the driver of a Level 2 vehicle is still responsible for responding to traffic signals, changing lanes, and scanning for hazards.[631] Level 2 features can help keep the vehicle in the correct lane on the road and maintain a safe distance from the car in front when in a traffic jam.[632] Tesla's autopilot function and Volvo's pilot assist are both examples of Level 2 system capabilities.[633]

The biggest transition is between Level 2 and Level 3 of autonomous systems.[634] A Level 3 system has conditional automation and can manage most aspects of driving, including monitoring the environment under the right conditions.[635] The driver is allowed to safely use his phone or watch movies, although they are required to be on-hand to intervene if necessary.[636] The system prompts the driver to intervene when it encounters a scene it is unable to navigate.[637] Examples of a Level 3 system would be Audi's Traffic Jam Pilot, which requires the driver to be available to take over at any time if needed.[638]

For a car to be "fully autonomous" it must be a Level 4 or 5 system by SAE standard.[639] Levels 4 and 5 do not require the driver to take over driving, and pedals or a steering wheel may or may not be installed in the car at all.[640] A Level 4 system has auto

---

628. *Id.*
629. Langridge, *supra* note 626.
630. CAR & DRIVER MAG., *supra* note 623.
631. *Id.*
632. Langridge, *supra* note 626.
633. CAR & DRIVER MAG., *supra* note 623.
634. *Id.*
635. *Id.*
636. Langridge, *supra* note 626.
637. CAR & DRIVER MAG., *supra* note 623.
638. *Id.*
639. Ian Bogost, *Can You Sue a Robocar?*, ATLANTIC (Mar. 20, 2018), https://www.theatlantic.com/technology/archive/2018/03/can-you-sue-a-robocar/556007/.
640. Shuttleworth, *supra* note 624.

automation capabilities and can operate without human input or oversight, but only under select conditions defined by factors like road type or geographic area.[641] The driver is not required to intervene at all, so sleeping is an option in the right conditions.[642] An example of this would be Google's now-defunct Firefly prototype, which had neither pedals nor a steering wheel and was restricted to a maximum of 25 mph.[643] Local driverless taxis or ridesharing vehicles would need to be at least a Level 4, as no driver override is needed.[644] Waymo vehicles have been operating driver free for some time, although a test driver is on hand just in case anything goes wrong.[645]

Finally, a Level 5 vehicle is fully autonomous.[646] The driverless car can operate on any road and in any conditions that a human driver could navigate.[647] The only human involvement with the vehicle is entering a destination.[648] As of October 2017, there were no Level 5 systems, but Waymo, formerly Google's project, was using a fleet of Chrysler Pacifica hybrids to develop Level 5 technology.[649] Similarly, Audi's Aicon concept is an example of a Level 5 vehicle, but it will be some time before Audi has it on the road.[650] Some skeptics think we are a long way from putting Level 5 vehicles into mass production; however, Elon Musk (Tesla's CEO) claims that Tesla will be ready to do so in the near future.[651]

---

641. Car & Driver Mag., *supra* note 623.
642. Langridge, *supra* note 626.
643. Car & Driver Mag., *supra* note 623.
644. Shuttleworth, *supra* note 624.
645. Langridge, *supra* note 626.
646. Car & Driver Mag., *supra* note 623.
647. *Id.*
648. *Id.*
649. *Id.*
650. Langridge, *supra* note 626.
651. *Id.*

## B. Predominated Ownership of Autonomous Vehicles: Companies (Uber) versus Individuals (Tesla)

Most fully autonomous vehicles are not likely to be owned by individuals but by auto manufacturers, tech companies like Google, and ridesharing companies like Uber and Lyft.[652] Until the cost of ownership for self-driving vehicles comes down, most people will experience driverless vehicles through ridesharing.[653] Lyft has already partnered with self-driving company, Aptiv, and has opened a research facility in Silicon Valley called Level 5, and Lyft already has some self-driving vehicles on the streets of Las Vegas.[654] Companies like Uber and Waymo are in the process of building their own fleets of self-driving cars.[655] Lyft is eagerly awaiting the introduction of fully autonomous vehicles because it will eliminate the most costly part of its business—the drivers.[656]

The biggest problem for Uber and Lyft with the transition to autonomous vehicles is that they will face several new competitors, including General Motors, Alphabet's Waymo, Tesla, and Ford.[657] Companies like GM have plans to launch their own self-driving car services.[658] BMW plans to sell cars directly to consumers and also sell "transportation as a service," meaning consumers will have the ability to rent "free floating cars, hail a car with a driver, or order a car without a driver."[659]

---

652. Gershweir, *supra* note 604.
653. Ins. J., *supra* note 608.
654. Sasha Lekach, *Lyft Investors Are Banking on Self-Driving Cars, Not Ride-Sharing*, Mashable (Mar. 29, 2019), https://mashable.com/article/lyft-ipo-self-driving-cars-investors/.
655. *Id.*
656. Eisenstein, *supra* note 605.
657. Jeremy Bowman, *Autonomous Vehicles Won't Save Uber and Lyft*, Motley Fool (Apr. 15, 2019), https://www.fool.com/investing/2019/04/15/autonomous-vehicles-wont-save-uber-and-lyft.aspx.
658. Lekach, *supra* note 654.
659. Raquel Toral, *Evolving Autonomous Vehicle Technology and the Erosion of Privacy*, 27 U. Miami Bus. L. Rev. 153, 163 (2019).

Tesla plans to enable its Robotaxi network, which would serve as its ridesharing app service.[660] Tesla will enable owners to add their properly equipped vehicles to its own ridesharing app, which will have a similar business model to Uber.[661] The Robotaxis owned by individuals would return home and automatically park and recharge once their owners called them back home.[662] Tesla will take 25 percent of the revenue from those rides.[663] Tesla estimates that Tesla owners can make $30,000 per year by adding their cars to the Tesla Network.[664] In places where there are not enough people to share their cars, Tesla would provide a dedicated fleet of Robotaxis.[665] Elon Musk said, "From our standpoint, if you fast forward a year, maybe a year and three months, but [2020] for sure, we'll have over a million robotaxis on the road."[666]

There are numerous liability questions raised in the Tesla scenario because new players are added into the mix. Could a Tesla owner who lent his car to be used in the Robotaxi Network be liable if the car was in a crash even though they were not present or even aware of the vehicle's location? Does Tesla instead assume liability over all vehicles in the Robotaxi Network while they are completing routes? Many of these questions have yet to be solved, but once the network launches, it will not be long before these questions are at the forefront of the analysis.

---

660. Fred Lambert, *Tesla Unveils "Robotaxi" Plan for Self-Driving Ride-Sharing Network Next Year*, ELECTREK (Apr. 22, 2019), https://electrek.co/2019/04/22/tesla-robotaxi-network-self-driving-fleet-ride-sharing-cars/.

661. Kirsten Korosec, *Tesla Plans to Launch a Robotaxi Network in 2020*, TECH CRUNCH (Apr. 2019), https://techcrunch.com/2019/04/22/tesla-plans-to-launch-a-robotaxi-network-in-2020/.

662. *Id.*

663. *Id.*

664. Dalvin Brown, *Can Elon Musk's Robotaxi Plan Help Tesla Owners Make $30,000 a Year?*, USA TODAY (Apr. 23, 2019) https://www.usatoday.com/story/tech/2019/04/23/elon-musk-says-tesla-owners-could-make-30-000-robotaxi-network/3549652002/.

665. Korosec, *supra* note 661.

666. *Id.*

## III. How to Address Liability

On March 18, 2018, a self-driving car operated by Uber struck and killed a pedestrian in Tempe, Arizona.[667] Initial investigations indicated that the pedestrian may have been jaywalking after abruptly stepping into the path of the car.[668] Similarly, in 2016, a Tesla operating in "autopilot" mode crashed into a tractor-trailer that made a left turn in front of the vehicle, killing the Tesla's driver.[669] However, the car had been warning its driver to disengage the autopilot mode and take control over the vehicle.[670] It is inevitable that autonomous vehicles will be involved in accidents, which raises new liability questions for who is responsible when systems fail. Litigation over self-driving cars is in its early stages, but we can expect suits for negligence, products liability, and even statutory claims as the government begins issuing regulations.[671]

### A. Legislative/Regulatory Approach

Regulatory changes have already begun with regard to liability.[672] For example, Michigan, a state with deep ties to the auto-manufacturing industry, passed a law stating that an auto manufacturer assumes liability and insures every car in its fleet when driverless systems fail.[673] Anticipating the impact that technology companies will have on the autonomous vehicle industry and specifically on the future of ridesharing, Michigan fashioned the statute's liability rules to (i) qualify machines as "drivers" for purposes of assigning responsibility to accidents, (ii) define liability for technology companies that supply autonomous vehicle software, and (iii) insulate car manufacturers from liability except where the damage was caused by a defect

667. Bogost, *supra* note 639.
668. *Id.*
669. *Id.*
670. *Id.*
671. Johnston, *supra* note 615.
672. Gershweir, *supra* note 604.
673. *Id.*

that existed when the vehicle was originally manufactured and before its conversion to autonomous.[674]

A bill was proposed in New York that would provide strict liability for manufacturers, owners, and operators of unmanned motor vehicles.[675] A new Florida law would exempt the operator of a self-driving car from laws forbidding the use of wireless devices or watching a video screen while the car is in motion as long as the automated driving system is engaged.[676]

Uber and Ford's Argo AI are both large autonomous outfits in Pittsburgh, Pennsylvania.[677] Uber began testing an autonomous vehicle service open to frequent UberX customers in Pittsburgh in September of 2016.[678] Uber requires that an engineer closely monitor the system at all times.[679] Aurora, another Pittsburgh autonomous vehicle company, says its autonomous technology is put through thousands of software simulations daily, similar to the rigor applied to the aerospace industry.[680] A spokesperson for Aurora said that to make autonomous vehicles better than human drivers "you need to drive something like 500 billion miles, maybe more" because autonomous vehicles "[do] not learn fast."[681]

As of April 2019, the federal government does not have any laws regulating autonomous vehicles, only voluntary guidelines.[682] At a national level, agencies like the National Highway

---

674. Michael Callier & Harly Callier, *Blame It on the Machine: A Socio-Legal Analysis of Liability in an AI World*, 14 Wash. J.L. Tech. & Arts 49, 63–64 (2018).

675. Gershweir, *supra* note 604 (operator meaning "any person who has control over the unmanned motor vehicle").

676. Blanco, *supra* note 606.

677. Ryan Deto, *Pittsburgh's Self-Driving Cars Were Supposed to Revolutionize Mobility and Transit. But Their Future Isn't What You Think*, Pittsburgh City Paper (Jan. 22, 2019), https://www.pghcitypaper.com/pittsburgh/pittsburghs-self-driving-cars-were-supposed-to-be-revolutionize-mobility-and-transit-but-their-future-isnt-what-you-think/Content?oid=13242378.

678. Stocker & Shaheen, *supra* note 603, at 13.

679. *Id.*

680. Deto, *supra* note 677.

681. *Id.*

682. Korosec, *supra* note 661.

Transportation Safety Administration (NHTSA) will have to undergo a major overhaul to be able to adjust to a world with Level 5 autonomous vehicles.[683] For example, the NHTSA would need to develop more refined techniques for gathering and systematizing accident data, hire better trained personnel in automotive design and statistical analysis, and lobby for greater funding from Congress.[684]

A "proposal put forth by the Obama administration in December of 2016 would have required all new [self-driving] cars and light trucks" to, "by 2023, [be equipped] with technology that" allows the vehicles to exchange data.[685] The data exchanged would have included the "vehicle's location, speed, and direction," and it would have been exchanged "between vehicles up to ten times per second."[686] However, in November of 2017, the Trump administration dialed back some of these regulations, making the data sharing between vehicles a secondary safety measure rather than the centerpiece of driverless vehicle technology.[687]

## B. Common Law Theories

If a human driver fails to exercise reasonable care in avoiding an accident, they would be liable under the principles of negligence.[688] The current insurance regime with regard to auto liability is driver-focused, because drivers are at fault for the majority of accidents, while products liability is a secondary source of liability.[689] Traditionally, car accidents are assessed through the lens of driver negligence, with the potential for product liability only

683. Abraham & Rabin, *supra* note 622, at 162.

684. *Id.*

685. Toral, *supra* note 659, at 163–64.

686. *Id.* at 164.

687. *Id.*

688. Niall Edwards, Nicholas Fox, Deborah Newberry, & Clare Johnston, *Who Is to Blame When Autonomous Vehicles Are Involved?*, KENNEDYS (July 30, 2018), https://www.kennedyslaw.com/thought-leadership/article/who-is-to-blame-when-autonomous-vehicles-are-involved.

689. Abraham & Rabin, *supra* note 622, at 130.

when a defect in the car causes the accident or is alleged to have exacerbated the injuries.[690]

Under general tort law principles, the element of control is likely to be determinative.[691] The question of how much control the operator had or should have had over the car at the time of the accident will determine whether the operator could or should have prevented the accident.[692] Although the owners may have no control if their completely autonomous car malfunctions, they may be liable for failing to update the software that operates the vehicle the same way drivers can be liable for failing to replace their brakes or tires if either cause the driver to crash.

Who is responsible if a driver falls asleep and the Level 4 autonomous vehicle's driver monitoring system fails to wake up the driver in the event of an emergency?[693] Should drivers truly rely on these systems and sue the manufacturer of the vehicle or the component parts when the car does not alert him or her of the hazard?[694] Can an owner of an autonomous vehicle be liable for loaning the vehicle to an operator unfamiliar with the automated features and an accident occurs?[695] Can a driver operate an autonomous vehicle while under the influence of drugs or alcohol?[696] What happens if a Level 3 autonomous vehicle prompts the driver to take over control because of inclement conditions but the driver fails to do so with sufficient time? These questions, and more, may arise in coming years. In the absence of governmental regulatory answers to these questions, courts will be tasked with defining which parties will bear responsibility for accidents involving automated driving systems.

---

690. Johnston, *supra* note 615.
691. *Id.*
692. *Id.*
693. *Id.*
694. *Id.*
695. *Id.*
696. *Id.*

### 1. Product Liability Theories

When there is no human driver to blame for an accident, focus will inevitably shift from driver liability to possible design defects in the car.[697] For example, if the automated features of the vehicle fail to note the presence of a pedestrian or another vehicle, the manufacturer of the vehicle could also be held responsible under a theory of products liability.[698] But, can or should a manufacturer be subject to liability for not preventing an accident, even if its technology did not cause the harm?[699]

Despite a few early examples, it remains to be seen whether or not vehicle manufacturers will take to self-insuring their autonomous vehicles.[700] In 2015, Google announced they would assume full liability if their self-driving cars cause an accident.[701] However, there is recognition that self-driving cars implicate the manufacturer of the vehicle more than its driver or operator.[702]

#### a. Component Manufacturers

Component manufacturers of parts for autonomous vehicles also face potential liability issues. Questions will arise as to whether or not these components are initially installed in the vehicle at the time it is manufactured, or if the components are installed as aftermarket parts. Some companies are already marketing parts for autonomous vehicles as aftermarket components. However, their capabilities may otherwise be limited, as they are not fully integrated with the automobile's other systems. As the technology increases, the potential for aftermarket autonomous components will only increase. Furthermore, there is also some question as to whether the component manufacturer may be held liable under a theory of products liability, when the component is integrated into a car prior to the car being manufactured. The theory is that if one sensor, manufactured by a specific vendor,

---

697. Gershweir, *supra* note 604.
698. Edwards, Fox, Newberry, & Johnston, *supra* note 688.
699. Johnston, *supra* note 615.
700. Gershweir, *supra* note 604.
701. *Id.*
702. Bogost, *supra* note 639.

fails on an automobile, the manufacturer of the sensor, and not the entire car, could be held liable under a theory of products liability.

Generally, there are three technologies that make autonomous vehicles possible: sensors, connectivity, and software and control algorithms.[703] An automotive industry professional noted,

> Most of the sensors required for autonomous driving are available today and are used in advanced safety features such as blind-spot monitoring, lane-keep assistance, and forward collision warning. Sensors for other features such as radar, ultrasonics, and cameras provide the input necessary to navigate the car safely.[704]

Connectivity means that cars have access to the latest traffic, weather, surface conditions, maps, adjacent cars, and road infrastructure.[705] This data is used to monitor the car's surrounding operating environment to anticipate braking or avoid hazardous conditions.[706]

Software and control algorithms are needed to capture the data coming in from the sensors and make decisions on steering, braking, speed, and route guidance.[707] This aspect of the autonomous vehicle is proving to be the most complicated because the vehicle must be able to handle complex situations seamlessly.[708] Google's lidar technology uses a radar-like system that uses light instead of radio waves to control the vehicle without the need for steering wheels or pedals.[709] Tesla's Autopilot uses high tech camera sensors that function as the vehicle's "eyes" and are already on the market.[710]

---

703. Gupton, *supra* note 607.
704. *Id.*
705. *Id.*
706. *Id.*
707. *Id.*
708. *Id.*
709. *Id.*
710. *Id.*

## C. Addressing the Problem through Insurance

It is predicted that the United States will see a decline in annual personal vehicle insurance policies as autonomous vehicles become the mainstream.[711] As a result, it is anticipated that the auto insurance industry will shift to a pay-per-use model.[712] However, it is more likely that insurance companies will morph into two distinct forms: negligence insurance for the driver for failing to update or maintain the vehicle and products liability insurance for any defects in the vehicle itself or its software. Traditionally, strict liability is prominent in product liability cases, including those involving vehicles, where some part of the vehicle malfunctions and causes a crash.[713]

One possibility is that autonomous vehicles are sold with a built-in insurance policy that is tacked on to the price, something some states have considered doing with firearms. An individual would pay more to own a self-driving vehicle, but their insurance policy covers negligence on their part for failing to maintain (up to a certain degree) their vehicle and products liability insurance should anything go awry with the software, sensors, or anything else in the vehicle in the event of an accident.

As self-driving vehicles become more mainstream and dominant on the roads, it is unlikely that the government will mandate that everyone make the change to autonomy. What is more likely is that the government will maintain that drivers are able to continue driving their ordinary vehicles, but the drivers are strictly liable for any accident they are involved in. Effectively, this would force the hand of many drivers who were not ready to make the switch. While this is certainly a possibility, the likelihood of it coming into fruition in the foreseeable future is relatively doubtful for the time being.

States that hope to attract autonomous vehicle manufacturers may institute special liability waivers to attract these companies. The special liability waivers would likely cap relief for any accident caused by an autonomous vehicle to a set amount.

---

711. Gershweir, *supra* note 604.
712. *Id.*
713. Edwards, Fox, Newberry, & Johnston, *supra* note 688.

Although such a number could be highly variable in any given state, it is likely that by offering damage caps, the cost of doing business and testing in these states would drop dramatically for autonomous vehicle companies.

## D. Ethical Dilemmas

Ethical questions are raised when thinking about the dilemma a self-driving car will confront when deciding about what hazard to proceed toward, if all paths are obstructed and without sufficient time to brake. Experts have raised questions like, "[w]ill a self-driving car recognize the micro-drama of an unsupervised toddler, or a professor lost in his smartphone?"[714] When self-driving cars arrive, they will be forced to decide who should die when they collide with members of the public.[715] In a research study regarding such a choice, it was found that people favored that fewer people die rather than more, older people are killed rather than younger, and that humans are favored over animals.[716]

Further, there are privacy concerns regarding autonomous vehicles that operate over a network. "[S]ecurity researchers have repeatedly demonstrated how easy it is to wirelessly hijack a car's electronic instrumentalities."[717] There are even significant privacy concerns about what information the government, other vehicle manufacturers, and the like will be able to access from and about an autonomous vehicle. The data from existing ridesharing services is invaluable in the creation of self-driving vehicles. For example, ridesharing services gather data on travel habits, schedules, and profiles of passengers and drivers, typically analyzing information with software to anticipate demand and improve service.[718] As of December 2018, "seventeen states

---

714. Bogost, *supra* note 639.

715. Andrew Griffin, *Self-Driving Car Survey Shows Who Exactly the World Wants Autonomous Vehicles to Sacrifice*, INDEPENDENT (Oct. 24, 2018), https://www.independent.co.uk/life-style/gadgets-and-tech/news/self-driving-car-autonomous-vehicle-survey-kill-death-road-crash-study-a8599981.html.

716. *Id.*

717. Toral, *supra* note 659, at 165.

718. Brian Wang, *Worldwide Ridesharing at $285 Billion per Year by 2030 Will Be Profitable When Self Driving*, NEXT BIG FUTURE, (Oct. 29, 2017),

ha[d] enacted state statutes related to data privacy issues of data retrieval from an event data recorder, (EDR) which serves as a 'black box' for recording critical sensor and diagnostic data prior to collisions."[719]

According to the National Conference of State Legislatures, the states that have enacted statutes relating to data retrieval have included provisions that the EDR data may only be downloaded with the express permission of the vehicle owner or policyholder, and with certain exceptions.[720] In *United States v. Jones*, Supreme Court Justice Sotomayor stated, "it may be necessary to reconsider the premise that an individual has no reasonable expectation to privacy in information voluntarily disclosed to third parties" as it is "ill-suited to the digital age, in which people reveal a great deal of information about themselves to third parties in the course of carrying out mundane tasks."[721]

## IV. Conclusion

Much about the future of ridesharing with autonomous vehicles is uncertain. Largely due to the fact that there is doubt about when and if autonomous vehicles will be commonplace on the roadways. If fully autonomous vehicles do come to fruition, there will quickly be a convergence of autonomous vehicles and ridesharing. Federal and state governments will have to adapt their respective statutes and regulations to address a multitude of issues. Of those issues, how to address liability will necessarily be at the forefront. There are limitless issues and rhetorical questions that can and will be raised in this area, which will be continuously changing with every technological step toward completely autonomous vehicles.

---

https://www.nextbigfuture.com/2017/10/worldwide-ridesharing-at-285-billion-per-year-by-2030-will-be-profitable-when-self-driving.html (last visited June 21, 2019).

719. Toral, *supra* note 659, at 169.

720. *Id.*

721. Toral, *supra* note 659, at 117 (quoting U.S. v. Jones, 566 U.S. 400 (2012)).

# Appendix A

Lyber Ridesharing Co.
145 Technology Blvd.
10th Floor
San Francisco, CA 94103

RE: Lyber Driver: John D. Jones
Our Client: Sally P. Person
Date of Injury: January 1, 2020

To Whom It May Concern,

Please be advised our firm has been retained to represent Sally P. Person in relation to her injuries and legal claims arising from a motor vehicle collision that occurred while she was a Lyber passenger. The collision occurred on January 1, 2020, in Someplace, Texas. The police report for this collision is enclosed and it contains additional information about the collision.

Mrs. Person has informed us that your company was previously notified about the collision shortly after it occurred. Accordingly, it is likely that your company has already taken steps to preserve evidence related to this collision. However, in an effort to make certain that this information is being preserved, please accept this letter as a formal request to preserve and retain all evidence and information related to this collision, the trip that was occurring prior to the collision, and all information you have regarding your driver, John D. Jones. This request includes all information that Lyber has, and any information or data in the possession of a related entity, such as the Lyber driver, John D. Jones, any subsidiary corporation, or related company that maintains records. If you have any company procedures regarding the time-based automatic destruction of information or data, those policies must be immediately suspended. If it is necessary that you forward this letter to other persons or entities, please do so.

The information that this preservation request pertains to includes, but is not limited to:

- Electronic data related to the collision or preceding trip, including GPS data;
- E-mail, messages, or other communications with the Lyber driver or any other party related to the collision or preceding trip;
- Information sent to, or recorded by, the Lyber driver's phone or Lyber's system for dispatching and tracking vehicles;
- "Black box," electronic data recorder, or similar information stored by a vehicle, smartphone, or other device;
- Photographs, video recordings, or audio recordings related to the collision or preceding trip;
- Information about the driver and his wireless communication carrier (e.g., Verizon, Sprint, etc.);
- Training materials or instructions given to Lyber drivers (including John D. Jones), materials concerning what to do in the event of a collision;
- Information relating to any special rewards programs offered by Lyber in which John D. Jones may have participated, and
- Lyber's "file"—i.e., the information in Lyber's possession—regarding John D. Jones, including all trips in the two weeks preceding the April 5, 2019, collision, all records of complaints or incident reports, and any information retained as a part of any background or driving record check that was performed.

Finally, while I do not anticipate that your company will fail to preserve this information, please be aware that failing to preserve this data and information could result in significant adverse legal consequences (case from your jurisdiction awarding sanctions for spoliation).

Thank you,
Steve Q. Attorney

# Appendix B

| | | |
|---|---|---|
| **Sally P. Person,** | ) | **CASE NO: 19 CV 12345** |
| | ) | |
| Plaintiff, | ) | **Judge** |
| | ) | |
| vs. | ) | **PLAINTIFF'S** |
| | ) | **COMPLAINT** |
| **Lyber Ridesharing Co., Frasier LLC,** | ) | |
| **and Jones D. Jones,** | ) | |
| | ) | |
| Defendants. | | |

<u>**COMPLAINT**</u>[722]

Plaintiff Sally P. Person ("Plaintiff"), by and through counsel, hereby alleges as follows against Defendant Lyber Ridesharing Co. ("Lyber"), Frasier LLC ("Frasier"), and John D. Jones ("Jones") (collectively "Defendants").

722. This sample is based in part on the Complaint filed in *Ang Liang Liu v. Uber Techs., Inc.*, No. CGC-14-536979 (S.F. Super. Ct. Jan. 14, 2014).

## PARTIES

1. Lyber Ridesharing Co. is a Delaware Corporation which runs a Transportation Network Company ("TNC") which provides a number of transportation options and vehicles for users of its service, through an online-enabled application (hereinafter "app"). Lyber has its principal place of business in and conducts business in San Francisco, California.
2. Frasier is a Delaware Limited Liability Company which is a wholly owned subsidiary of Lyber. Frasier has its principal place of business in and conducts business in San Francisco, California.
3. Frasier has been assigned Carrier ID 123456 by the PUC and that Lyber and Frasier use Carrier ID 123456 to operate its Transportation Network Company ("TNC") in California.
4. Plaintiff is informed and believes that Frasier is the insurance certificate holder for the insurance that Lyber is required to carry as a TNC by the PUC, which it uses for its Lyber operations.
5. Jones is an adult male and was the driver of the vehicle which hit and injured Plaintiff.
6. Plaintiff is informed and believes that on April 5, 2019, at the time of this collision, Jones was a driver/transportation provider who was operating his vehicle utilizing the Lyber App and as such was an agent and/or employee and/or partner of Lyber and/or Frasier.
7. Plaintiff is informed and believes that at all times material to this complaint, Lyber and Frasier were the employer of Jones, and/or his partner and/or an agency relationship existed between them.
8. Plaintiff is informed and believes, and on the basis of said information and belief allege, that there is a unity of interest and operation between Lyber and Frasier such that their separate and independent classification is but a fiction and that each is the alter-ego of the other.

9. Defendants are liable for the acts of each other through principals of *respondeat superior*, agency, ostensible agency, partnership, alter-ego, and other forms of vicarious liability.

## JURISDICTION AND VENUE

10. Jurisdiction is proper in this case in that the amount in controversy is in excess of the statutory requirements of this court.
11. Venue in this court is appropriate as the injuries to the Plaintiff occurred in East Dakota County.

## FACTUAL ALLEGATIONS

12. On April 5, 2019, Plaintiff was walking home in San Francisco.
13. Plaintiff approached the intersection of Main Street and Central Street. When the light was indicating she could walk, a vehicle driven by Jones turned right from Main Street and collided with Plaintiff.
14. The collision caused serious injury and bodily harm to Plaintiff.
15. The Lyber and Frasier service has been classified by the East Dakota Public Utilities Commission (hereinafter "PUC") as a TNC.
16. Lyber and Frasier, through its services, provides prearranged transportation services for compensation using its app or platform to connect persons wanting to procure transportation (hereinafter "users"), with those who, utilizing their own personal vehicles, want to provide transportation in exchange for compensation (hereinafter "drivers").
17. Plaintiff is informed and believes that Jones was logged on to the Lyber app at the time that the collision occurred and was appearing as a Lyber driver available for providing transportation services to users and/or was viewing, monitoring and/or interacting with his wireless

communications device/smartphone/GPS at or near the time of the collision.

18. Before users can utilize the app, users must become "partners" of Lyber and Frasier, and by logging into Lyber's app or web-based portal and provide information about themselves to Lyber including their name, e-mail, credit card number, mobile telephone number, etc. Only registered users can use Lyber's app to prearrange transportation service.
19. Before drivers can participate in Lyber and Frasier's prearranged transportation service, they must apply to be a driver by logging into Lyber's app or web based portal and providing information including but not limited to their name, phone number, address, e-mail, banking information, vehicle registration, insurance, vehicle description, and have their vehicle inspected. Lyber and Frasier are required to conduct a background investigation of their drivers including but not limited to their driving and criminal history (and thereafter conduct periodic reviews of their driving history).
20. Lyber and Frasier then evaluate the driver and only permit those drivers it finds suitable to become registered drivers on its app. Lyber and Frasier reserve the right to remove or delete drivers from their system at their discretion. Therefore, Lyber and Frasier are entirely in control of who can use their system as either a driver or user.
21. Users who chose a ride are shown a GPS looking screen which displays vehicles available to provide transportation services in their area. After requesting a driver, the app alerts nearby drivers who must timely indicate their acceptance of the users' transportation request by manually interfacing with the app. Once the driver accepts the user's request that driver's name, photo, vehicle description, user rating, and time from pickup are displayed to the user.

22. Drivers, in order to be available to provide users transportation services in exchange for compensation, must log onto the Lyber app and indicate their availability. Their location and information is then visible to users and drivers can access an aerial view screen on their electronic communication device/smart phone/GPS which shows them a map of where others in the system are located.
23. Lyber's brand and value to users, and potential users, is enhanced by having a significant number of drivers registered, visible to the users on the Lyber app, and available in close proximity to users so as to provide transportation services. Indeed, Lyber states on its website "When you ask for a driver, we'll find a driver fast." Your driver's name and car details appear in the app and you can message or call if you need to." Lyber and/or Frasier's competitive advantage in the transportation industry is fostered by having an app that shows both drivers and users where the other is, providing information and reviews about the driver and user, permitting communication by test and phone between driver and user and by demonstrating the large number of available drivers that are logged onto the Lyber app.
24. Lyber and or Frasier derive an economic benefit from not only having users transported by drivers collecting a portion of the charge for transportation, it derives an economic benefit, and competitive advantage, by displaying the location of available vehicles near the user's location. Users seeing the ready supply of Lyber vehicles have greater consumer confidence that they will be able to obtain one-to-one prearranged transportation services rapidly and are therefore more likely to be repeat customers. In this way, Lyber and/or Frasier enhance their business by attracting a larger number of users to their services and, therefore, increase their market share of the transportation industry and commerce in the busi-

ness sector in which they are providing service. Therefore regardless of whether driver actually has a user in their car, is on the way to a user who has engaged the driver, through the app, or simply logged onto the app as an available driver, Lyber and/or Frasier derives an economic benefit from having drivers registered on the service.

25. The nature of the app and its interface is both visual and tactile. Therefore, drivers must monitor their wireless communications device/smartphone/GPS as to be aware of the location of other Lyber vehicles so they can position themselves near areas of high user demand. The app provides for texting and phone calling and instant messaging between the driver and the user.
26. A Lyber driver, like Jones, must respond quickly to a user request for service by physically interfacing the app thereby leading to distraction while a driver monitors and/or used the app on their wireless communication device/smartphone/GPS. Defendants knew or should have known use of the app by drivers, including but not limited to Jones, in the manner intended and actually required by Lyber and/or Frasier, would be in violation of California Vehicle Code 23123 which, in subsection (a) states "A person shall not drive a motor vehicle while using a wireless telephone unless that telephone is specifically designed and configured to allow hands-free listening and talking, and is used in that manner while driving."
27. Defendants knew or should have known that use of the app by drivers, including but not limited to Jones, in the manner intended and actually required by the defendants, would be in violation of Code section 23123, which states "(a) A person shall not drive a motor vehicle while using an electronic wireless communications device to write, send, or read a text-based communication, unless the electronic wireless communications device is specifically designed and configured to allow voice operated

and hands-free operation to dictate, send, or listen to a text-based communication, and it is used in that manner while driving. (b) As used in this section, 'write, send, or read a text-based communication' means using an electronic wireless communications device to manually communicate with any person using a text-based communication, including, but not limited to, communications referred to as a text message, instant message, or electronic mail."

28. Pursuant to Vehicle Code section 5321 any portable GPS, may only be mounted in a seven-inch square in the lower corner of the windshield farthest removed from the driver or in a five-inch square in the lower corner of the windshield nearest to the driver and outside of an airbag deployment zone, "if the system is used only for door-to-door navigation while the motor is being operated." The Lyber app is, by its nature, a GPS.
29. Use by Lyber drivers of a GPS while engaged in the business activity of being a Lyber driver, is not door-to-door navigation and, therefore, violates Vehicle Code section 5321.
30. The status of Jones as a Lyber driver, including but not limited to the use and/or monitoring of the app and its interface, was a proximate cause of this collision including but not limited to its causing Jones to be distracted while driving.
31. The design of the Lyber app and driver interface requires drivers to use the app in such a manner as to violate the law, including but not limited to Vehicle Code sections 23123, and/or 5321, thereby causing distraction to drivers including Jones.
32. Jones' distraction was a substantial factor in causing the subject accident and resultant harm.

## COUNT I—NEGLIGENCE

33. Plaintiff alleges and reasserts all of the preceding paragraphs as if fully set forth herein.

34. Defendants owed Plaintiff a duty of reasonable care as well as statutory duties established in California Vehicle Codes, 23123 and/or 5321.
35. Defendant Jones, on April 5, 2019, while operating his vehicle in the scope and course of his employment/agency/partnership with Lyber and/or Frasier, was negligent and did breach one or more of the duties and said breach was the proximate cause of personal injuries to Plaintiff.
36. As a proximate result the negligence of Defendants, Plaintiff has suffered significant general and special damages in amounts to be determined at trial.
37. The conduct of the Defendant was done with fraud, oppression and/or malice, and was in conscious disregard of the rights and safety of others, including but not limited to the Plaintiff so as to warrant the imposition of punitive damages.

**COUNT II—NEGLIGENCE PER SE**

38. Plaintiff alleges and reasserts all of the preceding paragraphs as if fully set forth herein.
39. Vehicle Codes, 23123 and/or 5321 were laws implemented by the State of East Dakota to protect individuals from injury due to inattentive or distracted drivers. Plaintiff was a class of persons intended to be protected by these laws.
40. Defendants owed Plaintiff a duty to conduct their affairs in accordance with Vehicle Codes 23123 and/or 5321.
41. Defendants breached one or more of the duties established by Vehicle Codes 23123 and/or 5321. Such conduct constitutes *negligence per se.*
42. As a direct and proximate result, Plaintiff suffered significant general and special damages in an amount to be determined at trial.
43. The conduct of the Defendant was done with fraud, oppression and/or malice, and was in conscious disre-

gard of the rights and safety of others, including but not limited to the Plaintiff as to warrant the imposition of punitive damages.

## COUNT III—NEGLIGENT HIRING AND RETENTION

44. Plaintiff alleges and reasserts all of the preceding paragraphs as if fully set forth herein.
45. Lyber and/or Frasier owed the general public a duty of reasonable care in hiring, training and supervision of its drivers.
46. Lyber and/or Frasier breached the duty of acre in the hiring, retention, training and/or supervision of Defendant Jones who was unfit to be a provider of transportation, and who was not adequately trained or supervised in his driving and/or use of the app and the dangers inherent therein. Lyber and/or Frasier knew or should have known that Defendant Jones would be using the app in a manner which would distract him and lead to a risk of the very type of danger and harm that occurred on April 5, 2019.
47. The breach of that duty was the proximate cause of harm to the Plaintiffs causing them to suffer significant special and general damages in an amount to be proven at the time of trial.
48. The conduct of the Defendant was engaged in fraud, oppression and/or malice, and was in conscious disregard of the rights and safety of others, including but not limited to the Plaintiff herein so as to warrant the imposition of punitive damage.

## PRAYER FOR RELIEF

WHEREFORE, Plaintiff prays that the Court enter judgment in her favor against Defendants, containing the following relief:

A. An award for damages in an amount to be determined at trial, plus prejudgment interest, to compensate Plaintiff for all physical, monetary and/or economic harm; for harm to her professional and personal reputations and loss of career fulfillment; for all non-monetary and/or compensatory harm, including, but not limited to, compensation for mental anguish and physical injuries; all other monetary and/or non-monetary losses suffered by Plaintiff;

B. An award of punitive damages;
C. An award of costs that Plaintiff has incurred in this action, as well as Plaintiff's reasonable attorneys' fees and expenses to the fullest extent permitted by law; and
D. Such other and further relief as the Court may deem just and proper.

## JURY DEMAND

Plaintiff hereby demands a trial by jury on all issues of fact and damages stated herein.

| Sally P. Person, | ) | CASE NO: 19 CV 12345 |
|---|---|---|
| Plaintiff, | ) | Judge |
| vs. | ) | PLAINTIFF'S COMPLAINT |
| Lyber Ridesharing Co. and Jones D. Jones, | ) | |
| | ) | |
| Defendants. | ) | |
| | ) | |
| | ) | |
| | ) | |
| | ) | |

## COMPLAINT[723]

Plaintiff Sally P. Person ("Plaintiff"), by and through counsel, hereby alleges as follows against Defendant Lyber Ridesharing Co. ("Lyber") and John D. Jones ("Jones") (collectively "Defendants").

## PRELIMINARY STATEMENT

1. On the morning of April 5, 2019, Plaintiff, was raped by her Lyber Driver, Jones.
2. Jones had previously been convicted of felony attempted first-degree murder. Jones was sentenced to 20 years in prison.
3. After serving his prison term, Defendant Lyber Ridesharing Co. authorized Jones to drive Lyber customers for a fee as a Lyber driver.

723. This sample is based in part on the Complaint filed in *Doe v. Uber Techs., Inc.*, Case No. 1716-CV12741, Cir. Court, Jackson Co., MO.

4. Months before Plaintiff was raped, Jones assaulted a woman during a Lyber ride.
5. The assault victim submitted an incident report through Lyber's website in order to warn the company that Jones posed a serious risk to Lyber riders. The report contained Jones' full name, date of birth, a description and date of the assault, and the fact that Jones had a warrant out for his arrest. The report also included a warning to Lyber: "it is not safe for your riders to ride with Jones!"
6. The following day, Lyber informed the assault victim that an internal investigation had launched, and someone would be in contact regarding this matter. Jones was permitted to continue driving for Lyber.
7. Several weeks later, after Lyber failed to take any steps to protect the public from Jones, Plaintiff summoned a Lyber through the Lyber app, which paired Plaintiff with Jones. Once connected through the Lyber app, Jones raped Plaintiff Sally P. Person.

**PARTIES**

8. Plaintiff Sally P. Person is a resident and citizen of City 1, State of East Dakota.
9. Defendant Lyber Ridesharing Co. is a Delaware Corporation with its principal place of business at 1234 Lyber Street, Cityplace, State of West Dakota. Lyber operates throughout the United States and internationally in approximately 991 cities including Townville, East Dakota.
10. Defendant Jones D. Jones is a citizen of Townville, East Dakota.

**JURISDICTION AND VENUE**

11. This Court has personal jurisdiction over Lyber because it regularly conducts business in, purposefully avails itself of the privilege of conducting activities within East Dakota, and the wrongful acts giving rise to Plaintiff's claims arose from Lyber's transaction of business within East Dakota.

12. This Court has personal jurisdiction over Jones because he is a resident and citizen of East Dakota and is currently domiciled in Townsville.

## FACTUAL ALLEGATIONS

13. Lyber is a global online transportation company headquartered in Cityplace, State of West Dakota. Lyber is the creator and provider of a downloadable software application known as the Lyber application that allows customers to request a ride comparable to a taxi with the push of a button on a smartphone (the "Lyber app").
14. The purpose of the Lyber app is to connect Lyber approved drivers with members of the public in need of transportation. Once a consumer requests a ride through the Lyber app, an approved Lyber driver in the vicinity "accepts" the request and the app displays an estimated time of arrival for the Lyber driver to arrive at the consumer's pickup location. The Lyber app notifies the consumer when the driver is about to arrive and it provides general information about the driver's first name, vehicle type, license plate number, and driver rating. The rider then enters the preferred destination, which the rider can do before or during the ride. Upon arriving at the destination, the fare is automatically calculated and charged to the payment method linked to the rider's Lyber account, typically a credit card.
15. Lyber offers a variety of transportation options that are differentiated by the size and type of the vehicle or number of riders.
16. Lyber's business model requires an enormous pool of drivers in order to provide rides to customers quickly and efficiently. To accomplish this, Lyber solicits and retains hundreds of thousands of drivers. Lyber markets to potential drivers: "Lyber makes earning money easy. Get paid while driving your own car on your own schedule."
17. Lyber's business model depends on willing riders. Lyber has aggressively marketed itself as a more efficient and safer alternative to public transportation and traditional

taxis. Lyber has also targeted specific groups of vulnerable riders who place a premium on safety, including women and intoxicated late-night riders.

18. These efforts have proved to be wildly successful. Lyber is now a multi-billion-dollar company with operations around the globe.
19. Lyber requires the applicants to upload the required information through Lyber's website. Lyber does not verify the documents that are uploaded.
20. Lyber does not require any training prior to taking consumers on rides.
21. Lyber is a common carrier. Lyber offers to carry and transport members of the general public and holds itself out to the public as an on-demand form of transportation available to anyone who wants to use it.
22. Lyber has significant control over its drivers. Lyber drivers are required to follow numerous detailed requirements imposed on them by Lyber. Lyber drivers are graded and are subject to termination based on their failure to adhere to these requirements. These include rules regarding their conduct with customers, the cleanliness of their vehicles, their timeliness in picking up customers and taking them to their destination, and what they are allowed to say to customers.
23. Lyber's fare prices are set exclusively by Lyber.
24. Lyber processes the fare for each ride and then pays a fixed portion of the fare to the drivers directly.
25. Lyber attempts to impose uniformity in the conduct of its drivers. Lyber policy mandates that all drivers:
    a. Dress professionally;
    b. Send the customers a text message when the driver is 1–2 minutes away from the pickup location;
    c. Keep the radio either off or on smooth jazz;
    d. Open the door for riders;
    e. Pick up customers on the correct side of the street where the customer is standing.

26. Lyber can deactivate its drivers and make the Lyber app inaccessible with the push of a button. For example, Lyber retains the right to terminate drivers at will, with or without cause, and relies in part on rider feedback to discipline or terminate drivers. Once deactivated, drivers cannot be paired with riders seeking rides through the Lyber app.
27. Lyber aggressively markets its safety to increase its customer base and ridership. Lyber's business model is contingent on convincing its customers it is safe to get into a stranger's vehicle. To do this, Lyber makes a number of representations on its webpages and advertisements to create the impression that Lyber provides safe rides.
28. Lyber has also added an extra charge on the rider's fee for the ride labeled as a "Safe Ride Fee" in order to support Lyber's efforts to provide a safe experience to its riders.
29. Lyber's safety marketing targets females and intoxicated late-night riders. Lyber's website and marketing materials contain images of smiling women using Lyber, which are intended to convey an appearance of safety.
30. Lyber has spent millions of dollars fighting against enhanced safety measures. Lyber has provided funding for many lobbyists in various states to lobby against higher safety regulations such as a more thorough background check.
31. Lyber's safety representations are false and misleading. Lyber has been in multiple lawsuits due to lack of safety in its rides. Lyber drivers have committed numerous sexual assaults against riders that Lyber does its best to hide and cover up. Despite these lawsuits, Lyber continues to promote its safety. These public safety representations are inconsistent with the reality of Lyber's safety and corporate behavior in investigating such acts.

## FACTUAL ALLEGATIONS RELATING TO PLAINTIFF

32. Plaintiff is a young woman who recently completed her second year of college.

33. On the evening of April 4, 2019, Plaintiff planned to attend a social function hosted by peers of Plaintiff who attend the same college. The event took place at an event space less than two miles from Plaintiff's apartment.
34. Plaintiff used the Lyber app to summon a ride from her apartment to take her to the event. Lyber paired Plaintiff with a driver with the last name of Jones.
35. When Plaintiff got in the Lyber vehicle, Jones told Plaintiff he was a "professional driver" and that he was visiting the city temporarily while considering a permanent move.
36. Jones asked Plaintiff a series of questions about her personal life, including details about the event she was attending. Plaintiff told Jones where she was attending school and about the event she was going to. Plaintiff informed Jones she used the Lyber app because she and her friends would be drinking and would need a safe ride home after the event.
37. Jones capitalized on this opportunity and insisted that since he had an SUV, Jones would pick up Plaintiff and her friends after the event. Jones suggested they exchange numbers and that once he was in the vicinity, they could coordinate their subsequent rides through the Lyber app.
38. Plaintiff was dropped off at the event with her classmates. Jones later texted Plaintiff and asked if she was having fun and if Plaintiff and her friends were ready to be picked up. Plaintiff later responded in the affirmative.
39. Jones picked up Plaintiff and her friends, drove them to another location and then dropped them off at the second location.
40. Jones later picked up Plaintiff and she was visibly intoxicated. Jones drove plaintiff to her apartment. After arriving at the parking structure near the apartment, Jones raped Plaintiff.
41. The next morning, Plaintiff was hospitalized. Plaintiff reported to the police and provided official statements to local police detectives.

42. In addition to the physical trauma she experienced, Plaintiff continues to suffer severe emotional distress as a result of the rape. She has exhibited symptoms of post-traumatic stress syndrome, was prescribed multiple medications, and is currently in therapy as a result of the rape. Plaintiff has also struggled to complete her college studies as a result of the events of this rape, putting her professional career at risk.
43. Plaintiff was only introduced to Jones through the Lyber app. Plaintiff never would have accepted a ride from Jones had he not been an approved Lyber driver. Plaintiff believed that Jones was trustworthy and safe because of his affiliation with Lyber.
44. At all relevant times describes herein, Jones was logged in his Lyber app, held himself out as a professional driver with Lyber and represented that all rides he provided were in his capacity as a Lyber driver.
45. A basic background search reveals that Jones has a long history of violence and was convicted of attempted first-degree rape in 1997.
46. Lyber was put on actual notice that Jones was dangerous. From the aforementioned assault victim that received a ride from Jones in his capacity as a Lyber driver, this victim filed a report with Lyber explaining she was assaulted and specifically included that it is not safe to allow Lyber riders to ride with Jones.

**COUNT I—NEGLIGENCE**

47. Plaintiff alleges and reasserts all of the preceding paragraphs as if fully set forth herein.
48. Lyber owes a duty of care to all persons not to place others at a foreseeable risk of harm or create unreasonable risk of harm for others through its actions of inactions.
49. Lyber knew or should have known that its driver, Jones, had a violent history including a conviction for attempted first-degree rape.

50. Lyber knew of many sexual assaults that have occurred by Lyber drivers targeting passengers, and in particular, intoxicated females.
51. "Special circumstances" existed in that Lyber was in a unique position to protect Plaintiff after Lyber was put on actual notice that Jones had recently assaulted a rider and posed a serious risk to the safety of Lyber drivers. It was foreseeable likelihood that permitting Jones to continue driving for Lyber would result in harm or injury to a passenger.
52. Lyber owed Plaintiff a duty of care not to subject Plaintiff to a foreseeable risk of harm or create an unreasonable risk of harm by connecting Plaintiff with a driver that Lyber knew or should have known was dangerous.
53. Lyber breached its duty of care by permitting Jones to drive for Lyber and connecting Plaintiff with Jones for a ride.
54. As a direct and proximate cause of Lyber's breach of its duty of care, Plaintiff was raped by Jones. Plaintiff has sustained and will sustain physical injury, pain and suffering, serious psychological and emotional distress, mental anguish, embarrassment and humiliation. Plaintiff has also incurred medical expenses, professional expenses, lost future income, and other economic damages.
55. Lyber knew or should have known, based on the available information and surrounding circumstances, that its conduct created a high degree of probability of injury.
56. Lyber showed complete indifference to, and conscious or reckless disregard for the safety of Plaintiff and others that Lyber paired to ride with Jones. Plaintiff is entitled to punitive damages as the result of Lyber's egregious and unconscionable conduct.

## COUNT II—NEGLIGENT HIRING AND RETENTION

57. Plaintiff alleges and reasserts all of the preceding paragraphs as if fully set forth herein.

58. In transporting members of the public, Lyber operates in a critical position of public safety and has a duty to hire drivers that are skilled and competent to provide "safe reliable rides."
59. Lyber failed to exercise reasonable care in hiring Jones. At the time Jones was hired as a driver for Lyber, Lyber knew or should have known that Jones was dangerous as the result of his prior conviction for attempted first degree murder.
60. Lyber was either unaware of Jones' prior violent felony conviction, or was made aware, and failed to take additional precautions such as conducting an in-person interview, reviewing third-party references, or performing a fingerprint background check on Jones to determine whether he posed a risk to the safety of Lyber's riders prior to being hired.
61. After hiring Jones, Lyber negligently retained Jones after Lyber was put on actual notice that Jones assaulted a Lyber rider.
62. Jones was unfit to perform the work for which he was hired to perform. It was reasonably foreseeable to Lyber that Jones would expose riders to an unreasonable risk of harm.
63. As a direct and proximate cause of Lyber's failure to exercise reasonable care in it hiring and retention of Jones, Plaintiff was raped and has sustained and will sustain physical injury, pain and suffering, serious psychological and emotional distress, mental anguish, embarrassment, and humiliation. Plaintiff has also incurred medical expenses, professional expenses, lost future income, and other economic damages.
64. Lyber knew or should have known, based on the available information and surrounding circumstances, that its conduct created a high degree of probability of injury.
65. Lyber showed complete indifference to, and conscious or reckless disregard for the safety of Plaintiff and others that Lyber paired to ride with Jones. Plaintiff is entitled to

punitive damages as the result of Lyber's egregious and unconscionable conduct.

## COUNT III—NEGLIGENT INFLICTION OF EMOTIONAL DISTRESS

66. Plaintiff alleges and reasserts all of the preceding paragraphs as if fully set forth herein.
67. Lyber subjected Plaintiff to a foreseeable risk of harm and created an unreasonable risk of harm by pairing Plaintiff with a driver that Lyber knew was unsafe.
68. Lyber knew or should have known that its conduct put Plaintiff at risk and created a high degree of probability of injury.
69. As a direct and proximate cause of Lyber's failure to exercise reasonable care in it hiring and retention of Jones, Plaintiff was raped and has sustained and will sustain physical injury, pain and suffering, serious psychological and emotional distress, mental anguish, embarrassment and humiliation. Plaintiff has also incurred medical expenses, professional expenses, lost future income, and other economic damages.
70. Lyber's conduct and failure to act was extreme, outrageous and utterly intolerable in a civilized community.
71. Plaintiff's emotional distress and mental injuries, including symptoms of post-traumatic stress disorder and severe anxiety, are medically diagnosable and of sufficient severity so as to be medically significant.
72. Lyber showed complete indifference to, and conscious or reckless disregard for the safety of Plaintiff and others that Lyber paired to ride with Jones. Plaintiff is entitled to punitive damages as the result of Lyber's egregious and unconscionable conduct.

## COUNT IV—INTENTIONAL INFLICTION OF EMOTIONAL DISTRESS

73. Plaintiff alleges and reasserts all of the preceding paragraphs as if fully set forth herein.

74. Lyber subjected Plaintiff to a foreseeable risk of harm and created an unreasonable risk of harm by pairing Plaintiff with a driver that Lyber knew was unsafe.
75. Lyber should have realized that its conduct involved an unreasonable risk of causing distress to Plaintiff.
76. As a direct and proximate cause of Lyber's failure to exercise reasonable care in it hiring and retention of Jones, Plaintiff was raped and has sustained and will sustain physical injury, pain and suffering, serious psychological and emotional distress, mental anguish, embarrassment and humiliation. Plaintiff has also incurred medical expenses, professional expenses, lost future income, and other economic damages.
77. Plaintiff's emotional distress and mental injuries, including symptoms of post-traumatic stress disorder and severe anxiety, are medically diagnosable and of sufficient severity so as to be medically significant.
78. Lyber knew or should have known, based on the available information and surrounding circumstances, that its conduct created a high degree of probability of injury.
79. Lyber showed complete indifference to, and conscious or reckless disregard for the safety of Plaintiff and others that Lyber paired to ride with Jones. Plaintiff is entitled to punitive damages as the result of Lyber's egregious and unconscionable conduct.

## COUNT V—ASSAULT AND BATTERY
**(Against Lyber)**

80. Plaintiff alleges and reasserts all of the preceding paragraphs as if fully set forth herein.
81. Under State law, Lyber is a common carrier and has a duty to provide the highest degree of care to its passengers. A common carrier is absolutely bound to protect a passenger from unlawful assaults by its drivers.
82. Lyber's duty is nondelegable. As a common carrier, Lyber is liable for its agents' intentional torts, whether or not such acts were committed within the scope of employment.

83. The duty described above arises where there is a "special relationship" between the parties or "special circumstances" exist such that an act or omission exposes someone to an unreasonable risk of harm through the conduct of another.
84. The relationship of a common carrier-passenger is a "special relationship" in which a party entrusts himself to the protection of another and relies on that person to provide a place of safety.
85. Lyber and Plaintiff had a special relationship in that Plaintiff was a passenger of Lyber and Lyber was in a unique position to protect Plaintiff. Plaintiff entrusted herself to the protection of Lyber and relied upon Lyber to provide safe transportation.
86. "Special circumstances" existed in that Lyber was in a unique position to protect Plaintiff and members of the public after Lyber was put on actual notice that Jones assaulted one of Lyber's riders. It was a foreseeable likelihood that permitting Jones to continue driving for Lyber would result in harm or injury to a passenger.
87. Lyber violated its nondelegable duty by failing to provide Plaintiff with a safe ride home. Jones used his position as a Lyber driver to case Plaintiff while in transport, and then take advantage of her while Plaintiff was in a highly intoxicated state, which resulted in Jones' rape of Plaintiff. A reasonable person could have foreseen that injuries of the type suffered by Plaintiff would be likely to occur under the circumstances.
88. As a direct and proximate result of the aforementioned conduct, Plaintiff sustained and will sustain physical injury, pain and suffering, serious psychological and emotional distress, mental anguish, embarrassment, and humiliation. Plaintiff has also incurred medical expenses, professional expenses, lost future income, and other economic damages.
89. Lyber showed complete indifference to, and conscious or reckless disregard for the safety of Plaintiff and others

that Lyber paired to ride with Jones. Plaintiff is entitled to punitive damages as the result of Lyber's egregious and unconscionable conduct.

**COUNT VI—ASSAULT AND BATTERY**
**(Against Jones)**

90. Plaintiff alleges and reasserts all of the preceding paragraphs as if fully set forth herein.
91. Jones leveraged his status as an approved Lyber driver to pursue Plaintiff and take advantage of her in an intoxicated state.
92. After Plaintiff sought a safe ride home, Jones intentionally manipulated Plaintiff in order to get Plaintiff alone at the end of the night. Jones presented himself as someone tasked by Lyber with assuring Plaintiff's safety. Jones took advantage of Plaintiff's trust in Lyber by using a ruse to get inside Plaintiff's apartment while Plaintiff was in a highly intoxicated state, and then raped Plaintiff.
93. In doing so, Jones attempted to injure Plaintiff and did in fact intentionally injure plaintiff by raping her.
94. Jones' conduct was unlawful and unjustified.
95. As a direct and proximate result of Jones' conduct, Plaintiff sustained and will sustain physical injury, pain and suffering, serious psychological and emotional distress, mental anguish, embarrassment and humiliation. Plaintiff has also incurred medical expenses, professional expenses, lost future income, and other economic damages.
96. Plaintiff is entitled to punitive damages as the result of Jones' egregious and unconscionable conduct.

**PRAYER FOR RELIEF**

WHEREFORE, Plaintiff prays that the Court enter judgment in her favor against Defendants, containing the following relief:

A. An award for damages in an amount to be determined at trial, plus prejudgment interest, to compensate Plaintiff for all physical, monetary and/or economic harm; for harm to her professional and personal reputations and loss of career fulfillment; for all non-monetary and/or compensatory harm, including, but not limited to, compensation for mental anguish and physical injuries; all other monetary and/or non-monetary losses suffered by Plaintiff;

B. An award of punitive damages;
C. An award of costs that Plaintiff has incurred in this action, as well as Plaintiff's reasonable attorneys' fees and expenses to the fullest extent permitted by law; and
D. Such other and further relief as the Court may deem just and proper.

**JURY DEMAND**

Plaintiff hereby demands a trial by jury on all issues of fact and damages stated herein.

# Appendix C

| | | |
|---|---|---|
| **Sally P. Person,** | **)** | **CASE NO: 19 CV 12345** |
| | **)** | |
| **Plaintiff,** | **)** | **Judge** |
| | **)** | |
| vs. | **)** | **PLAINTIFF'S FIRST SET OF** |
| | **)** | **INTERROGATORIES TO** |
| **Lyber Ridesharing Co. and** | **)** | **DEFENDANT LYBER** |
| **Jones D. Jones,** | **)** | |
| | **)** | |
| **Defendants.** | **)** | |

Now comes the Plaintiff Sally P. Person ("Plaintiff"), by and through counsel, and propound the following Interrogatories to be answered by Defendant Lyber Ridesharing Co. within twenty-eight (28) days pursuant to Rule 33 of the Federal Rules of Civil Procedure.

<u>INSTRUCTIONS</u>

Please answer each Interrogatory in full. If you cannot do so, answer to the extent possible, specifying the reasons for your inability to answer the remainder and stating whatever information, knowledge or belief you do have concerning the unanswered portion.

In answering each Interrogatory, identify each person who assisted or participated in preparing and/or supplying any of the information given in answer to or relied upon in preparing answers to these Interrogatories.

These Interrogatories shall be deemed continuing so as to require supplemental answers when and if Plaintiff obtains further information subsequent to the filing of her answers up to and including the time of trial of this action.

## DEFINITIONS

Except where the context indicates otherwise, the following definitions shall apply to these Interrogatories:

1. "Person" means natural persons, corporations, partnerships, sole proprietorships, unions, associations, federations, government agencies, or any other kind of entity.
2. "Documents" means any printed, typewritten, handwritten or otherwise recorded matter of whatever character, whether a copy, preliminary draft or original, including but not limited to letters, correspondence, memoranda, notes, statements, notebooks, minutes, reports, worksheets, handbooks, manuals, pamphlets, brochures, diaries, desk calendars, stenographic notes, analyses, forecasts, announcements, publications, press releases, photographs, video and/or audio tape recordings, motion pictures, tabulations, graphs, charts, maps, telegrams, agreements, contracts, affidavits, transcripts, printouts or other stored information from computer software or hardware or other information retrieval systems, and any copies of the foregoing that are different from the original or other copies because of notations or markings.
3. The word "identify" when used in reference to a natural person, means to state his or her full name, present address, telephone number, employer and position or job title at the time of the transaction, occurrence or event covered in the Interrogatory. If any of the above information is not available to Defendant, provide any other available information with or by which such natural person can be identified.
4. The word "identify" when used in reference to a person (as defined above) other than a natural person, means to

state (1) its full name, (2) the nature of its organization, including the name of the state in which it was organized, (3) its address(es), (4) the address(es) of its principal place of business, and (5) its principal line(s) of business. If any of the above information is not available to Defendant, provide any other available information with or by which such person can be identified.

5. The word "identify" when used in reference to a document means to state (1) its date, (2) its author, (3) the type of document (e.g., letter, memorandum, receipt, invoice, schedule, report, telegraph, chart, photograph, sound reproduction or note), and (4) its present location and the name of its present custodian. If any such document was, but is no longer in the possession of Defendant or subject to its control, or is no longer in existence, state whether it (1) is missing or lost, (2) has been destroyed, (3) has been transmitted or transferred voluntarily or involuntarily to others, identifying such others, or (4) has been otherwise disposed of. In each such instance, explain the circumstances surrounding the authorization for such disposition and state the date or approximate date thereof. If any of the above information is not available to Defendant, provide any available information with or by which such documents can be identified.
6. "You" or "Your" or "Defendant" means Lyber Ridesharing Co. and/or any of its agents, representatives, investigators, and all other persons, including government investigators, acting for or on its behalf.
7. "Plaintiff" means Plaintiff Sally P. Person and/or any of her agents, representatives, investigators, and all other persons, including government investigators, acting for or on her behalf.
8. "Defendants" means Lyber Ridesharing Co. and John D. Jones.
9. "Complaint" means the Complaint that was filed in this matter on July 15, 2019.
10. "Date," when used herein, shall include the day, month and year of the occurrence to which the Interrogatory

refers. Defendant is to provide the exact date or inclusive dates if known, or if not known, an approximation together with an indication that the date or dates supplied may not be exact.

INTERROGATORIES

1. Identify each person supplying information used to prepare answers to these interrogatories, and as to each person so identified, indicate the number of the interrogatory, or part thereof, as to which the person supplied information.

   **ANSWER:**

2. Identify all persons with knowledge of each of the allegations contained in Plaintiff's Complaint.

   **ANSWER:**

3. Identify all persons who have discoverable information regarding this lawsuit, including witnesses of the incident that serves as the basis for the Complaint. For each person so identified, please indicate the following:
   (a) a general description of the individual's knowledge which is discoverable;
   (b) the manner in which the individual had the opportunity to gain such knowledge.

   **ANSWER:**

4. Please identify any statements you have given or any statements you have access to or in your possession regarding the claims asserted in this lawsuit, including the name, address and telephone number of each person who has given a statement, the date each statement was

given, and the name and address of the person presently having custody of each statement.

**ANSWER:**

5. Please identify any experts you have retained, or expect to retain, for purposes of this litigation. For each such expert named, please identify the following:
    a. The date on which the expert was first contacted regarding this engagement;
    b. All cases or engagements for which the expert has previously been retained or consulted by Plaintiff's counsel or anyone in the same law firm as Plaintiff's counsel;
    c. The expert's credentials, by providing a current resume and/or curriculum vitae;
    d. A detailed summary of the subject matter upon which the expert is expected to testify, by providing a report from such expert;
    e. An itemization of any amounts paid to each expert to date, and the hourly rate the expert expects to charge the Plaintiff for testimony.

**ANSWER:**

6. Please state the name and address of each individual you expect to call as a fact witness at trial, and the subject of each individual's expected testimony.

**ANSWER:**

7. Identify all contact or communications current or former employees, agents or representatives, have had with the Plaintiff or any agents of Plaintiff, and with respect to each, state the following:

a. the identity of the person with whom you or your investigators, agents or family members had the contact or communication;
b. the date(s) of their contact or communication;
c. whether the contact or communication was initiated by you or any of your investigators, agents or family members; and
d. the purpose of the contact or communication.

**ANSWER:**

8. Please identify when John D. Jones began driving for Lyber.

**ANSWER:**

9. Please identify the number of trips completed and total number of hours spent logged on to the Lyber application by John D. Jones within the two weeks preceding the April 5, 2019 accident.

**ANSWER:**

10. Please identify all internal investigations and their contents resulting from the April 5, 2019 accident.

**ANSWER:**

11. Please identify any disciplinary response or communications from Lyber to John D. Jones, including, but not limited to, any response or communication related to the April 5, 2019 accident.

**ANSWER:**

12. Please identify any and all rewards, loyalty, guaranteed rate or other compensation programs offered by Lyber in which John D. Jones may have participated.

    **ANSWER:**

13. Please identify all documents which were used to answer these Interrogatories or that were reviewed prior to answering these interrogatories.

    **ANSWER:**

| | | |
|---|---|---|
| **Sally P. Person,** | ) | **CASE NO: 19 CV 12345** |
| | ) | |
| **Plaintiff,** | ) | **Judge** |
| | ) | |
| **vs.** | ) | **PLAINTIFF'S FIRST SET OF** |
| | ) | **REQUESTS FOR PRODUC-** |
| **Lyber Ridesharing Co. and** | ) | **TION TO DEFENDANT** |
| **Defendants.** | ) | **LYBER** |
| | ) | |
| | ) | |

Now comes the Plaintiff Sally P. Person ("Plaintiff"), by and through counsel, and propound the following Requests for Production to be answered by Defendant Lyber Ridesharing Co. within twenty-eight (28) days pursuant to Rule 34 of the Federal Rules of Civil Procedure.

**REQUESTS FOR PRODUCTION OF DOCUMENTS**

1. All non-privileged documents identified, referenced or relied upon in formulating responses to Plaintiff's answers to Plaintiff's First Set of Interrogatories.

   **RESPONSE:**

2. Any and all documents the Defendant Lyber intends to produce at trial.

   **RESPONSE:**

3. Any and all reports prepared by any expert Defendant Lyber anticipates calling at trial.

   **RESPONSE:**

4. Any and all material reviewed by any expert you intend to call at trial, including but not limited to billing doc-

umentation, correspondence between counsel and the expert, all electronic communications made by the expert pertaining to his or her involvement in this case, all telephone notes and all tangible material generated or reviewed by the expert.

**RESPONSE:**

5. All communications between Lyber and Driver.

**RESPONSE:**

6. All communications between Lyber and Plaintiff.

**RESPONSE:**

7. All records of communication between Driver and Passenger.

**RESPONSE:**

8. All internal records of written or oral communication between or among Lyber employees dated between April 5, 2019 and the present date that mention or discuss the April 5, 2019 trip and motor vehicle accident.

**RESPONSE:**

9. All electronic data related to the Driver's trips within two weeks of the April 5, 2019 trip and motor vehicle accident, including GPS data, including but not limited to:
    a. information sent to, or recorded by, the Lyber driver's phone or Lyber's system for dispatching and tracking vehicles;

b. "black box," electronic data recorder, or similar information stored by a vehicle, smartphone, or other device;
c. photographs, video recordings, or audio recordings related to the collision or preceding trip;
d. information about the driver and his wireless communication carrier (e.g., Verizon, Sprint, etc.);
e. detailed trip records including, but not limited to, date, time, pick-up and drop-off locations, duration, route taken, fare rate, and any rating or review.

**RESPONSE:**

10. All information contained with the Driver's "File"—i.e., the information in Lyber's possession—regarding Driver including all trips in the two weeks preceding the April 5, 2019 collision, all records of complaints, reviews of Driver, and/or incident reports.

**RESPONSE:**

11. All Lyber user guides and other policies, procedures, guidelines, rules, and protocols given to Lyber drivers (including John D. Jones) about what to do in the event of a collision.

**RESPONSE:**

12. All records retained as a part of any background or driving record check that was performed relative to Driver.

**RESPONSE:**

13. All vehicle information, including number of vehicles registered to the Driver's account, make, model, year, and any additional information for each.

**RESPONSE:**

14. All insurance information provided by the Driver to Lyber and by Driver to Lyber.

**RESPONSE:**

15. All records of communications between Driver and Plaintiff.

**RESPONSE:**

16. All data and information kept by Lyber that relate to Plaintiff and were created as a result of Plaintiff's use of Lyber's application.

**RESPONSE:**

17. All records of communication between Driver and Passenger.

**RESPONSE:**

# Table of Authorities

## Cases

## Statutes and Regulations

# Index